It Was Long Ago
It Was Yesterday

It Was Long Ago
It Was Yesterday

Felicia Altman Gilbert

Copyright © 2011 by Felicia Altman Gilbert.

Library of Congress Control Number: 2011919341
ISBN: Hardcover   978-1-4653-8777-6
               Softcover   978-1-4653-8776-9
               Ebook   978-1-4653-8778-3

All rights reserved. No part of this book may be reproduced or transmitted in any form or by any means, electronic or mechanical, including photocopying, recording, or by any information storage and retrieval system, without permission in writing from the copyright owner.

This book was printed in the United States of America.

To order additional copies of this book, contact:
Xlibris Corporation
1-888-795-4274
www.Xlibris.com
Orders@Xlibris.com
84785

For My Family

Contents

Chapter 1 The Bungalow on Miramar Street...13

Chapter 2 The Family Enclave at Occidental Boulevard 34

Chapter 3 A Pleasant Evening and a Nasty Headache 48

Chapter 4 Recovery and Back to Art..56

Chapter 5 A Weighty Decision and a Great Outcome.......................62

Chapter 6 Adventures with Helping Hands 66

Chapter 7 Hard Work and *Business is Business*..................................71

Chapter 8 Striking Out on Our Own 77

Chapter 9 A Dugout on Brandon Street, 1952 79

Chapter 10 Lapeer Drive 84

Chapter 11 Altman Antiques and a Crucifix 87

Chapter 12 A Paradise with Animals...107

Chapter 13 Landing at the Boy's Club..117

Chapter 14 A Chinese House in Pasadena...124

Chapter 15 Coffee at Altman Antiques and a New Job for Gil 127

Chapter 16 The House on Cerro Gordo...130

Chapter 17 Mother's Panic Brings Family Togetherness..................136

Chapter 18 A Curious Bird and a Costume Party 140

Chapter 19 A Letter from the Past 147

Chapter 20 That's When They Left Us 150

Chapter 21 At The House of the Giant Hibiscus 173

Chapter 22 Going in New Directions 185

Chapter 23 A Small Cottage, A Panther in the Tree 190

Chapter 24 Losing My Brother 196

Chapter 25 Meeting Up With Synanon 200

Chapter 26 A Wedding and an Earthquake 209

Chapter 27 Gil Retires 216

Chapter 28 The Olive Mill House Was Ours 220

Chapter 29 The Wedding at Tomales Bay and Zachary is Born 233

Chapter 30 Ursula, the Flood and Gil is Ailing 246

Chapter 31 Respite at Hedgebrook 252

Chapter 32 Loss and Sorrow 262

Chapter 33 Atlanta 270

And sometimes it does feel like yesterday. I had a rich and colorful childhood surrounded by people who took loving care of me. I was nurtured by books and often submerged in a fantasy realm of my own, quite unaware of the outside world, of turmoil and of lurking dangers. I was in my early teens when I became more conscious of what really concerned the people around me. I heard heated discussions among family members and sometimes guests and saw worried faces around the dinner table. The radio brought news of bank closings and the rapid rise of the Nationalist Socialist Party. Arabs attacked Jews in Palestine. The rise of anti-Semitism in our country was discussed. Only Father and I had concerns about our own special endeavors. Nothing could have been more important to our *Herr Direktor* then his theatre, the rehearsals for an upcoming performance of Shakespeare's *Othello* at the State Theatre in Hannover, where we lived. My attention was focused on my German literature teacher, Mr. Wollenberg, whom I had a crush on and also on my lively circle of girlfriends that met every Saturday afternoon for lemonade and cookies, knitting and sewing, and also reading and discussing favorite books from time to time.

And then in 1933 our country erupted in great turmoil and the catastrophe of Hitler's reign began. My mother drummed us out of bed one night in April of that year and we drove across the border to Belgium to escape. I had just turned sixteen. We traveled in Belgium, France, and Italy for a year in search of a place to settle, then lived in France for three years before boarding the Manhattan, a big ocean liner that brought us to our final destination, the United States.

My brother, who was eight years older than I, left his medical studies in Berlin and followed us to California where we all settled in San Francisco. I was twenty by then, not a child anymore, but I think it still took me a long time to fully mature into adulthood. The experience of being uprooted so suddenly and then traveling with only my parents' company for so many years turned me into a very lonely, introverted young woman. I started to come out of my cocoon when I went to New York on my own and studied at the Art Students League for three years. Going back to San Francisco I was caught by the irresistible magnetism of a special young man and the first volume of my memoir ends with the event of a joyous wedding.

Liegt dier Gestern klar und offen,
Wirgst du Heute kraeftig frei;
Kannst auch auf ein Morgen hoffen
Das nicht minder gluecklich sei.

—Johann Wolfgang von Goethe
Weimar, 15 June 1826

If yesterday shines clear and open
You'll live free and strong today
And you can hope for a tomorrow
That will be happy in every way.

My father had a replica of this poem in Goethe's handwriting hanging in a little silver frame close to his writing desk for as long as I can remember. It accompanied him during all of our wanderings and in every house we lived in, and it now hangs in mine. It conjures up the image of my father sitting in his favorite leather armchair, a book in one hand, cigar in the other. He looks at me over the rim of his glasses. He is about to say, "We'll have a big celebration," the proclamation he made without fail preceding every family birthday or other festive event, and he meant it. A little smoke from his cigar drifts in the slim streak of sunlight that steals in through the tree-covered window behind him. And there are books, thousands of books covering the walls around him from top to bottom.

When my parents died, Father in 1962 and Mother in 1963, I had to go through the painful task of dissolving their household. I rummaged around in one of my father's closets one morning. I was alone. My husband was out of town again and the boys in school. I pushed the heavy coat aside and various jackets and rain gear, found a tennis racket and the sturdy cane that had accompanied him on walks in mountainous Switzerland. My God, I thought, these had not been used in years.

Now I know from whom I inherited the desire to hold onto things for the sake of memories. I looked up at the top shelf. I took two large cardboard boxes down and peeked in. Up to the rim they were filled with old letters, it seemed like hundreds of letters, some yellowed and slightly crumpled, some quite pristine and tied with ribbons, almost all written by family members. I spread my find out on the dining room table and breathed a deep sigh. I thought it would take weeks or even months to sort and read through all of those voices from the past, and it did. I got to work sorting and reading and it was not really a chore, but quite a moving experience.

Two of those letters, two short romantic notes, stood out. They were dated back to my parents' courting days in 1907 when my father, Dr. George Altman, was proud of his first job as Assistant Director of the main theatre in the city of Mannheim.

The very young charming actress Alice Hall had been hired to join the company at the same time, and as father told us many times during his lifetime, he took one look at her and knew that she was to be his wife. The first somewhat faded letter I held in my hands was dated January 24, 1907.

Highly esteemed Miss Hall,

I am unexpectedly required to be at the theatre tonight and will consequently not be able to keep our dinner engagement. Therefore I would like to be able to ask your forgiveness this afternoon while taking a walk with you or by meeting at a café.

Please send me a few lines back via this messenger as to whether and when I may ring your doorbell.

Things must have been progressing, but not too fast. A short note turned up dated February 19, 1908.

Good morning my overtired little darling.
Ten o'clock, Rose Garden.

The majority of the letters contained writings of parents and children corresponding with each other and friends, painting a valuable picture of happenings throughout the years until almost to the end of my father's life in 1962. It took months to read and sort this unexpected treasure that ultimately and so enormously enriched my memory of times past. I am including some letters in this volume just as they were written at the time.

Here now is the second book about my life. I have recalled what took place, what I thought and felt, how I fought for strength, conquered despair, loved and relished life from the start of my marriage until now, almost to its end. And that, alas, will not be too far away. Although if I can make it for another six years or so, to a mere one hundred years, book number three might still be born. I'd like that.

Chapter 1

THE BUNGALOW ON MIRAMAR STREET
November 1944

I pushed the screen door open and leaned against the doorframe. A light November drizzle misted the little courtyard and polished the red tile roofs of the bungalows that surrounded it. They were all alike, these small houses hugging each other tightly from wall to wall. They had one bedroom, a tiny living room and kitchen, just like ours. I let my eyes wander from one closed door to the other. It was early morning and the occupants were still asleep. They were mostly elderly and had lived there for many years. Their window curtains drawn, some little nightlights not yet extinguished, wrapped in soundless sleep, they seemed to stay that way forever, never moving, never going anywhere. I took a deep breath and tilted my face out into the mist. To me this small house, this door that I had opened felt like a gesture towards a new and wondrous life.

I thought back to that special night two months before in October. Gil and I were sitting in the dimly lit restaurant of a hotel in San Mateo. Only a few other guests were still eating. It was quite late. We had left our wedding party in San Francisco and there we sat looking at each other and holding hands across the table. Who was he, this man who had drawn me to him so strongly that it seemed inevitable that our lives would mesh together? We had met less than five months ago. We were still strangers, but we knew that we belonged to each other.

"Wear this for your wedding night and your honeymoon." My mother had proudly spread a beautiful silk nightgown and embroidered robe on my bed. Her happy smile just barely veiled the teary moisture in her eyes. That had been two days before my wedding, and there I stood in the rose-tinted light from above the garish gold-framed mirror in the

"Honeymoon Suite" bathroom of the San Mateo Hotel. I unpinned my long dark hair and shook it loose over the silken white of the lavish gown. I hesitated. I was afraid to go to him, go to the one that waited for me impatiently beyond that door. The few encounters I had before we met were forgotten, meaningless. Was my life going to be fulfilled and loneliness banished forever with the one I loved? Was it real? It had to be. I opened the door, and that was the last moment that I wore the silken robe for quite some time.

Our honeymoon was spent in a peaceful little motel in Palm Springs, a small vacation village in the desert that might then have had hopes, but certainly no knowledge of its future tremendous growth. I believe it had one or two big hotels, some smaller establishments like ours and various nice tourist shops to browse in. That is how I remember it.

And I remember the birds. Every morning early—that is early from the viewpoint of a loving couple on their honeymoon—the birds would greet the day enthusiastically, a warbling and twittering assault. "What kinds of birds are those that wake us every morning?" I asked as the man at the desk handed us the mail.

"They belong to the ambiance of this place," he said. "Our guests do enjoy them." He looked at our bleary eyes. "Well, if you don't like them . . . ." He reached under his desk and pressed a button. Heavenly quiet reigned in the mornings from then on for the rest of our stay. But every time we passed the reception desk a pair of narrowed eyes followed us, signaling hurt and disgust at our lack of appreciation.

We rented bicycles and explored the desert. We had elegant dinners by candlelight in one of the hotels at night and lounged around our small motel's swimming pool in front of our room during the day, arms linked across adjoining deck chairs, enjoying the desert sun, dozing a little off and on and feeling close to each other. And then we talked and talked. We talked of childhood and family, of growing up and aspirations we had and hopes for the future we now shared. We talked about books and art and music we liked, but certain parts of our past adult history did not get touched.

I wanted to ask *what went on in your life before we met? Tell me about your first marriage. Why did it end?* Whenever that subject seemed close Gil's face turned rigid and I knew not to persist. Much later he mentioned that his wife wanted to be an actress and went to New York. That was all. I felt shut out of a part of his life and felt that he did not want to know too much about mine, though I was so ready to open up to him and give him all I was. Yet he never asked.

As happy and content as we were in our marriage it took a long time until the last barriers fell, and we were completely close and open with each other without reservations.

I believe that Gil's mother's insensitive tyranny in concert with the economic struggles of his youth had much to do with the development of his iron will to succeed, to seem unshakably strong and to withhold as much as possible any expression of strong emotion and outward signs of weakness. In reality he was a warm and sensitive man in need of the love and affection he did not get in his parents' home while growing up.

As far as I was concerned the struggles and confusions of my student days in New York were slowly left behind in the weeks and months that followed. Gil's obvious love and care for me reassured me in the years to come and helped me to overcome some of my insecurities and to value myself as he valued me.

I had left my family and friends in San Francisco. Our home was to be in Los Angeles. Gil was working for the Santa Fe Trailways Bus Company and was involved with the scheduling of troop transports for the war, a job that kept him out of active duty in the army, thank God.

Shortly after our marriage the Trailways Company transferred him, and we had to move to Los Angeles. That was the town where Gil spent most of his youth and his parents and brothers still lived there. It was 1945, a year of uproar throughout much of the world. Roosevelt died and Truman became president. In April Hitler committed suicide and Mussolini was killed. And atomic bombs were dropped on Japan in August. World War Two came to an end.

While we were conscious of the times we lived in we were very much wrapped up in our own lives. Gil's salary was barely adequate. Finding a place to live that we could afford due to the scarcity of available housing due to the war presented quite a problem. So when we found this small bungalow on Miramar Street we were overjoyed. Our elderly neighbors nodded to us from behind their screen doors and probably remarked to each other on what a relief it was to see some young faces around for a change. Mr. and Mrs. Tillotson lived right next door to us, and we could not help getting to know them soon after moving in.

Gil had left for work as usual one morning when I heard a little knock on my door and Mrs. Tillotson introduced herself with a tray of cookies in her hands. "I just want to welcome the new neighbors," she said. Her pale little wrinkled face seemed to disappear behind the barrier of large horn-rimmed glasses that allowed her bright eyes to peer out at the world with good will and endless curiosity.

I stepped aside and asked her in. As she looked around our small space her eyebrows rose in astonishment. Very lightly her dry old hand admiringly stroked the smooth blond wood of the round table in the middle of the room and she let her eyes roam over the golden wood framed and flowery silk upholstered sofa and the two imposing wingchairs. She gazed at the tall secretary desk and the corner cabinet.

"What beautiful furniture. Where does it come from?"

"My parents sent it down from their home in San Francisco," I said. "It's early ninteenth-century German Biedermeier."

"Meant for a big home, isn't it?"

I nodded and we both laughed. With the addition of a book shelf and an old upright radio and record player from the Salvation Army we had managed to stuff that little room with our heavy period furniture to a point where we had to navigate sideways rather then walking in a straight line when we were at home. Fortunately we were both slim.

The record player had been our first purchase together. How could we have lived without music? While I had gone to concerts and to the opera with my mother, it was Gil who taught me to love and really listen to music, not only to Bach, Beethoven and Mozart, but also to very early works, those of Josquin des Pres, di Lassos and Heinrich Schuetz. Through the open window on summer nights Monteverdi madrigals as well as Bela Bartok's violin concerto and Stravinsky's *Petrouchka* could all be heard outside, among the geranium pots in the little courtyard. I don't remember any complaints from our neighbors. We also liked folk music, blues and jazz. John Jacob Niles, Roland Hayes, Pete Seeger and the Weavers were some of our favorites. We adored Marian Anderson and Paul Robeson. Music became a strong extra element of bonding between Gil and me.

I can see us quite clearly on a late winter evening. It was wet and dark. We were standing in the street, standing in a line that moved ahead towards the entrance to a bar on Melrose Avenue. The pace was slow, a step at a time. We were to hear the pianist Art Tatum. The crowd was patient and obviously in a good mood. The streetlights glittered through the drizzling rain and brushed across Gil's black curly hair. He stood next to me wearing his dark green woolen sport jacket. I still feel his presence with an almost physical intensity.

Having been admitted at long last, we sat squeezed together at a little round table in the overcrowded, smoke-filled room. Nursing the drinks in front of us, whisky for Gil, a Manhattan for me, we studiously avoided the eager eyes of the bustling waiters who hovered over us, ready to snatch the empty glasses, prodding us to order a second round. We were poor. We resisted. We listened to Art Tatum playing Eric Satie's compositions and all kinds of jazz. We listened shoulder to shoulder with an incredibly mixed, sweating, enthusiastic crowd in this small room.

Settling down to an orderly home life was not completely easy. My heretofore-pampered existence had not prepared me for housework or any knowledge of the culinary arts, except for preparing endless servings of spaghetti and scrambled eggs in my student days in New York. I recite here, as exactly as I can remember, Gil's frequently repeated account of his nightly return home from work.

I found my very nervous young wife with grease splatters on her blouse and drooping strands of hair that had escaped the bobby pins. The kitchen was a mess. Every pot we owned had been used and spread across the counter. I took her by the hand and pulled her out of the kitchen. Then I mixed us a couple of strong martinis and settled her down. After the second martini everything was fine and dinner proceeded without a care in the world and was even edible.

I knew that my parents, who were still living in San Francisco, were always eager to hear from me.

Dec.1, 1944
My dearest Mutti,

If you had only the slightest idea about how busy we are, you would be at least 60% less mad at us for not writing. The remaining 40% I will allow to rest on my shoulders.

Moving into our new place was really very hard work. We had to run all over the landscape to find a stove, refrigerator, bookshelves and kitchen equipment. As you know there are obstacles galore due to the war restrictions. We were not able to obtain the priority to purchase a refrigerator. We could have gotten a used one for $100.00. It was huge, terribly unpractical and noisy, unbearable in our little place. As luck would have it some people we know sold us a small, used ice chest that is in good condition for $30.00. After having hunted for a stove with heat control in scores of second hand stores all over the city, I finally gave up and bought one without it for $85.00. It is of medium size, has four burners, an oven and a grill.

I am so glad that I took my bookshelf along. No carpenter is allowed to build one of a similar size. The regulation size is ridiculously small, only a quarter of what we need. Again I made the rounds of endless numbers of junk shops. No success.

In spite of the fact that Gil cheerfully eats everything I cook and it actually seems as if he enjoys it, my culinary art has far from reached its zenith. I have not really ruined anything yet, but some of my output could have been termed "Just barely edible." It was difficult with a new stove and without heat control. The day before yesterday I made my first roast. The oven was probably too hot and I had put the meat too close to the flame. I saved it just before it got burned. It tasted good, but was quite hard. That could have been the fault of the meat, of course. I served potatoes with it and squash with tomatoes. Both were good, thank God. An excellent bakery in the next block contributed the desert.

Now it is already ten minutes before five o' clock. Gil comes home at six and dinner must be ready, because we are invited afterwards.

Mutti, I'll write more tomorrow. I want to mail this quickly now. Pappi, Ralph and Pat will get their own letters. I am happy and love you as always. Kisses.

Fe

Dec. 20, 1944
Dear Mutti,

Just a quick note: This morning I received a little package from San Francisco. It was from your friend Elisabeth Philipp. I did not believe my eyes: an oven-thermometer. A lifesaver. A Treasure! I bet you know about it and are the instigator, as always.

Love, Fe

At the end of November soon after moving into our little house I became a student of the sculptor Bernhard Sopher. He had a storefront studio on Sunset Boulevard that you entered through a curtained glass door and left the noisy street behind. Class began at nine thirty three days a week and ran until far into the afternoon.

There were four of us who worked in this wonderful place, an oasis removed from any outside interference. Aside from myself there was black-haired Marsha—energetic, creative and elegant—whose husband was a film writer. Young Emmy was a delicate beauty, just recently married to the violinist Henry Temianka, who later became a friend of ours and was considerably older than she was. He was a well-known musician and the first violinist of the Paganini Quartet. Bemi Debus was the most outspoken personality among us. With her strong body, her bright round face and the long braids that were wound around her head, one could have imagined her walking along a meadow in the Swiss Alps. She had a deep sonorous voice and made a living as a radio announcer, supporting her husband Louis until he earned his degree in psychiatric social work. Louis, for his part, served as a model for our class with his well-muscled athletic body to pay for Bemi's tuition. They were quite poor and lived in a trailer near the ocean.

We were a very happy family and Mr. Sopher filled the father role to perfection. At lunchtime we unpacked our brown bags and he brewed us strong black coffee in his little Turkish coffeemaker, served in tiny cups. We sat cross-legged on dusty, fat pillows on the floor. Dust from clay was everywhere. How our teacher managed to keep himself so neat and clean was a mystery to us.

"Old Man Sopher," as Gil and I called him between ourselves, was not really so old. He might have been in his early sixties. He was a delicate man, pale skinned, with sparse gray hair the color of his clay. One did not expect any particular physical strength in his slight body unless one had seen him work. He had strong muscular arms and hands that were used to pouring heavy plaster into molds and kneading large chunks of clay into a workable consistency. In these large and capable hands lay great strength and much of his sensitivity as well. Whether it was a figurative piece that grew from the clay he was shaping, a portrait bust for a client or just a human face whose form and expression interested him, it almost seemed as if he stroked it to life.

A sofa bed way in back of the room was discretely hidden from view by a heavy old velvet curtain. Once I stole a look behind this barrier. Some nails in the wall held hangers with a few pieces of clothing on them. There was a small washstand and a heavy rough wooden box that had an antique iron clasp that held the massive lid down. I imagined that sailors of Long John Silver's time carried their belongings in such a box when they boarded ship to take off on their treasure hunt. Here it obviously served as a table holding the remains of a small repast accompanied by a few rumpled pages of a newspaper.

Did he ever leave his studio? He seemed to be a part of it, with his sparse gray hair, pale skin and gray artist's smock. One could imagine that he might one day disappear into the gray walls and mottled ceiling.

Disappear? Oh no. When his sharp blue eyes were trained upon you they showed that he was very much on deck and had no intention of fading away. He remained a mystery to us, though. We never learned whether he had a family, where he actually lived, or what country he came from. We just kept on guessing and he never answered our carefully veiled questions. He was a sweet man and an excellent teacher.

My classmate Bemi and her husband Louis Debus grew to be close friends of ours for many years. Louis became a parole officer for delinquent youth and Bemi devoted herself to the rearing of her children, a task that she was admirably suited for with her education and her intellect. "We study life in other countries," she told us. "Once a month we prepare a special meal for the family that belongs to the people and the culture we have been studying." I really admired her.

Many years later when we lived in Santa Barbara and had been out of touch with Louis and Bemi for a long time we received a special invitation to celebrate Bemi's seventieth birthday in Los Angeles. We knew that Louis had died years ago.

It was a terribly hot summer day, but the happy expectation of seeing Bemi again made us forget the heat and the long drive to Los Angeles on the crowded freeway. We arrived at a rented hall in Santa Monica and struggled through a crowd of celebrants, none of whom we knew. Where was Bemi? We recognized the heavy braids slung around her head. She stood next to her daughter, her face averted.

"Bemi!" Gil and I rushed up to her, ready to fall around her neck. She turned and looked at us. We stopped in our tracks. Her bloated face showed no expression, no sign of recognition. She stared across the crowd with empty eyes like someone lost in the desert. Not a sound came from her lips.

Her daughter raised her hands and called for attention.

"My mother will say a few words and then we'll have the birthday cake."

A space opened around mother and daughter. Following whispered instructions, a toneless almost inaudible, "Thank you," fell from Bemi's lips, succeeded by "For coming," a few seconds later. Everyone clapped and shouted. Gil and I slipped out. No jubilation for us. We drove home in silence. We were in shock and indescribably sad.

Gil had lived in Los Angeles with his family since his early teens. He still had friends with whom he had gone all the way through high school and two years of college. It was a strange and uncomfortable experience for me when we visited Bernard and Ethel Garey for the first time, because I knew that they had known Gil's first wife Lil, who had also gone to school with them and had been a close friend. Gil's mother, with her usual lack of sensitivity, had described her to me at length as Lil the beautiful and Lil the adored, and so the shadow of Lil hovered all around me. I felt that I was on display and probably not measuring up to the ghost of my predecessor.

Bernard, or Barney as we called him, and Ethel embraced me with genuine warmth. Years later they told me, "You were pretty and elegant, obviously ill at ease, shy and very, very silent." Silent? Of course. I had often been silent in company ever since I can remember. I just observe and listen for the most part without joining the conversation, a trait I've never been able to conquer completely.

Barney was bright and lively, interested in many things and loved music as much as did Gil. He was always ready for a heated discussion and animated arguments about books, music, or world events that never allowed a flicker of boredom to enter our relationship. Ethel tended to be more relaxed. She observed her young enthusiastic husband with her sweet, indulgent smile, not always comprehending what his excitement was all about. We did many things together, we four friends. We picnicked at Griffith Park, went on bicycle trips and played badminton at the Sports Palace on indoor courts.

We became friends for the rest of our lives from that time on. I recall sitting on their terrace on many hot summer nights discussing the pros and cons of religious education for our children among other topics.

While Gil and our friends had been brought up in the Jewish tradition my Lutheran indoctrination at school had been expunged thoroughly by my early realization of not only the Germans' hypocrisy but also by a persistent mistrust of any dogmatic religious beliefs.

The one thing that we agreed on was that our children should learn about the world's diverse peoples, their cultures and their beliefs, so that they would be capable of deciding how to lead their own moral and meaningful lives. We grieved with the Gareys when they lost a child, and we all shared heartbreaks and joys in the years to come.

"Why don't you come and visit my studio?" Dorothy Royer smiled at me and obviously wanted me to come and see her work. She was an artist, I had been told. We were guests at a dinner-party that evening. She sat next to me, and we liked each other immediately. Contrary to my usual difficulties in opening up to new people and carrying on a halfway reasonable conversation, I felt at ease with her. In her early sixties, her very white, smooth skin and her light gray sparkling eyes gave the impression of a much younger person. Her face spoke about someone who was thoughtful but at the same time alert to her surroundings and the people she encountered.

She had already understood that I was a young woman in search of an occupation that suited her capabilities and added to her family's income.

"I lead an art workshop for children and young people. Come see us. You might find it interesting." A few days later I walked down La Cienega Boulevard in Hollywood, turned down a side alley and found a little door at the back of a gray, nondescript commercial building. Over the entrance a child's drawing in black outlines on a white metal plate with a few wild splashes of red, yellow, and blue color across it proclaimed that this was the entrance to Dorothy Royer's Children's Art Workshop. It looked like a small bouquet of flowers on a big man's drab overcoat.

I entered a room that was suffused with energy. There was no extraneous noise, a little chatter here and there drowned quickly again in the concentrated hub of activities around the three large tables in the middle of the room.

About twelve or fifteen children ranging in age from five to eight or nine years old were engaged in a multitude of activities. Some painted, some drew, some worked with clay and others were engaged in manipulating unlikely materials into strange constructions with glue, string, toothpicks or wire.

"Do you give different assignments to the children? They do not seem to be striving towards any one project." I was confused. This was not the kind of art activity I had observed in my boys' public school.

Dorothy laughed, "I do not give assignments. Each child follows his own ideas. I provide the environment and give them the opportunity to discover how to implement those ideas. I am a facilitator and co-worker more then a teacher. You see little Amy over there? She is just four. She loves colors. All I showed her was to wash her brush each time before dipping into a new paint pot, but on her paper she can use her colors any way she wants. Soon she found that if she mixed all the shades together in one big puddle, gray mud would be the result. So now she tries each color separately and will no doubt soon find out how to create new tints by just mixing two or three of them. Robert came in very angry this morning. He is seven. I do not know what had annoyed him so, but you can see that the spitting cat he draws and the long claws he has given her with his black charcoal stick really expresses his feelings. And there is Howard. He wants to build a castle for his tin soldiers, so he is going to dig around in our Treasure Boxes for material to implement his plan."

"What treasure?" I was intrigued.

"It's right over there." Plastic bins and cardboard boxes were lined up against a long wall. They were filled with an incredible assortment of scraps, bits of colored paper, corrugated cardboard pieces, spools of wire, all kinds of found objects and even a few shoes and hats. On tables stood jars with sand or shells or little rocks in them next to trays with dishes of paints in muffin tins. Bottles of glue and hammers and nails stood on a shelf against another wall.

"You see," Dorothy swept her arm in a wide circle over all as if to say *this is my world*, "they can use all of these things whenever and in whatever manner they wish. Now, tomorrow morning I am going to scavenge around town to find some more goodies. Do you want to join me?"

The next day found us driving all over Hollywood and parts of Los Angeles. A lumberyard yielded boxes of chips, sawdust and odd-shaped pieces of wood, remnants of various construction jobs. We were given empty, heavy cardboard spools by a knitting shop and bags full of woolen yarn-ends in every color imaginable. A frame shop gave us discarded pieces of picture matting and a number of broken frames.

"Do you really never teach them anything?" We had added our loot to the rest of the bins against the workshop wall and collapsed onto the small, dilapidated sofa, wiping our sweating faces. It had been hot, and we had been on the go all morning.

"Of course I do, but in a very subtle way. I show them how to use their tools, of course, and I teach them to have courage, to believe in themselves, to be curious and enterprising, to express their feelings and go after what interests them. That big bunch of flowers we just bought, I've put it in the middle of the painting table. Some child might fall in love with it and get excited by those wonderful colors. Who knows, maybe we'll have a Bonnard in our midst."

I became Dorothy's apprentice, after a while her paid assistant and very good friend. She gave me books to read, especially one by the philosopher John Dewey who wrote much about education. His book *Art as Experience* that came out in 1934 had influenced her the most. It fascinated me.

Here I quote from an article on Dewey's philosophy. It is short and to the point:

> *The educational process must begin with and build up on the interests of the child; that it must provide opportunity for the interplay of thinking and doing in the child's classroom experience; that the school should be organized as a "miniature community"; that the teacher should be a guide and co-worker with the pupils, rather than a taskmaster assigning a set of fixed lessons and recitations; and that the goal of education is the growth of the child in all aspects of its being.*

In the midst of this I always made sure to keep writing letters to my parents. I wrote a letter to San Francisco on the occasion of Mother's birthday.

April 10, 1945
Dearest Mutti,

> *I am sitting here on the roof of our garage in the most beautiful sunshine you could imagine. I wish I could send you some of its warmth via railway express to San Francisco as a special birthday surprise. Instead: Kisses, love and the best wishes available. Come*

to think of it—in the light of my own egotistic and incredibly happy existence, I thank God that the born Thurston, namely my Oma Hall, gave life to you. Was it 35 years ago? Or 39?

We are making big plans to celebrate you when you come to visit us next. When? I am curious how you like your presents.

Gil and I are very busy as usual, although today and tomorrow I savor my monthly rest days and spend them dutifully by doing absolutely nothing. An ideal state of affairs.

For this evening we got passes to see the show "Blackouts of '45." On Sunday afternoon we will go to the first of two concerts where our friend Henri Temianka is going to play. Works by modern composers for violin and piano will be performed and, believe it or not, each composer will be the pianist for his own work. There will be Stravinsky, Ernst Toch, Korngold and Castelnuovo-Tedesco. Quite an affair.

Last Sunday we heard THE most beautiful concert: Joseph Szigety. If you ever have the chance to hear him play do not miss it. He can put three Heifetz and several Menuhins in his vest pocket. In spite of that, we will consent to listen to Menuhin on the afternoon of my birthday next.

Since we finally filled the piggy bank that Pat had given us and in addition sold an old chest of drawers for $5.00, we were able to add quite a bunch of new records to our collection. Among others a Prokovieff concerto with Szigety, which is fantastic. Do you listen to the Philharmonic and Rodzinsky from New York on the radio? If not, you miss a lot. Every Sunday from 12 to 2, with first class soloists. It belongs to our special Sunday pleasures and usually coincides with our last cup of breakfast coffee.

On Saturday we had the parents Gilbert, Aunt "Big Behind" and Uncle George and another couple for dinner.

I have a new model, a young black man. Gil saw him at a cafeteria and liked his looks so much that he thought that I would like to paint him, so he brought him home to me. His name is Charlie. He is 18 but looks like 16. He speaks with such a strong Southern accent that I am sometimes unable to understand whole sentences. Nevertheless Gil prophesizes that if I listen to him long enough I will develop a Southern accent as well. Charlie's job is dishwashing. At 5 o'clock I drive to pick him up from his work to save time. He sits quietly and follows my progress with great interest. He is terribly shy, but we notice daily that he relaxes more and more. When Gil comes home we all have dinner together and both men compete at who can complement me more about my cooking.

By the way, I have not thanked you yet for the last parcel you sent me. The Crisco container was squashed, but everything else was in good shape. I did not dare to use the roasting pan yet.

Pappi has probably told you that I went to the doctor. I got liver injections to combat anemia and iron pills that I seem to tolerate well. Otherwise the doctor is very satisfied about my health. As a result I have already gained 3 pounds.

Birthday kisses from—whom else?

April 27, 1945
Dear Ones,

I am trying to start this letter since one hour. I pulled a chair out in front of my door to get some fresh air. All of the neighbor ladies have congregated around me and I am being inundated by gossip, recipes and well-meaning, impossible advice about all kinds of things. One of the ladies, Mrs. Marine, "Mrs. Submarine," called by us privately, is very pregnant, ready to burst any minute. She is the youngest and nicest of the whole bunch. We regard her protrusion with mixed feelings though, since she lives right across from us and will probably condemn us to purchase ear stoppers galore in the near future. Another neighbor is Mrs. Hall, but I refuse to research any connection between her and our family tree. Heaven save us! (My mother's maiden name was Hall). And then there is my favorite, Mrs. Tillotsen.

The family Fennichel appeared. They are excited people who use their voices only at crescendo level. To make matters worse, they have a son-in-law who is visiting from San Francisco. He is a cantor who does not seem to do anything else while he is here than to intone and practice to keep his voice limber.

I escaped.

Now I am sitting in my living room feeling cool and refreshed. I have not disassembled my birthday table yet, of course. The presents *from you are still on display and gave me great joy. Mutti, you are amazing. The hat looks very good on me and Gil approves. The jacket is almost too pretty to wear with slacks. I do recognize what a sacrifice it was for you to relinquish the cigarettes since they are so hard to find these days. Even Pop Gilbert with his tobacco stand is not able to get Pall Malls anymore* (War shortages still occurred for many products).

You have already seen the jade pendant that Gil gave me. Gil also gave me a record of Brahms "Lieder," sung by Lotte Lehmann and another with a Bach sonata played by Yehudi and Hephzibah Menuhin. From my parents-in-law I also got records and a cocktail apron. My teacher Mr. Sopher gave me a little piece of sculpture. Since it was Sunday we celebrated thoroughly. We slept late. We had our traditional breakfast: grapefruit, waffles, this time with ham (a luxury), honey, jam, a criminal amount of butter and poisonous, strong coffee.

Afterwards I opened my presents. A beautiful jade pendant from Gil was wrapped in a very small package and was left to the last, because Gil said that it was of small importance. The surprise and pleasure were that much greater. After that we sat around, played our new records and sunned ourselves. We went to another Menuhin concert in the afternoon. Dinner at home and in the evening, a concert at the university, a Beethoven trio and a Faure quartet.

Otherwise I worked a lot last week, especially on Charlie's portrait. Yesterday I finished it. I would also have liked to sculpt a clay model of his head, but he is going to his mother in Stockton. He wrote such a sweet note into our guest book. Next week I'll finish the copy I am making of one of Sopher's pieces and he promised to personally sit and model for me afterwards.

Now I shall start to concentrate on my dinner preparation. Meatloaf. That, by the way, took my last ration stamps, the red ones for meat. Catastrophe! I hope we'll get some from the parents Gilbert. Otherwise we eat vegetables and eggs. If we could get chicken at least . . . We are eating so much fish. We'll develop scales, but at least we do not stink. Kisses, Love.

April 28, 1945
Dearest Ralph and Pat,

My husband is sleeping. We have been out rather late last night. There was a goodbye party for a friend who has been drafted. Pray for us day and night, will you? (Because of his job Gil had not been drafted thus far.) *It is 3 o'clock in the afternoon, beautiful, beautiful weather and everything is joyous and good, at least for us. But when I lift my blinders foolishly enough at breakfast time and open the newspaper or the latest* Time *magazine the world comes crushing in. Commentary superfluous, I guess.*

My dear ones, thanks for the Middle Ages *book. I've wanted to read it for some time. My birthday was awfully nice. You'll have read about it in the parents' letter. So much music, you'll say, heaven forbid! Well, tomorrow we will hear Rubinstein and then make a dash for it and try to hear the last part of the second concert Henry Temianka and his Paganini quartet is giving at the First Congregational Church. Otherwise, I am really working on my painting most continuously when there is good light.*

I have to tell you what our little Charlie wrote into our guest book without having been prepared for it and without hesitation and, as you will see, without punctuation. Charlie, you must know, has been brought up on a farm in Clovis, New Mexico and his encounters with the U. S. education system have been rare and infrequent.

He wrote, "To Mr. and Mrs. I. E. Gilberts—it is and has been more then a pleasure to me being with you all and it have gave me some inspiring ideas in life that I had not seen it would take more then inauguration to tell how much I like being round you all no one has been any nicer to me in my whole life than you.

The doom of me hear I have said
I will always think of you instead.

Yours Truly, Charlie Johnson"

I think you'll appreciate this. We are honestly proud of it. Inauguration, we guess, is supposed to be imagination, but the last two lines still puzzle us no end. Pat, have you met up with anything in your literary excursions that sounds remotely like that?

> *Talking about literature, Pat, your cookbook craze got me. Would you by any chance lend me the* Gastronomical Me *and* Serve It Forth *by M. F. K. Fisher? Return guaranteed. Go to see the new movie,* A Tree Grows In Brooklyn. *We liked it very much. Did you read the book? How did you like our pictures? Now I'll wake my sleeping beauty. I love you both. Long to be with you.*
>
> > *Kisses and a pinch on each one's cheek,*
> > *Fe*

Here I would like to mention a small interlude from that time. We were invited at Hephzibah Menuhin's house. I do not remember how we got there, but someone must have taken us along. A lively group sat around the living room after dinner. There was talk about concerts and musicians and Gil joined in, highly animated as usual when it came to topics that interested him. It so happened that just for a moment there was a lull in the conversation. Only Gil's voice could be heard loud and clear, "For me the greatest violinist of them all is Szigheti."

He had forgotten that he was in the house of Yehudi Menuhin's sister. After a suppressed gasp of shock the general talk resumed, even livelier than before in an effort to eradicate the offending remark. We left the party somewhat early.

At the end of May I stood in Dr. Steinberg's office, gazing up at him and holding my breath.

"Congratulations," he said, "You have started your family." He put his hand on my shoulder and smiled at me. I looked at him and felt that he was some sort of relative of mine, an uncle maybe. At the same time, I could imagine him to be a wise rabbi or a distinguished philosopher with his high forehead, large dark eyes in his long face that was strong and sensitive. He was of average height and certainly far from old.

"Now listen," he said, "For the next three months I want you to be careful. No strenuous exercise, no overtiring. You and my wife have the same problem. You were both born in Germany at a time of great food shortages during World War I and your organs show the effects of it. Your uterus is small and will be asked to carry quite a load in time. If you take care of yourself for the next three months there won't be any problem."

It was a month or so later. The euphoria of having been told of my new status had by no means diminished. Ralph and Pat came to visit from San Francisco at the start of May. One day they asked us to accompany them to the home of Bill Moore. He was a single man living with a male partner, a fact that was carefully hidden and was considered extremely scandalous at that time. He taught art and design at the famous Chouinard Art Institute and was known and feared by his students as an uncompromising taskmaster.

He was very friendly when he greeted us, but just looking at him, at his tall body held erect and at his pale, elongated and rather handsome face that did not seem used to smiling much, one felt that this man was a fortress that was not easily breached.

Moore's home was like a museum. He showed us his collection of African art, marvelously displayed throughout the spacious rooms. There were masks and weavings on the walls, sculptures on tables and shelves. The displays themselves were masterpieces of design. Everything was clean and polished, tasteful and irreproachable. It scared you to touch one of his beautiful tables for fear it might leave a mark.

He took us out to his garden. The sun was warm, the air smelled of spring, a feeling of beginning. The plantings of trees, bushes and the flowerbeds all spoke of the gardener's impeccable taste and care. There was a gazebo on a hill. We started to climb the steep steps that led up to it. We almost reached the top when all of a sudden something warm and moist started to trickle down my legs and quickly turned into a gushing stream of blood.

They laid me down on the delicate little flowers that framed the steps. Someone ran to the house and returned with a towel. They pressed it between my legs and Gil and Ralph carried me to our host's living room and placed me on one of his white leather sofas. I was too horrified to notice, but I am sure our poor host's face turned green and he was close to fainting. More of his luxurious towels were packed around me and a phone call to Dr. Steinberg resulted in my being taken home.

Dr. Steinberg was already there when we arrived and the injection he gave me and his calming voice settled me down. Finally he gave orders in no uncertain terms: The foot end of my bed was to be raised by two feet. I was to lie slanted and flat on my back, head down, and legs up for the next three months to save the baby. After that time it would be safe. He did not think that I lost it.

Lonely, dreary weeks followed. Gil had to be away on his job during the day. He helped me to stuff pillows under my elbows so my arms could hold a book up for awhile. There I lay helpless and alone until dear Mrs. Tillotsen discovered my plight. She recruited several ladies of the court, resulting in regular visits by one or another gray-haired Good Samaritan each day, bringing me lunch, tea in the afternoon, and more or less effective good cheer.

Poor Gil. He worried and tried so hard to make me comfortable. One evening after dinner that consisted mostly of ready-made food from the deli he was sitting next to my bed and read to me. He lowered the book.

"How would you like some tea?" He asked and, "How do I do it?" was his next question.

I knew that cooking had never been a part of his education. "All right," I said, "I'll direct you from here. Go to the kitchen, put water in the pot and wait until it comes to a boil." I heard him fumbling around in the kitchen that was very close to the bedroom in this small place. He came back in and sat down again.

"I did it," he said and picked up his book again.

"It can't take that long. Better check it." No sooner had I spoken than I heard an ominous, high, cracking noise from the kitchen. Gil rushed towards it and returned amazed and horrified with the handle of a dripping, jagged porcelain Chinese teapot, what was left of a beautiful wedding gift. He had put the water to boil in it and set it directly on the open gas flame. Never after that experience was I able to get him into the kitchen.

Finally Pat came from San Francisco and stayed with us for many weeks. I wrote to my parents.

> *May 29, 1945*
> *Dear Ones,*
>
> *I am sure that Ralph has already told you what goes on with me, so there is not much that I can add. I am being pampered by Pat and Gil. The service is excellent. I read from morning to night, yawn, eat, start numerous letters and am most grateful for Pat's company. You should see us right now. Pat is curled up in the big old Biedermeier chair next to my bed where I lie on a slant, legs up,*

> head down. That's how we spend many hours together, reading and talking. A lot of talking, in fact.
>
> The whole Gilbert family is very excited. Gil's brother Paul will be released from the army in Alaska and is due home later this summer. I look forward to meeting him.
>
> How is Putzi getting along? (Putzi was the successor of Bella, the little poodle who had been an important family member and had emigrated with us from Germany, traveled all over Europe and finally decided in San Francisco that she had enough and gave in to old age in spite of all the loving care and Mother's streaming tears.)
>
> Let us hope that things will go all right here and that your grandchild will behave properly. I am very optimistic, but it is always better to be also aware of other possibilities. I feel well, but often very sleepy, which comes from lying around day and night without moving.
>
> *I kiss you,*
Fe

At the end of July I was released from my imprisonment. The baby had taken hold. Now we were faced with looking for a larger house. Children were not allowed where we lived. Finding an affordable rental that would accept a child was a daunting project, especially during these wartime housing shortages. My parents came to the rescue.

At the beginning of August mother called me from San Francisco.

"We are coming down tomorrow. We will buy a house for all of us. Ralph and Pat will follow later." There was not even a hint of a question, such as *would you like us to*? At first Gil and I were somewhat leery. Were we giving up our independence? On the other hand, we did not really know what else to do.

The parents arrived and we sat in our little living room discussing this momentous decision.

"I promise," my mother said, "We will never interfere in your family affairs. You will have complete privacy. We'll look for a house that can be easily divided into separate residences." They stayed at the Rossmore Hotel in Hollywood and went house hunting. They felt that it was a new lease on life for them. They were going to stay together with their children and their future grandchildren. That they were going to lose all of the many friends in San Francisco and that it would not be so easy making new acquaintances in Los Angeles did not occur to them.

Mother especially was often lonely after that and tended to lounge on the settee in her room bemoaning the loss of her creative life in the theater, without making any attempt to find another outlet for her energy or stimulus for her intellect. She read the newspaper every morning, following not only the reports of the Nuremberg trials, which were certainly fascinating, but also decrying every accident and murder that happened on that day in California. We patiently teased her a little about her penchant for catastrophes. I do not know what else she read, but I recall her going on passionately about a book by the philosopher Oswald Spengler, *The Decline of the West*, in which he predicts the rise of the people in the East and grueling wars to come between the different cultures. That was in about 1947 or 50. Would we still belittle her today?

Chapter 2

The Family Enclave at Occidental Boulevard
September 1945 to August 1952

A big house was found at 403 South Occidental Boulevard near La Fayette Park in Los Angeles and purchased on September 11, 1945. The stucco walls were white. A red tile roof extended over the windows of the second story. A wide well-kept lawn pushed the front of the building back from the sidewalk and defended it from gawking people walking by and the traffic noise of the broad boulevard beyond. A small backyard was dominated by a large, gnarled Australian tea tree and flanked by a sturdy two-car garage.

It was decided that the parents would reside downstairs and our family would occupy the second floor. Since the war had ended on August 14th, my brother Ralph was able to leave his job at Bethlehem Steel in San Francisco, where he had worked in order to avoid the draft. Now the garage in the garden at the back of our new home was going to be rebuilt as a studio apartment for Pat and him.

Gil and I moved in during the first days of October. We had to wait until then because one of the two upstairs bathrooms had to be converted into a kitchen for us. A staircase rose up from the lower story and led to quite a spacious area that flowed into a good-sized alcove. The remaining space had doors that opened to three large rooms and one small one. The biggest of these became our living room, another was meant for the eagerly awaited new addition to the family that was due to arrive in two months.

There were built in benches on all three sides of the alcove in the large entrance hall at the top of the stairs. Here we decided was going to be our eating area. It was close to the new kitchen. From a second-hand store we acquired a beautiful dark brown solid walnut table that we placed between the seats. It was nearly eight feet long and extended from the depth of the alcove into the large open space that led to the bedrooms. This area became the hub of our family life, where we took our meals, had friends in for dinner and in the years that followed watched our boys spread their toys, play with little cars and fight for crayons and coloring books.

The parent's huge moving van arrived on the 8th of November 1945 and they commenced to occupy the downstairs. As in all of the houses where they had lived before, they transformed their new home into a colorful and interesting place. Two large rooms extended along the whole depth of the house from the front clear back to the garden. They combined their living room area and Father's library and study by removing two wide glass doors that separated the two rooms. Where the doors had been there were two steps down to the sunken second room where Father's desk stood, looking out into the garden. Every wall was covered with bookshelves up to the ceiling. I still have his indispensable Art Nouveau library steps.

The first room had a round table in the middle that could be extended to seat many guests and was surrounded by red leather armchairs. There were books, ethnic masks and sculptures throughout both rooms and even the hallway. Everything Father coveted and owned was somehow related to performance and the theater. There were pieces from Africa, Indonesia, India and Melanesia. Also American Indian art was represented and works from China and Japan. In between one might find an engraving of a Shakespeare portrait hanging against a bookshelf or a small antique model of a Baroque stage that stood on a table in the hallway. There was an impolite visitor one day who murmured under his breath, "What a clutter."

Father heard him and laughed, "What are rooms and walls for, except to display the things I love."

On the other side of the hallway near the foot of the staircase where the ascent to our domain began, Mother had established her sitting room. Her door was always kept open so that anybody who entered the house or left it would have to parade past her vigilant eye. As promised, she was not "meddling" and she just made perfectly reasonable comments, as she assured us, such as *Where have you been? Where are you going? My, you are home so late. You should really wear a coat. Is THAT what you are going to wear? Aren't you going to comb your hair?*

At that time, happy to have a beautiful home and being basically very fond of my family, we either laughed at or ignored these little encounters. We did not realize that they were only the forerunners of tensions that would grow throughout the following years.

In November, at the same time as my parents, Ralph and Pat left San Francisco to join us. The building of their new quarters in the garden had just begun and promised to take quite some time, so they moved in with Gil and me. After all, we still had plenty of room to spare. The four of us lived together for nearly three months, from the beginning of November until just before Rick was born the following January and their house was completed.

We had a wonderful time together. Never was there a cross word spoken or a misunderstanding between us. We kept house. We cooked and ate together. We were all busy during the day and shared our experiences when we got together at dinnertime. There was much laughing and kidding when the two men tried to out do each other by fishing for the biggest piece of the roast on the platter.

Christmas came, then New Year's Eve and big belly or not I felt wonderful. We had a party at home and I danced with Gil, to my mother-in-law's delight. It prompted her to make the unforgettable pronouncement, "She looks like a proud ship in full sail." Her poetic image was not sustained much beyond that. Two weeks later on January 15, 1946, at 1:35 a.m. according to the official logbook of one Dr. Steinberg at the Cedars of Lebanon Hospital, the ship unloaded its cargo, groaning and heaving mightily for fourteen hours.

"Go home," Dr. Steinberg had put his arms around shaken, white-faced Gil's shoulders, as I was later told. "Go home and rest. It will be hours yet. I'll call you when it's time."

"Here," my good doctor said. He was standing at my bedside as he took the watch off his wrist and gave it to me, "Keep checking the minutes carefully each time the spasms occur and note how long they last." What a great device to distract from utter misery. It helped a little, but not too much.

Poor Gil. I remember that he sat next to me in the delivery room and the pain made me pound him with my fists just before they put the mask on my face and the ether did its work. Next I saw a bundled baby dangling somewhere above my head. Oh, I thought, they show me someone else's baby to give me courage.

"There is your boy," I heard. Gil's face swam into focus. He had just been allowed back into the room. "It's all over," he beamed, "You've done it."

The next day Grandpa Gilbert came to visit at the hospital. I was sitting up in bed. The sheet covered my lap, but it must have been obvious to anybody else that I was sitting on the bedpan, trying to keep my balance, weak as I was. He noticed nothing. He glowed with joy and pride.

"It's a boy!" He shouted, "A boy!"

Even in my feeble and compromised position I found myself bristling, "What would have been wrong with a girl?"

"Oh, a boy is so much better," he crowed. I rang for the nurse, sank back onto my pillow and closed my eyes.

A booming voice roused me from a deep sleep.

"We want breakfast!" A red-cheeked nurse rolled her massive girth towards my bed, my tiny baby held in her arms, sunk into the pillow of her soft and ample bosom. As he was handed down to me his eyes were closed and his lips moved softly up and down like the mouth of a baby carp.

"Well now, let's see *if* we can do it." This cheerful statement promptly introduced the possibility of failure in nursing my child. After trying to coax the milk to flow and to gratify the vigorously sucking child for perhaps fifteen minutes, the nurse's patience was at an end.

"I knew you could not do it. You are much too skinny. Never mind. He'll get the bottle. It's so much simpler anyway." Swooping the baby up without a look at my distraught face, she kicked the door shut behind her.

My husband came flying into the room. "Why have you been crying?" He had been waiting impatiently to get off work and for the evening visiting hours each day of the week so he could see his wife and son. And now my tears burst forth as I answered his question.

All I could do was sob, "What was *wrong*?" I don't know, I don't know". The nurse who brought my dinner tray just shook her head.

"Most of them get weepy after giving birth. It won't last. Try some orange juice, honey." I now know that the feeling of inadequacy caused by the failure in breastfeeding my child was intensified by the depression that sometimes assails young mothers, but in 1946 you were just called hysterical. Gil calmed me in his arms and when we brought our child home a week later the sun shone and a peaceful time awaited us.

We named our son Eric, for the sole reason that the sound of that name aroused in me a feeling of light and clarity. Only much later did it occur to me that sensual reaction to sound could generate a host of feelings and stir the imagination. *Eric and airy*—bright and breathing freely—happy.

My life and time stood still. The rest of the world was on vacation. There was just Gil and I and the little body of our child in my arms. There was the sour smell of upchucked milk, the sweet smell of soft skin and the feel of a moist little face tucked between my shoulder and my cheek, all seeping into my storehouse of remembered sensations, never to be forgotten.

My initial objections had not prevented my dear Mama from hiring a nurse to take care of the baby and me for the first two weeks at home and I must admit that I gratefully and gracefully submitted to being pampered. The elegant silk robe my mother had lovingly supplied for my wedding night and honeymoon and that had been so impatiently tossed aside now finally found a worthwhile place in the annals of our family's history as symbol of luxury and first-time motherhood. A lady photographer came to the house and I still share her pictures with my grandchildren. They can see Gil gazing proudly at his son and his wife's young face. Her long dark hair flows down the white robe and Ricky peers across her shoulder, clutching her tightly like a baby monkey.

Ralph and Pat had moved into their new home in the meantime, with their books, art collection and various cats. Their second-hand bright red VW bug stood in the driveway. They had been in quite a quandary since the war ended and Ralph left his job at the Bethlehem Steel shipyard. What could they do now? Sadly, a family with children was not to be for them; they had been told that a pregnancy would be very dangerous for Pat since she had a kidney removed several years before. One thing was clear, they did not want to be apart most of every day for the rest of their lives. How could they make a living without working at separate jobs?

Finally the solution occurred to them: A store. They could work in a store together. They both loved antiques. They were going to sell fine old furniture and perhaps also some art on the side. It was settled.

How they were able to pay the initial expense of setting up their business I do not know. I suspect there was help from both sets of parents. Right after the New Year they went on a buying trip.

A day after baby Rick and I came home from the hospital Gil and I received their letter from Boston. It was funny, silly and very sweet.

January 17, 1946
My very beloved children,

You can't imagine how happy and proud our new aunt—and uncle-dom makes us—although it would be most difficult for me to decide whether the proud uncle or the relieved brother has preponderance in my soul this minute. We are inexpressibly happy in any case and wish both of you all the best in the world with and for "him. We received the long-desired wire only this morning. We celebrated—unknowingly, I admit, but enthusiastically—his birthday in Boston's Museum of Fine Arts, a circumstance which influences my wishes for him—as it will influence his life no doubt: I safely substitute "he will" for "may he," therefore. Well, here it goes:

He will be: as tough as a net-like ceremonial gown of an Egyptian 3-D Dynasty priest, but

He will be: as delicate and fine as Indian and Persian miniature paintings

He will be: of a peacefully strong mind as some magnificent Khmer Buddha's.

He will be: as glowing with life as Rubens' "Head of Cyrus Brought to Queen Tamyris".

He will be: as colorful and radiant as Renoir's very best painting, "Le Bal a Bougival" (No reproduction could show you what I mean in either of these astonishing paintings.)

He will be: as ageless as the unique Minoan Snake-goddess of ivory and gold who looks as if made yesterday.

He will be: as desired as American Colonial furniture at this time, but

He will be: as desirable as a divine gold bowl from the Greek island of Chios and

He will be: as fertile as the Tanagra figures—within reason of course, because:

He will find a wife as nice as either his grandmother or mother or aunt.

We miss you terribly and wait impatiently for details about you all.

Kisses from Ralph and Pat.

Two months passed and I started to take care of household and baby, fixing formula to feed my hungry offspring. I walked the floor with him trying to calm his frequent howls and protestations to various disturbances in his budding life. Exhaustion started to creep in from time to time, but tended to be forgotten when Gil and I, the proudest parents ever, gazed at our boy. He actually seemed to look at us and know us and practically produced a ghost of a little smile. The insensitive clod who mentioned that that kind of smile just signified the rumbling of a bit of gas in a baby's bowels was disdainfully ignored. The presence of our child marked a high point in our lives. It was a wonderful time.

"You need relief." Gil studied my tired face. "I have an idea. We can't afford full-time help, but what would you think about trying to find a woman who would assist you part time in exchange for room and board? We have two extra bedrooms. You set one of them up as your studio and let her have the smaller one."

The ad in the local paper brought immediate success and the first of many ladies that joined our household throughout the coming years presented herself. She was an elderly, very tall and gaunt African American lady. Her name was Vallena, which prompted Gil, whose specialty it was to play with people's names, to christen her Vanilla, of course not within her hearing range. We tried hard to befriend her. She was angry when she came and remained angry all the time, no matter what we did. Vanilla was no joy to have around and when she dropped Ricky near the staircase one day we parted company.

Next came Mrs. Kreidler and she was a delight. She was a widow in her early sixties, a nurse by profession who worked the nightshift at a hospital. She was kind and helpful and we loved her. She stayed with us for a long time until she retired and moved away.

When I had fully regained my strength and new baby and household had settled down, I followed Gil's prodding and enrolled at the Chouinard Art Institute for several hours per week. I took drawing and painting classes with Herb Jepson and Millie Rocque. I celebrated by painting an array of period furniture and art objects whirling madly about on a large sheet of paper that we hung across the display window of Ralph and Pat's new store. It proclaimed the opening of *Altman Antiques* on La Cienega Boulevard in Beverly Hills at the end of 1946.

The store developed and its owner's reputation grew from year to year. Actors from the Hollywood film community discovered the unusual and varied collections of interesting objects. Soon Ralph found that the African mask or the Melanesian warrior's shield that he had hung among the furniture attracted much more attention then the Renaissance chest or the set of Victorian chairs. It did not take long before *Altman Antiques*, specializing in ethnic arts, became famous and Ralph and Pat held court on La Cienega Boulevard for nearly twenty years. They eventually sold to museums not only in the states, but also in Europe and other countries overseas.

In the middle of August 1947 I discovered that I was pregnant again. I felt well and vigorous and continued to study at Chouinard, work at Sopher's studio twice a week and watch baby Ricky develop into a happy, boisterous little boy.

My rather limited experience in housekeeping and cooking did not keep me from hosting dinner guests at the long table in our upstairs hallway. One evening we gathered the actor Vincent Price and the Italian painter Rico Lebrun, along with Ralph and Pat and two or three other people for a meal at our house. Everyone was in a great mood and little two-year-old Ricky crawled under the table investigating everybody's shoes. Tall Vincent, the sinister ogre of horror movies, who was a very handsome, sweet and gentle man in reality, was delighted with him and got down on hands and knees trying to win the child's trust and to coax him to play. He rolled on the floor, pushed a little car around and pretended to have a conversation with a teddy bear. But nothing worked. Ricky would not have any of him. Rico turned around in his seat and looked down on the now scowling toddler.

"Eh, bambino, come stai?" he stretched his hand out to him and smiled. It only took two seconds and Ricky ran to him, climbed on his lap and put his arms around his neck. Poor Vincent was devastated.

Still today I am amazed at my youthful temerity that allowed me to serve a big dish of Italian lasagna that same evening to the Neapolitan, Rico, who was known to be an excellent cook. Nevertheless, let it be said that it was a big success and declared *"Molto bene."*

Later, when Ricky was almost three, I had to prepare a dinner that took more courage, because it involved hosting Gil's boss, the head of the advertising agency he worked for at that time, a very stern and humorless gentleman. I had also met his wife on one occasion and found her to be cold as ice and barely civil.

I had prepared most of the food the day before the event and was quite proud of that organizational accomplishment. All I had to do when I came home from my drawing class at Chouinard was to shove the meat in the oven, reheat the stuffed potatoes and wash the salad greens. The guests were due at seven.

I dashed home at 5:30. I had forgotten that the sink was still full of dirty dishes from the day before. So much for my organizational skills . . . In haste I turned the hot water on full blast. The sink filled and muck rose and rose from the drain and spilled to the kitchen floor. If ever there were a chance of submitting to panic in my life that could have been the moment. In several trips to the bathroom I loaded the dishes into the tub, rinsed them, probably not too well, and washed the kitchen floor. It was by now quite close to seven, with just barely time enough to tend to the food. No chance to change clothes. Seven o'clock, the doorbell rang and there they were with politely smiling Gil in tow. I hated them. Why couldn't they be late like perfectly decent people could be sometimes? I sweated and I smiled and they smiled also, but their smiles sat so shallow on their faces that I thought a quick flick with a handkerchief could remove them immediately.

The evening was pure torture and boredom for me. First of all, they picked at their food, which was really quite good. The conversation consisted of business talk and never-ending discussions about baseball and cars. A few racist remarks were dropped here and there that made my blood curdle. Gil shot a warning glance in my direction from time to time and I obediently bit my tongue. The only bright moment of the whole evening came when we were sitting in the living room after dinner and unexpectedly three-year-old Ricky had climbed out of his crib and came scampering in. He headed right up to the dignified gentleman, looked at him intently and asked, "Would you like to see a tiger make pee pee?" By God, neither the man nor his lady fainted. For the first time they became almost human. They actually laughed, played with the little guy and his toy tiger and the visit ended fairly well.

At least once a month Gil and I and Ralph and Pat gathered maybe six or eight of our friends for an evening out. We piled into our cars and drove to a most uninviting section of downtown Los Angeles. The streets were bleak, the gutters full of debris. Hungry cats were slinking about. There was a gas station and a few dimly lit bars competed for attention with the red neon bulbs that illuminated two Chinese restaurants that sat next to each other. Our destination was Man Fook Low, the bigger of the two.

"Ah, yes, yes," our friend and favorite waiter, Paul, came rushing out from behind the bar, tucking a towel into his apron pocket, his round and shining face suffused with pleasure. I believe Paul was actually the owner of the restaurant. He would never permit any of the other two waiters to serve us. We were the honored guests and his alone. Seating us at one of the large round tables, he immediately stifled any attempt on our part to look at the menu or voice a preference for a certain dish by raising both his hands in the air and protesting, "No, no! I choose. I make fine meal for you. You'll see."

And we trusted him completely. We had to wait quite a long time, but it always turned out to be a culinary masterpiece. Dish after dish of delectable surprises was brought to the table and circulated among us, stopping any conversation while we savored what was before us with absolute concentration. At last happily satiated, drinking Jasmine tea, nibbling on little kumquats and breaking our fortune cookies to extract the slips of wisdom within, we were able to socialize again and had a wonderful time.

On one of these evenings Rico Lebrun, Vincent Price and Howard Warshaw joined us. With great ceremony Paul led two of his waiters parading through the restaurant to our table. They carried a platter between them that held a huge steamed fish that was maybe three feet long. It was beautifully decorated with mushrooms and fresh herbs and other goodies. I will never forget the way Rico's face lit up with surprise and pleasure. He stood up, rolled his sleeves above his elbows.

Nobody could have prevented him from serving the fish by artfully separating the flesh from the bones and laying portions on our plates with solemn reverence. Rico was a great cook, so we all understood that his gesture bestowed the supreme order of culinary excellence upon Man Fook Low.

One day a letter arrived that jarred us in all our rich and comfortable lives. It came from war-torn East Berlin and was written by mother's former brother-in-law. Albrecht Berger was a young opera singer when he married Mother's older sister Florence, who died in childbirth after just one year of happy married life. Eventually Albrecht married again, this time to a rather unattractive, small-minded lady whose name was Gertrude. Albrecht remained devoted to my mother and when I was small Uncle Albrecht was a regular visitor to our home at Christmas and family birthdays. Knowing about the food shortages in Germany after the war mother mailed supplemental packages to Albrecht in Berlin from time to time.

> *Berlin-Steglitz, November 16, 1947*
> *My Dear Alice,*
>
> One of the two packages has arrived already, the one that had the lard in it. Oh, is that good! Hardly ever can one find fat here! It is not available with food stamps, only on the black market at incredible prices.
> We just received notice that the second package arrived. Gertrude let me pick it up, but not share in it, since it is addressed to her. Oh well!
> We are always so tremendously happy when mail comes from you! You cannot imagine how much it helps us and how much we need it. For example, I took my coat to the tailor to have the collar turned and the cuffs stitched up so I can wear it some more. He asked, "Did you bring thread and yarn?" I looked at him askance. "Well," he said, "I don't have any."
> So it is with everything. If we did not have friends to help us with medicine for Gertrude, the poor thing would suffer even more with her arthritis. On Friday and Saturday I stopped at ten

pharmacies to find some aspirin for her. No luck. Almost all of the chemical factories that are still in operation are in West Berlin.

The other day I needed paper for my manuscript and got one sheet, the last one in the store. For months I have been hunting for light bulbs. There are none to be had. On top of it, we have constant electrical outages. Last Friday I gave a lecture and the minute I started the lights went out. By candlelight I deciphered my handwriting. It went all right, since I had prepared well. A discussion of an hour and a half followed. Afterwards I was exhausted, but happy. I felt a little more alive.

What was formerly self-evident seems like a stroke of luck now. One becomes strong when there is no way out and the seemingly impossible sometimes turns to reality. If someone had asked me years ago to pull a little wagon and walk for over an hour to fetch one or two zentner of coal and drag it for at least another hour on the way back home, I would have thought he was insane. Today? Albrecht does not squawk and is grateful that he is allowed to do it and--is able to do it. The last words should be written in capital letters! You should have seen me in 1945 when I had to lug bomb debris, sweep the streets and give a talk on Babel and the Bible at night. (Albrecht was a Gentile German, not Jewish. Babel was a Russian writer who died in exile in Siberia in 1941.)

I am quite a sight today, when I can be seen lugging ashes, coal or potatoes down or up the stairs, wearing a big, old blue apron over my worn out suit and a dust cap on my head. I then trot from one store to another, market basket on my arm, trying to buy bread and vegetables and carrying the milk pail in addition. One hour after returning home I emerge, cleaned up, almost a dignified gentleman. The same transformation every day! That's just how it is! One gets used to anything. I hardly ever get to concerts or the theatre, not even to a movie. Four or five times a week I am busy at my lodge, either in the afternoon or the evening. The other day I gave a very successful speech.

Why don't you send us a little of your warm weather, please. We could use it well. Daily heating is not possible; we do not receive that much coal. I can't use my desk. My office is too cold, so I often tuck my work under my arm and go to a friend's house and do it there for *a few hours. Gertrude is doing her best to prepare for my birthday and visitors. Oh, well! I guess one only gets to be seventy-five once. So enough for today. I have been on the go since early morning and now it is after midnight. I'd love to tell you much more, but--the censorship!*

A thousand greetings to all. For you a kiss.

Your faithful and devoted
Albrecht

Of course we where very moved and shaken by this letter, a message from the world my family and I had left. I do not think that it is ever possible to divorce oneself completely from the threats and horrors one has escaped and from the country where one grew up. It was such a potent reminder of not only the life we had escaped, but of unpredictability itself and of the turmoil of nature and human existence throughout the world. We witnessed horror and upheaval while others lived in calm and peace. And then the pendulum swung back and our own lives were peaceful while much of the world lived in need and danger.

I wrote to San Francisco, where Father had gone to have minor surgery.

Occidental Boulevard, April 15, 1948
Dear Ones,

Everybody, including the born and the unborn, is doing well. I saw Dr. Steinberg again and he is extremely pleased with me. You'll have your second grandchild soon. Ricky loved his postcard and ate it immediately. He is peaceful and happy.

You asked what I want for my birthday. A fascinating book came out last year, The Diary of Ann Frank, *written by a Jewish girl who died in a concentration camp. Also there is a new book on childcare by a Dr. Spock that is supposed to be excellent and very up to date. Just right for us now.*

By the way, the news about the incidents of polio here is becoming more and more disturbing. They are really calling it an epidemic now. I know it's been around for several years but not

> as virulent as now. The hospitals are running out of beds and the shortage of nurses is severe. They are now shipping them in from other parts of the country to cover the emergency here. The public swimming pools are all closed to prevent the spread of infections. I am glad that Ricky is still too small to go to school. Children seem to be the main victims.
>
> Ethel Garey gave birth to her child, a healthy eight-pound boy. Thank God! What a relief after the terrible disappointment with their last child. On Sunday we have to go to the circumcision. I won't like that. I will get lost in some other room at the proper time.
>
> Your grandson is shaking his crib to pieces. That means I have to stop. He is screaming with laughter.

According to all private and medical calculations my second child was to be born in the middle of April 1948. It was big and lively inside and bounced around mightily, but seemed to be perfectly happy and comfortable where he or she was. The date for the arrival came and he showed no intention of making his appearance. One week passed and then another.

"Well," said Dr. Steinberg, "Let's try a little persuasion." I was presented with a horrible full glass of castor oil. There was a result, but no baby. Strenuous walks, exercises, nothing worked. Another two weeks passed. On May 17 my dear doctor informed me, "My patience is at an end. That child is getting too big. I reserved the operating room for tomorrow. We'll just go and get it." That meant a caesarian section. That scared me and I decided to knuckle under, and so started labor on the morning of May 18, 1948. I gave birth towards evening. Here now was Ralph, named after my beloved brother, strong, kicking and ready to face the world.

He was an unusually sturdy child. "Look, look how strong he is!" It was Gil's great pleasure to show how his tiny son would clamp his little hands onto both of his papa's thumbs, hang on tight and get lifted into the air squealing with delight.

CHAPTER 3

A Pleasant Evening and a Nasty Headache

It happened three and a half months later on a hot evening in early August 1948. The air was perfectly still. Even the little garlands of lights that were strung up from tree to tree above our heads did not move.

"Oh these miserable beasts!" Elizabeth had just lit another cigarette and blew the smoke towards a mosquito that was about to land on her bare arm. "You do not know the nasty diseases these things carry."

That we lived during a big polio epidemic did not really occupy our minds on that pleasant evening. My friend was visiting from New York and we were sitting in the garden of a restaurant on Melrose Avenue in Los Angeles. She had finally obtained her medical degree and was planning to go into psychiatry. We were celebrating getting together again after almost four years since I left New York. I still remembered our farewell at Grand Central Station.

"How is our Dr. O?" I asked.

Elisabeth laughed. "*Our* Dr. O? You are almost right! He sure loved you. Maybe I should be glad you left." She reached for my hand across the table. "You know that I'm kidding, right? Sam and I are still together. Now here you are, a handsome husband and two little kids. Life is good?"

I nodded, "Very, except I wish we would have a place of our own. Living with my mother is not without problems. Let's not get into that minefield now. Let's be peaceful."

Gil was away on one of his frequent business trips and my parents watched the boys, who were asleep in their cribs. What a rare chance to get out of the house and enjoy a quiet meal with a friend.

Another glass of wine. We talked and reminisced about my nice shabby studio on Fifteenth Street and the parties we had where people had to sit on the floor when the only couch and the one lonely chair were occupied.

"I hope you shipped all of your paintings home when you knew that you were not coming back. I looked but saw none in your house." Elisabeth was horrified when I shook my head.

"Look, I'll do much better work now. No, I have not had time to paint much for the last few years, but as soon as the boys are in nursery school . . ." I had to admit that Ricky was only two and a half years old and Ralph three and a half months old. The great masterpieces I would produce had to wait awhile before they came to fruition.

A little headache started to creep up on me. "I guess it's time to go home,' I said. "The wine seems to be getting to me a bit, or maybe it's the heat." I only had two small glasses, yet I rolled all of the car windows down. The pain grew. It crept up from the back my neck to the top of my head and lay there, pressing down like a sheet of iron. Why did it feel so strange driving home through the dark streets that I knew so well? Everything seemed to be eerily alive, filmed in slow motion. Oncoming cars crawled menacingly towards me with blurry, colored headlights that shimmered like rainbows. The pavement moved in gentle undulation and the buildings on either side swayed slowly back and forth, their lighted windows bending down on me like piercing flashlights searching the dark.

"Why are you driving so slowly?" I heard Elisabeth, but could not answer. I don't recall how we got home. I awoke in my bed the next morning. Something was moving around on top of my chest. Swimming in front of me I saw a little face, its wide eyes gazing down at me almost touching my nose.

"Ricky, how did you get in here?" I heard someone exclaim and the lump on my chest was gone. I became aware of Elisabeth standing next to my bed. "You are making yourself sick because you hate your mother. The sooner you realize that the better it will be. Come on now, get up." She helped me to a sitting position and immediately a strong stream of vomit shot like a projectile into the room.

I sank back and the next sensation I remember was the bumping and swishing of wheels under me as I was being rolled along a hospital corridor. Passing the open door of a waiting room I thought I saw Pappi through a swirling and shifting gray haze. I tried to wave but could not lift my arm. And then bright lights came pouring down on me and I felt pressed against the top of a cold, hard steel table. Two men were there, their jackets white, their faces just a blur.

"Don't move, Miss. We are taking fluid from your spine." They bent me sidewise, crescent fashion, and someone lay on top of me pinning my head and arms down with one of his arms and my knees with the other. A searing pain bored into my lower back.

I must have blacked out, for next I found myself lying on the floor on a mattress, one in a long procession of people on mattresses like mine lining the walls of a hospital corridor. I gazed up to a high gray ceiling that seemed to undulate like a gently moving sheet on a washing line. A constant parade of hurrying legs passed by my face, white shoes and whiter pants and nurse's skirts came flying by, a dizzying procession.

I lay there for a long, long time. It seemed that it was night, then day and night again, until they found a bed for me. And this bed was not much softer than the floor. It had a thick board of plywood that rested directly on top of the springs and was covered by a skinny one-inch thick mattress. There was one tiny sheet that covered the mattress from my head to my waist From the waist down I lay on a rough horse blanket and was then covered by another scratchy blanket, without sheets and without a pillow.

"You must press the soles of your feet flat against there at all times," said the nurse who bedded me down and pointed to a small board that was propped vertically at the foot of the bed. "If you don't, you'll get drop-feet. Now, that's all I have for you, Honey. At least we found you a bed. We've run out of everything, pillows, sheets and blankets and more people are coming in. Where will we put them?" She shook her head and raised her arms as if in prayer and shuffled out as fast as her tired feet allowed.

Then two more white coats assembled around my bed. I felt myself lifted up and my head dropped helplessly backwards like an apple falling from a tree, quickly caught by two supporting hands. It was in the heat of August and still they wrapped a steaming hot, wet blanket around my body up to my chin. Then they left me there, a helpless mummy. Perspiration was streaming down my face.

This procedure was repeated four times a day, the only way they had to relieve the pain and, as they thought, to keep the muscles from stiffening. There was no medication.

Water, please. I am thirsty, I tried to call, but no sound came out of my mouth. I had no voice. I tried to turn my head. It would not move. There was no nurse. I was abandoned in utter misery.

Night came. The lights were lowered, but the noises of suffering in the ward had not abated. I could not sleep. I drifted in and out of consciousness. Pain was flooding through the room, the walls, the ceiling, over everything. Pain suffused my head, back and limbs in wavelike succession. I could not move my left arm and there was a syringe tied to the crook of the other one. A feeding tube gurgled and dripped above my head.

Rattling moans from someone's throat close to my ear bored into me as if they were my own. Was she dying? Was nobody there to help? I heard children scream in terror and pain. Little ones like Ricky cried, *Mummy, Mummy* all night long and I ached all over for wanting to go to them and pick them up. That ache was almost worse than the pain in my limbs. I could not even pick up my own head.

Several days passed and a nurse held a spoon of Jello to my lips. "Let's see if you can swallow this," she said and made encouraging little smacks with her lips. I sucked and it went down my throat. It was cool and sweet but felt heavy once it landed. Two spoons were all I could get down.

"All right, we are ready for the next ward. You'll feel better there, you'll see." She patted my hand and winked at me with one eye. The first friendly human contact and I started to weep.

Another ward, another bed in a long row of beds alongside mine and across the aisle as far as I could see. At least my eyes could move, although my sight was blurred and there seemed to be two of everything around me. I blinked, I stared, but nothing changed. At least my right arm was liberated from the feeding tube and, lo and behold, I could move it. I could wipe a tear from my face. And then I discovered something else: I could not feel the touch of my fingers on the left side of my face. It was stiff as a board and the corner of my mouth seemed to be sagging. I tried to move my legs. The right one felt normal, but the left just lay there like a piece of wood.

It was quieter in this ward. People were still very ill but there was no screaming, no panic, there were no children. Some groaned, some whimpered and many just lay there in quiet desperation. I fell into a deep sleep.

Being handled and unwrapped from a wet blanket woke me up and I found myself surrounded by several people whose faces and eyes gazed down on me with obvious curiosity. There were maybe five or six of them, all young except for one tall, bearded old man with glittering glasses who seemed to lecture them. They all wore white jackets, had pads of paper tightly held with anxious fingers and took notes.

"This is the interesting case I told you about," old Greybeard said and then turned to me. "Now, young lady, will you please wrinkle your forehead for me? OK, now squint your eyes. Wrinkle your nose. Follow my finger with your eyes. How well can you read these letters?" He held a printed page up for me to read, but all the letters showed in double images, overlapping and unreadable.

"See what I mean?" he turned to his audience, waved them on and they all left. There was not a word of explanation in my direction, not even a *thank you* or *good by*. The next morning old Graybeard came again. This time new faces surrounded him. "Wrinkle your forehead, squint your eyes." I felt like a circus dog. Another performance was held in the afternoon with another audience. When they showed up again the next morning I went on strike. I simply closed my eyes and did not budge.

There were always one or two nurses running around the large ward trying their best in utmost haste to tend to the needs of their many patients. They were never able to fully accomplish the tasks satisfactorily because of ever increasing demands on their time.

"There should be at least six of us here," sighed the young woman relieving me of my wet, itchy wrap. She tried to dry me with a piece of cotton that was obviously torn off an old bed sheet. "Now they even ran out of decent towels. Do you know that patients are still lined up on mattresses along the corridors down below? Some will be shipped off to Corona Naval Hospital tomorrow. They opened a whole floor there to our people. County is just overflowing. Did you get something to eat yet?"

I produced a croaking sound that was meant to say *no, I did not want anything*. The thought of food was unappealing and swallowing was an effort.

I had barely opened my eyes the next morning and there stood a gurney next to my bed. "You are going on a trip to Corona Naval Hospital,

Miss. Takes about one hour to drive down the coast. You'll be nice and comfy," an orderly announced cheerfully and wheeled me into an elevator and then out of doors. The sudden light hurt my eyes. There stood an ambulance and I was slid onto the top bunk with my stretcher like a loaf of bread into the oven. And it was as hot as an oven. I tried to push the blanket off my chest, but I was so tightly strapped down that even my good arm could not function. Of course I could not ask for help.

"We can't quite leave yet, miss. There'll be another passenger. You'll be riding with young mister Roosevelt, our president's son." The man's voice calling up to me from below sounded very proud and also seemed to admonish me to realize what an honor it was for me to be allowed to ride in the same car with such an illustrious personage. He probably had no idea how little that meant in my present wretched state. I surmised that the young man who was deposited in due time on the bunk below mine also had interest only in his aches and pains and couldn't give a hoot about his father's fame. When we arrived he was unloaded first. I never saw his face.

Oh what a different world I entered. There was a soft bed with sheets, pillows and a light summer blanket and a smaller room with fewer beds and sunlight coming through tall windows.

"You'll be here for two more weeks then you'll go to the big ward when you are not contagious any more." The elderly woman smiled down on me and smoothed the blanket. Light grey curly hair escaped the confines of her nurse's cap and framed the dark brown skin of her forehead. "You'll feel better soon," she said, and I croaked a little something, almost wanting to say *Yes, Mommy*. From her I felt love and concern, the best medicine in the world.

It was heavenly quiet in this room. We were allowed to sleep and rest without the constant noise and atmosphere of desperation. I started to eat a little, but the kitchen was obviously used to sailor's appetites. Hotcakes and sausages, omelets and bacon for breakfast did not go down well for me. I yearned for a piece of plain toast. But there was coffee and fruit juice six times a day and chicken on Sundays, as I later wrote to my parents.

We had a doctor whose name was Dr. Gutekunst, which in German means *good art*. I do not recall what he looked like, but I know that he was young, energetic and very kind and he did his name proud. I remember one of my darkest days of desperation in the first weeks in Corona. He stood at my bedside looking down at me.

"I have to get well!" I managed to whisper, "I have two small kids at home."

"You will," he patted my hand, "I know you have the will power. You'll make it." The same Dr. Gutekunst once allowed Gil to slip into the ward. It was late one evening when many patients were already asleep and most nurses were having their supper. Unannounced, a tall figure tied into a surgical gown and wearing a face mask hiding a broad nose and cheek bones appeared next to my bed.

It was the first time that we had seen each other since they took me from our house. He had been away on business in Texas at the time and when he was summoned home I was already at County Hospital and he was not allowed to see me. So now, weeks later with his famous powers of persuasion he had managed to reach my good doctor and was able to sneak in against all rules and regulations.

"We have ten minutes," he whispered. We talked of the boys. Baby Ralph's chances of progress, that was uppermost in our minds. I had not been told until very recently that he too had been diagnosed with polio at the same time I had. Thank God they kept him at home in our quarantined house. He would have perished at the hospital. Ricky, we thought, was safe and happy at Gil's parents house, out of harm's way. Ten minutes felt like ten seconds.

"I am not allowed to touch you," Gil said and tears were glinting in his eyes.

"Time is up, the nurses will be back." Dr. Gutekunst's hand was on his arm. Only with our eyes were we able to say good-by. He slowly turned away and I looked after him as long as I could.

It was a few nights after my arrival at Corona. I awoke from a deep sleep and realized that I needed to use the bedpan. I had not yet noticed the bell that hung right next to my head. How could I call for help? I looked up and down the long row of beds and the sleeping bodies in their white sheets all around me. A few small nightlights illuminated the large room leading towards a tiny, brightly lit cubicle at one end of it. There I knew two nurses sat, chatting happily away and probably sharing confidences and a cup of coffee.

How could I call them? Make my needs known? I still had no voice beyond a whisper. Carefully I supported my almost useless, paralyzed head with my hand until I was able to sit up and slowly lower my feet to the floor. I knew on which wall the closest bathroom was to be found and tried to gingerly head towards it. To my distress I found myself landing on the opposite wall, careening against it and crumbling up in a heap on the floor. Another patient must have noticed me and rang her bell. I was returned to bed, relieved but also very confused and upset. My whole world was out of balance. Right was left and left was right and the floor tilted up to the ceiling.

Another night for some reason my bedside bell was not answered. I had not been able to sleep and became aware of strange noises from one of the beds along a row on the opposite side. I knew that the young woman there had a tube in an incision in her throat. A growling, rattling sound welled out from the direction of her bed. I rang. I guessed the nurses laughed too loudly to hear. In desperation I grabbed the full glass of water that stood on my bedside table and threw it as far as I could out onto the middle of the floor. It shattered with the conviction of its mission and brought an immediate result. It turned out that the woman's tube had gotten dislodged and brought her dangerously close to asphyxiation.

Slowly, slowly I improved. My eyes started to focus again and I could read for half an hour at a time without tiring. From sitting on a regular chair next to my bed for a short while I graduated to a wheelchair that allowed me to roll myself around on the ward and pay visits to the beds of other patients. We played checkers, wrote letters home for those who could not hold a pen and talked about our families and what the future might bring for us. One young woman with a thick blond braid slung over her shoulder was only twenty-one. She already had three small children at home and no husband. With useless legs how would she manage later on? The fifty three year old woman next to my bed had painful spasms several times a day. I never saw her sit up during the time that I was there.

It was a happy day towards the end of September when some of us were able to wheel ourselves onto an elevator and down to a big cement yard, breathing fresh air and lifting our faces to the sun. We felt giddy and attempted to stage little races. Luckily nobody's chair tipped over and all that happened was that we were exhausted after a short time and glad to get back to bed.

Chapter 4

Recovery and Back to Art

By the beginning of November I was back at home. Gil carried me into the house like a new bride in the movies. Promptly I was put to bed again, against my protestations.

"No, first I want to see the baby. Where is Ralphy?"

His pale small face looked up at me from the bundle of blankets they put into my arms. He was now nearly 6 months old.

Gil looked over my shoulder, wrapped his arms around the two of us and said quietly: "Do you know what the first thing I did was when I returned from Texas? I dashed upstairs to the nursery and bent over the crib. By God, I think he recognized me. There was a weak little smile and I breathed a big sigh of relief. *You'll make it*, I told him."

The baby's face started to pucker up. We knew that he was crying but no sound could be heard. He had no voice.

"That's enough. It's time to rest." A command came booming down on our heads and there she stood before me, Nurse Bowman, tall, voluminous, white-uniformed and absolutely invincible. We were her charges, baby Ralph and I, and there was no escape. Even Mother obeyed her, occasionally.

When the diagnosis of polio had been confirmed for me as well as for my three-and a half-month-old baby we decided to keep Ralph at home and nurse Bowman moved in to begin her reign. "If you send him to the hospital he'll die. He won't get the proper care." Our Dr. Abraham's warning was heeded and the whole household was officially under quarantine. Nobody was allowed to leave or to enter. The only exception was granted to my father. He was allowed to go to the market once or twice a week, but nowhere else. How my dear impractical father managed that is a mystery to me. We had no car at that time, so he must have walked and carried his bundles.

Three-year-old Ricky was sent to Gil's parents on the day I was taken to the hospital. It was a miracle that he had escaped infection in spite of having been so close to me on the morning of the outbreak of my illness. He had climbed onto my chest and pushed his face close to mine. The nearly four months he spent with his strict and insensitive Granny Gilbert proved to be traumatic ones, experiences that he has remembered ever since. She spanked him when he wet his bed, which was frequently, of course; he had so suddenly been shoved out of his home without understanding the reason. He could not easily fall asleep at night, so Granny gave him big pieces of sugary Halvah when she tucked him in, hoping to calm him down. This of course had the opposite effect. More scolding did not help. The sugar pepped him up and sleep was delayed even further.

These are Rick's recollections of that time as he recounted to me not long ago.

"Grandpa was sweet and gentle, he sometimes read to me but he never attempted to save me from Granny's ire. I suppose years of strife with her made him so tired he did not want to battle anymore. I can still see myself trotting behind her on the way to the market. I must have been about four years old by then. She walked fast and my small legs had trouble keeping up. It never occurred to her to take my hand. She did acknowledge my presence though by talking about me, even to strangers in the street and then to old cronies at the market. 'Oy vey, what a bandit this is. He is bad, a very bad boy,' she would complain to one and all. 'He wets his bed. He never obeys his grandma. May the Lord strike me dead, this is a bad boy!' And then a litany of all of my misdeeds was reeled off while I stood there looking up at all these big people staring at me in disapproval. Why was I a bad boy? I was completely bewildered.

There were children in the neighborhood. They were black. 'They are too rough', she said, and would not let me play with them."

In defense of Granny, most of her neighbors were black and she told us frequently what good friends she had made among them and how nice they were to her. I believe she meant that Ricky was too small to play with older kids.

Here is Rick again.

I was lonely. The unused garage in the backyard was one of my retreats. There were tools hanging on the walls, my favorite playthings. I found a small hammer and hammered nails into pieces of wood and anything else that would accept them.

The cement incinerator in the drab back yard became a castle. I climbed on top of it, surveying the neighboring yards, houses and streets and felt like I governed all. When Granny discovered me there I was scolded, of course, and told to stay away from my domain. But since she rarely watched what I was doing outside, I promptly returned to my perch.

The highlights in my memories of those days belong to the visits by my uncle Paul. He came often, not to see his parents, but just to visit me. Being Granny's middle son and having endured much hardship from her in his youth, he did not harbor any love for her. He brought me toys and once a little box with child-sized tools that I treasured and never forgot. He often put me on his shoulders and walked the neighborhood with me. It was a higher perch then my incinerator and felt wonderful."

Poor Ricky. When he came home there was Nurse Bowman of the iron hand. After a jubilant reception by the whole family, tearful hugs and kisses by his still bedridden mom, there came a whole roster of new rules and restrictions. He was not to be noisy and wake the baby. The baby, the baby, the baby . . . Everybody cared about the baby. He got to see me at certain times but not as often as he wanted to. They stopped him from busting into my room and jumping onto the bed whenever he had an overwhelming need to see me. A bolt was fastened to the outside of my door, high enough so he could not reach it. Of course being an enterprising and determined fellow he pulled a heavy chair to the door, added some books to extend the height, climbed up and nimbly flipped the lock.

Slowly we both gained strength, Ralph and I. Little creaky sounds announced that his voice was coming back. At one year of age he started to drag himself along the carpet, pulling with one good arm, weakly assisted by the other one. One leg was unaffected and pushed vigorously ahead, dragging it's thin and lifeless partner along behind it. As the years went on the determination in this small child was amazing to watch. He refused to stay on the floor. He pulled himself up on whatever he could reach, resulting in many a spill. There may have been a minute of two of wailing and protest that spoke more of annoyance than pain, but beyond that he was unfazed.

So when on one such occasion Gil's mother and mine were present an otherwise small incident turned into high drama. Both ladies, seeing the child tumble, broke into screams of horror and rushed to his aid from different parts of the room. They both bent down at the same time and their heads collided with a resounding crack. Not a sound was heard from the startled baby. He sat there looking up at them with wide eyes, obviously wondering what the matter was with those two big women on either side of him, holding their heads and moaning. He forgot to cry.

An excerpt from a letter Mother wrote to my father who was in Austin, Texas, lecturing for two months at the university.

> *Little Ralphy is getting sweeter and sweeter. He sometimes repeats a word that he hears. Fe told me that she said bicycle, and he repeated bicyki. I could not believe it when Fe told me about it, so I tried it myself and heard it loud and clear. Ricky is getting to be difficult. Three years is supposed to be the worst age. He does not obey any more at all.*

I entered the newly opened Jepson Art Institute. Herb Jepson, with whom I had already studied at Chouinard, was the director and Rico Lebrun was the star teacher. He influenced and inspired not only me, but in the years to come a whole generation of artists. I sat in his classes glued to my hard drawing bench, even more so to his words and fired on by his enthusiasm. He would give a lecture once a week. Students of all the other classes would flock to hear it and soon brought friends and families to listen.

Even Gil escaped from his job whenever it was possible and drove in from far out of town to attend the lectures. "Wouldn't miss it for the world," He said. Rico talked not only about art, but also about history, philosophy and humanity. I don't recall what the theme of one of his lectures was, but I will never forget a particular occasion. Rico's talk progressed from holding forth about the painters Gruenewald and Goya, then went to Leonard Baskin and ended up with Robert Motherwell. Now the utter, deep contempt he harbored against that last gentleman was unforgettably expressed when Rico mentioned the name in his unmistakable Italian accent, "Now we come to

MEESTERRR MOTHERRRWELL," rolling his R's and his eyes at the same time. Mr. Motherwell was buried immediately, once and for all. This is a very unimportant incident, but it is somehow indelibly stuck in my memory.

Rico was a very charismatic speaker and while we followed his words with rapt attention he also admonished us to formulate our own ideas. In those days he was not yet as famous as he became two years later in 1951, when he exhibited his enormous triptych *The Crucifixion*. Gil and I attended the opening of that show and it was a gala occasion at the Los Angeles County Museum. So called *High Society*, art lovers and collectors, museum directors, critics and journalists where all there. Rico was beleaguered. He was not a tall man, but he looked particularly small in the midst of all of that fawning humanity. He saw us across the room, elbowed his way out of the crowd, came over and put his arms around us, "What a relief to see my own good friends," he sighed.

Two young men were in my class who were well on their way to becoming good teachers in their own right. Rico made them his teaching assistants. One was William (Billy) Brice. I'll never forget witnessing the first time that Billy gave a talk to the class at Rico's insistence. He was very tall and slim. His short black hair accentuated the whiteness of his face, which seemed to turn even whiter as he mounted the podium. The paper he held in his hand trembled. We all held our breath and then relaxed as he slowly gained control. His eyes darted several times across our heads towards the back of the room and then returned again to the notes he held in his hand. We were all intensely aware of the presence behind our backs. There stood Rico in his black turtleneck sweater, his large eyes intent and his head slightly cocked as if to hear better. He was leaning against the wall, his hands in his pockets, maybe thinking that he was inconspicuous. That, of course, he could never be; he was a small man, but his presence was large.

The other young man was Howard Warshaw, who had come from teaching at the university of Iowa to join the Jepson School and to study with Rico. He had the stature of a prizefighter and when he looked down at your drawing from under his large, black eyebrows that jutted out like an awning above his brooding eyes you knew that you better take your work seriously. No fudging, no triviality escaped Howard's merciless judgment.

My friend Pat Carey was a very talented and fiercely dedicated student, so when Howard on his rounds from one student's drawing bench to the next came to her work and growled his displeasure poor Pat exploded. She lifted her foot and kicked him square in the shin. It seemed like the whole room broke out in one communal gasp of horror, but Howard just stood still, looked at her, turned on his heels and continued on his rounds. This to Pat was more devastating then if he had killed her. To her it meant that she, her actions and her work were of no importance. Thank God the two of them later reconciled.

A contrasting little incident. One of the students, Teresa Sorce, served as a model from time to time in exchange for tuition. Wrapped in a large piece of drapery, her statuesque figure posed quite a challenge. I had set myself the problem of showing the structure of her body in conjunction and through the planes of the covering cloth. Rico came by and looked over my shoulder, "*You* did that?" he asked, then, lingering for a few more seconds, nodded his head and smiled. This approval meant more to me then if I had won a coveted prize in a major competition.

Chapter 5

A Weighty Decision and a Great Outcome

It was the month of April, 1949. Dr. Steinberg's eyes searched my face from across his desk as he leaned back in his chair. "We have to make a grave decision," he said. I held my breath. "Your suspicion was right. Another child is on the way." I let my breath out, straightened my back and smiled.

"However," he continued, "I don't want you to have it. You are not strong enough yet. It is early enough to interfere. I am not allowed to do it myself, but I'll send you to an excellent man who will. No," he held his hand up when he saw me rise in protestation, "Don't say anything. Go home and talk to Gil. Take a few days to think it over. You know what I advise, but it's up to you."

We walked around the lake at Westlake Park. We held hands, Gil and I. The first crucial decision in our lives together was confronting us. "Let's sit for a while," Gil led me to a bench at the water's edge. A duck burst out from under the bench and quacked its annoyance. We laughed, but then I sighed and put my head on Gil's shoulder.

"How do you feel about it?"

He held me tight and looked into my face, nodding his head in confirmation. "I feel that Hugo knows what he is talking about." Dr. Steinberg, a friend since Ricky's birth, was now plain Hugo to us.

Through a sleepless night I stood at the window and looked down at the garden and the bent crown of the tea tree below, its leaves shimmering silver through the April drizzle. My arms were folded across my chest as I hugged myself for reassurance. I closed my eyes. The being that grew in me—I knew I would not give it up.

The year went on. I realized that Dr. Steinberg, Gil's *Hugo*, had been right, I was not as strong as I wanted to be and I became exhausted from dealing with my two little boys and trying to help our financial situation at the same time. I was in my sixth month of pregnancy and our dear Hugo ordered a vacation. The small resort of Laguna was chosen and I found myself to be the proud and single occupant of a tiny bungalow at the beach for two glorious weeks.

September 1949
An entry from my diary.

Here I am sitting very peacefully in front of a nice crackling fire, poking around in its embers, drinking tea, smoking one cigarette after another, having no other obligation or duty then to replace a small plate with the sad remains of a cream puff in my small kitchen. But since this token of my solitary evening feast does not offend anybody's esthetic senses but mine and since all of my senses at the present moment are exceedingly relaxed and keyed to a perfect state of Mañana, I have no duties and no obligations. In short, the plate remains on the funny little side table, which is shaped like a clumsily fashioned ear in a child's drawing.

My small room is all friendliness and warmth in a plush and doily atmosphere and filled with all kinds of horrible bRic-a-brac.

The ocean outside is sounding off its constant rhythm with sovereignty and dignity. From time to time its impact upon the shore sends my windows rattling and the floor trembles slightly under my feet. I have been sitting on the beach for hours this afternoon. At first I read a little, Turnabout, by Thorne Smith. Just the right thing if you don't want to think and are on vacation. But the ocean is a demanding companion. It wants undivided attention. So I sat and watched the fog drifting in and the sun setting behind the fog, sending small coppery rays down through the liquid transparency of the horizon. The waves lapped higher and higher up onto the shore and the sand seemed to become alive with millions of crawling and hopping little beasties whose family names are not known to me. Four or five men were fishing in the surf, their bodies dark against the sky with the graceful, slender curves of the rods in their hands forming a pattern, like in a great Japanese wash drawing.

It grew chilly and gray and timeless. And then suddenly a thought crept up in me and I hunched my shoulders and shivered. Timeless, unchangeable? Can man now even change this?

"Russ to blame if atomic warfare breaks out." Those were the headlines. What a curse is there on our generation. We can't loose ourselves and rejoice in the beauty of our world in peace. We can't look upon our children with undiluted joy without fear for their future seeping into our very guts.

December 6, 1949

The baby wanted out, there was no doubt about it. At the time of Ricky's and Ralph's births I had been unhappy at the noisy and impersonal atmosphere of Cedars of Lebanon. So this time we had decided on the Queen of Angels Hospital and its kind and caring nuns. My roommate was an Irish Catholic lady.

"What would you like, a boy or a girl?" She asked, eying me critically. "I'll be going home with my ninth girl," She continued.

"I have two boys," I said, "I so hope for a girl this time."

She looked at me with narrowed eyes and shook her head. "You'll have another boy, Honey. Your only way to get a girl is to change husbands." This pronouncement immediately threw me into such strong labor-pains that I was wheeled into the operating room without having to take the customary shower and without having to undergo the insult of getting my lower quarters shaved. What a relief that was. The anesthetic procedures did not have enough time to work fully either.

Strong lights were crashing down on me. White-robed faceless people were moving about on either side of me and from somewhere beyond my feet I heard and recognized our Hugo's voice. Someone kept telling me *don't push*, over and over again, *don't push*.

And I kept yelling, "I can't help it," and then I felt him coming out. There are no other words that come to mind then *bringing forth*. Quite biblical, a piece of nature erupting and bringing forth a piece of itself, an unforgettable experience. I am still so glad that the anesthesia did not work completely.

At home Bruce was received with great astonishment and probably mixed feelings by his two not so big brothers. For Ricky there was another intruder, such a short time after the first one had temporarily dislodged him from his home and then from his place as the one and only prince of the family realm. Ralph's reaction seemed to be one of more benign curiosity. Maybe this was a *something to play with* attitude. We wrapped Bruce as a Christmas present with a big red bow around his blanket and took a photo of all three boys for our Christmas cards. It turned out to be a family-history document. Bruce looks up to those two guys crowding in on him with a rather worried expression. Who are they? Will they be friendly?

I was at home for three days and still in bed when I received my first visitors. Rico Lebrun and Constance, his wife, came carrying a three-foot long roll of paper that was tied with a gold ribbon and had a most incongruous, sentimental paper angel from a five and dime store dangling from it. I was almost scared to open it. It turned out to be a marvelous silk-screen print from a series of designs that Rico had done for a New York Ballet performance. It showed a strutting figure that had a piano keyboard incorporated into its richly colored, fantastic costume. What a lavish gift that was!

Chapter 6

Adventures with Helping Hands

The next years, from 1950 to 1955, were so full of happenings, so crowded with people appearing in our lives and disappearing again that I have a very hard time putting them in some kind of chronological order. There were the various household helpers that paraded through our home at different times while we still lived with my parents at Occidental Boulevard.

Myrene was a young African-American, about my age and very intelligent. She had been a teacher on a Navajo reservation before she came to us. I still think of her sometimes, even after so many years. We became such good friends that we were heartbroken when she left to go into the army, joining the WAC. Just like our Charlie a few years before, she said, "What else is there for me? In the army I can better myself." She wrote us once from camp and then we lost track of her, to my great regret.

Following her departure we put another ad in the paper, but this time we did not get a satisfactory reply. "Why don't you inquire at Social Services?" someone suggested. "They sometimes know of special young people that need work and a home."

"Veronica is a good girl." The harried looking social worker let her eyes roam all around our living space. "She will do good work for you. She goes to school until 2 o'clock. You must insist that she is home by 2:30 and that she starts work for you at 3. She is not allowed to go out by herself at any other time. It is important that you are very strict with her."

"Why is she under your care? Is there a problem?" I asked, feeling a little nervous. "After all, a fifteen-year-old girl is not a baby anymore. Why shouldn't she have some freedom?"

"Well," the lady hemmed and hawed a little, clearly somewhat embarrassed and finally came out with it, "We suspect that her father molested her and we removed her from his home. She is a good girl, though. You'll see. Try her and if any difficulties arise call us and we will take her back."

Veronica arrived, a little shabby suitcase in her hand and an anxious expression that could not be missed in her gray eyes. She was sturdy and already quite well developed, looking older than fifteen. It took only a week or so for her to relax. She adored the boys and they in turn clung to her when she played with them. We heaved a sigh of relief, deciding after all that we had not made a mistake. Every day she returned promptly at 2:30 after school and took great care with our boys and she seemed to be increasingly sure of herself and more secure within our family.

A month or two passed until, several times a week, Veronica arrived home late from school with a variety of excuses. One day she returned way after dinnertime looking hot, tired and disheveled without any explanation. That was when we lowered the boom.

"You straighten up or we'll send you back," we told her in no uncertain terms. Tears and promises followed.

"Oh please, please, don't do that. They'll put me in juvenile detention." For the next several weeks she was a good girl again. We thought we had convinced her of our best intentions for her and that she had decided to reform.

Then a letter arrived, in an official looking envelope. The school inquired as to the continued absence of one *Veronica So and So*, who had not attended school for several months. We confronted her until it finally came out: she had been seeing her father.

That evening Gil and I had to attend one of his important business dinners, one that we could not miss. We told Veronica that we would talk about the situation when we got home. Knowing that my parents were downstairs and could be asked to keep an eye on the upstairs, we left.

Around midnight we returned. Everyone was asleep. The children slumbered peacefully and loud snoring came from Veronica's room.

"My God," said Gil, "Listen to that racket. Try to turn her over or something. I can't stand it." I went in and gently shook her shoulder. She did not move and kept on snoring.

"I'll try again when we go to bed," I told Gil. We had a little snack and talked and then, for some reason that I still can't explain, I went into the bathroom, opened the cabinet door above the sink and stood there for a few seconds. *What was I looking for*? I scanned the shelves and then I saw it. A pillbox minus its cap was lying on its side. It had been filled with sleeping pills that I had never touched and now it was empty.

Panic grabbed us. We dashed into Veronica's room and shook her in desperation. She would not wake up. We threw coats on over our nightclothes. Gil picked the heavy girl up, loaded her into the backseat of our car gunned the engine and we raced towards the emergency hospital. Thank God the streets were quite empty at that time of night.

What we had not figured on was the fact that our good old car did not like to run without gas. In the seediest and darkest part of the city it simply decided to stop. We were at least another thirty or more blocks away from the hospital as far as we knew. In helpless horror our eyes searched the forbidding fronts of the silent houses and the empty street and then we both yelled *There!* It was a cry of relief. Around a far corner two headlights cut the darkness and came our way. We jumped into the middle of the street and waved wildly for it to stop. Luck was with us. It was a police car and after explaining our situation to the rather suspicious guardian of the law, the officer and Gil loaded our unconscious passenger into the police car.

"You come with me," the man said to Gil, "And you, lady, stay in the car. Lock yourself in." Why on earth did he not want to take me? I have never understood that. I could not lock our old car. Gil had the key in his pocket. I was scared to death all alone in those deserted streets. I decided to run and find my way to the hospital on foot, and so I did.

Sweating and panting I found Gil in the emergency ward and clung to him for the next miserable hours until the police decided that we had not committed a crime and Veronica was out of danger. Afterwards the poor girl was handed over to the juvenile authorities. How much therapy and kindness did she receive there?

What a relief it was after that experience when we found Karen as a replacement through the employment agency at her high school. Karen had just turned 16 and came from New York, leaving her parents behind. Did she run away? She seemed too young to live all on her own. "We did not get along," was all she said about her parents, and that was that. Here we had a happy, slightly plump little Jewish girl who moved in with few clothes, a radio, a teddy bear, schoolbooks, movie magazines and a lot of enthusiasm and good will. We liked her immediately and the boys adored her. She was still enough of a child to become a big sister to them.

She was fond of all the three boys, but her highest devotion went to Ralph. She exercised his leg, massaged it with infinite patience and tried to make him walk. She brushed his long blond locks and took him to the park, pushing his stroller along with pride. "You know," she confided in me one day, "When we are out there, I always pretend that I am his mother and every one admires him."

But there came a day when her motherly pride received a jolt as my son Ralph's penchant for humor and individualism emerged at the age of three. On one of their outings an old gentleman came down the street leaning heavily on his cane and stopped next to the stroller. He put his hand on Ralph's head and smiled down at him,

"Well, well, well, and what is your name, little girl?"

Before Karen could reply, Ralph's serious eyes looked up at the gentleman.

"Agnes," he said.

"No, no, he is a boy!" Karen was furious, as if the poor old man had insulted her and the child. He hobbled away, muttering and shaking his head in confusion. Karen returned home sputtering with indignation. "The time has come. We have to cut his hair." And we agreed. Goldilocks had to become a boy. From where or whom Ralph adopted the name Agnes will be a mystery forever.

Young Karen was all dressed up early one evening, ready to go out to a party. The jeans were traded for a flowery skirt and blouse combination and a big pair of dangling earrings framed her little pudgy face. We had never seen her wearing lipstick before.

'How do I look?" She presented herself to us with obvious pride.

"Great, just great," we said, "But aren't you forgetting something?"

"Am I?" She looked herself up and down, shook her head and stared at us in bewilderment.

"Might some shoes be useful?" We inquired delicately.

She was all dressed up and she was barefoot. She returned fairly early that evening.

"How was it?" I asked.

"Oh, they were all old people, all over twenty." Nevertheless an old person of probably just about twenty years of age rang our doorbell one day and asked for Karen. He seemed exactly the kind of guy we did not want our Karen to be involved with. He was pale and a little grimy. His long black hair was slicked back behind one ear and allowed to fall across his eye on the other side. A glittering earring and a tight fitting leather jacket completed the picture. His motorcycle was parked at the curb.

Romance blossomed in spite of our considerate, tactful attempts to advise and warn her. Karen buzzed off on the back of her swain's motorcycle after school let out and whenever we did not need her services. Months passed before she announced her plan to marry and she moved out with tears and hugs, assuring us of her undying love.

From time to time she came to visit and seemed to be quite happy.

"I miss the boys," she kept saying, so when we asked her to babysit she was delighted. Late that night we returned home and found everything quiet in our quarters upstairs. The kids were fast asleep and so was Karen. She was sitting in a chair in the middle of the hall, bound up and wound with yards and yards of string.

"Karen, what happened?" We were aghast and shook her awake. She looked up and her sleepy, happy face beamed up at us in utter delight.

"We had such a nice time," she giggled. She called us a few years later. She had married the boy, but he left her as soon as she got pregnant. We were eager to help, but without letting us know she moved on and we could not find her again.

CHAPTER 7

Hard Work and *Business is Business*

Gil's job at the Santa Fe Trailways Bus Company terminated after the war. He found employment at the West Coast Trailer Company, only to leave there for a position at a high priced advertising agency that held out promise for a great future. He became a proud young executive with an office on Wilshire Boulevard.

It only took a few months before Gil came home, his newly purchased and elegant jacket carelessly slung over one shoulder and his tie stuffed into his pocket. He had lost his job. The firm was bankrupt.

That was when we made our big decision. We too, like Ralph and Pat, did not want to be separated for most of every day, leading separate lives and having our children see their father only at night and weekends. So we decided that we would go into business and produce ceramic giftware, capitalizing on my talent for designing and painting and Gil's affinity for working with his hands and his obvious gift for salesmanship.

Gil signed up to attend the Frank Wiggins Trade School to learn cabinet making and we both took night classes in ceramics at City College.

At about that time Ricky and Ralph together attended Paul Brodsky's Nursery School and Bruce, who was still too young to go, stayed at home with me or with a part-time babysitter. I looked forward to Ricky entering first grade at public school with very mixed feelings. I was sure that Ralph would refuse to go back to nursery school without his big brother and that would have curtailed my work time considerably.

The fateful day arrived. I pulled the car up to the curb at the school, expecting a fight with my little offspring, having to drag him kicking and screaming across the pavement. But no, I did not believe my eyes.

Ralph slid out of the car, yelled "By Mom" and limped into the building as fast as his bad leg would allow. On that day I learned a very important lesson and Gil's exclamation *you never know what they'll do* stuck with me. I learned to sit back and observe, instead of predicting the future.

The garage became our workshop. We bought a medium-sized kiln and started to experiment by decorating and firing tiles to be set into trays and tables that Gil would eventually build.

One day we stopped at a very elegant gift shop in Beverley Hills and met the owner, whose name was Bill Alexander. We showed him some of our tiles and he expressed great interest and high approval of my design talent. He was a designer and an architect. We became friends and he promised to help us in any way that he could with counsel and referrals to stores and interior decorators.

My letter from Occidental Boulevard to parents who again were away on a lengthy trip.

December 10, 1950
Dear Ones,

It is Sunday morning and the wild horde is on the way to Gil's parents. Heavenly quiet. Only Brucey is crawling around my legs. He has four teeth now, waves and says bye bye" *Yesterday he climbed out of his playpen in the garden. All of a sudden he sat in the grass and munched on weeds. Nobody knows how he got there. The children are all well. Ricky graduated from nursery school and now turns the whole house into one hazard zone.*

We are working like crazy. Brother Paul is teaching Gil to work with wood and machinery and soon Paul's equipment will be set up in our garage. Gil painted two rooms in Nat's new apartment and repaid some of our debt to him that way. Otherwise there is nothing new. I baked two cheesecakes, your recipe, Mutti, and also the chocolate squares. It was a tremendous success. Howard Warshaw found them sensational. We are now giving our very large tiles out to be fired and they return to us without a flaw. Our kiln is just not big enough for them.

From next week on we'll have a very busy program. Gil will probably go to a trade school to learn cabinet making from Monday to Friday for six hours per day. No tuition!

> Aside from working on my commercial designs I still go to Rico's drawing class on two mornings a week and Gil and I take a ceramics class at adult education on two evenings.

We acquired the agent Meyer who got us into a big gift show at the Jewelry Building in downtown Los Angeles. Then one day we visited the buyer at the Bullocks Wilshire department store on our own and met with tremendous approval and a very large order of the *Jester* design on big platters and bowls.

I had by now sculpted my own shapes of free-form bowls and smaller dishes in clay. Gil made molds of them and we gave them out to be fired. Finally it became necessary for us to relinquish our garage shop and look for larger quarters. A store was found on a rather shabby part of Glendale Boulevard that was just perfect for us. We bought a larger second-hand kiln and found big tables at the Salvation Army. One of them even had a revolving top, perfect for decorating dishes in rotation. We were pleased with our finds, like children on an Easter egg hunt.

The next problem we had to face was that we could not produce all the orders we had gotten by ourselves. So our ad in the Los Angeles Times asked for an artist, part time. It was not easy to find a person who could copy my designs to my satisfaction. They were, after all, so individually mine, done in my own *handwriting*. We needed someone who had the skill and sensitivity to reproduce them. After trying several people we finally found Carol, a young art student who stayed with us for some time.

We gave up on the agent Meyer and the whole cheap line. We had too much trouble with his orders, too little profit and it kept us from following up on bigger things. We had trouble with Carol. The Parvin order included two of her designs and when the time came to do them, she refused. All of a sudden she did not want to give us the designs. And in addition she was the one who kept records on Meyer's orders. I kept asking her if things were going to be ready for Sunday.

"Oh yes, easily," she said. So Friday night I checked up, with the result that I sat up Friday and Saturday night painting Meyer's orders frantically. She was far from ready. Her work had gotten very bad. She was moody with a long face all day. We also employed another girl.

Then we met a man who came from Denmark. He was a potter who had worked in Danish potteries since he was fourteen and he was highly skilled. He worked for us for one dollar an hour. He threw big bowls on the potter's wheel at the rate of seven or eight pieces per hour, a task that would take two weeks if pouring to a mold. He made big vases and finished a complete coffee set in one day.

We had three people working for us then. Carol's long face, the fact that they all started to have a fine time together chatting, going out to lunch for an hour and a half and at the last minute franticly rushing to complete Meyer's orders was enough to make us stop. We decided it was insane. We needed to reap the benefit of our labors instead of paying other people wages. The Dane remained and did as much work as three girls combined.

Bill Alexander was working for us with great energy. He called everybody in town and many people said they'd come after the week of the show. Lord and Taylor in New York, Neiman Marcus in Texas and Marshall Field in Chicago all wrote us. Some let us know that they would not come to the California gift show, but since Bullocks Wilshire recommended us so highly, please send them photos and samples. The buyer from Wanemaker's department store in Philadelphia came, sent by Miss Strobel of Bullocks Wilshire, and ordered ninety pieces, $ 328.00 worth to us. She raved and said that it was only the beginning. All the pieces were to have the *Jester* with the yellow rose design. She said she had been to the New York shows and had seen nothing as good as our stuff.

Again we needed more help in our business. Two young women answered our next ad, presenting themselves as a couple that lived together. One called herself a designer and the other said that she was a writer. They both looked rather down on their luck, hungry and clad in dilapidated jeans and T—shirts. There was something unconventional and interesting about them and they were friendly and outgoing. We liked them.

It turned out that we could not pay them as much as they needed, but after some discussion they confessed that they had no place to stay. We came to an agreement. We would give them room and board and a salary that we could afford and they would work for us. So they moved in with a few bags containing their meager belongings. It turned out to be an excellent arrangement. Jean Buckley was the taller one of the two. Her dark blond hair was pulled tight behind her ears and folded into a long, thick braid that she wore slung over one shoulder or tossed across her back. She wore large rings on both her hands and an Indian turquoise necklace dangling down her worn T-shirt. She was gentle and alert and adjusted quickly and intelligently to our way of working, copying my designs with great skill and speed. I could not have wanted better help and she was pleasant to be with.

Her friend's first name I cannot remember, since she hated it and only wanted us to call her by her last name, Louthian. Louthian was short and stocky and proved to be strong enough to be excellent help for Gil. She heaved heavy sacks of cement, learned to mix and pour it and to make molds of the bowl and platter shapes I had sculpted in clay. Thank God, with Louthian on board I was released from the frequent emergency calls from Gil's woodshop in the garage: *Hand me the saw, no, not that one, can't you see where I am pointing? Hold that board still. Hold it, I said. Don't move. No, you are tilting to the right. Keep it straight, damn it!* I heard such words many times.

Poor Gil. It was still all so new and, as for most men, admitting that he was not completely sure of what he was doing was humiliating. So his frustrations landed on my head more often than not. I knew what was eating him and I did not take it to heart, but I dreaded the call for help from the garage. Now there was Louthian, patient, efficient, strong and she could not be yelled at. She was a gift from heaven.

During our shared home life and dinners we became well acquainted and we learned quite a bit about their unconventional lives, their searching and their wanderings. I cannot recall much of it, except the overriding concern that was shaping Louthian's life.

The third glass of wine one evening dissolved her in tears and we learned of her long held plans to effect a change of gender.

"I am not a woman, I just look like one."

She and Jean had saved their money for years, working wherever they could find gainful employment, barely spending any of it on housing and food. Now the two of them felt that since they had a home with us they could go ahead and complete their plan. And so they did. How could we object? It would have taken hearts of stone and ours were made of butter. They both assured us that their work would not suffer.

Neither Louthian nor Jean knew how to drive, so it was mostly Gil or I who undertook to transport the patient back and forth to the hospital for treatments, a daunting enterprise in view of all else that lay on our shoulders. They stayed with us for nearly two years yet I don't remember when the actual surgery took place. It must have been quite some time before the transformation took hold. Louthian's reddish hair succumbed to the barber's shears and was cut so close that the skin of his skull emerged a shiny pink. A small moustache appeared on his upper lip and he often stroked it lovingly as if to coax it out into the open. His voice descended a few octaves and his formerly soft and round woman's face seemed to harden to emphasize the bone structure. The ending of that saga though is very clear in my mind.

We left the front door to our shop open hoping the fresh air would pep us up. It was only seven o'clock and we were already working feverishly. We had gotten a very big and important order from Gump's, a large gift store in San Francisco. The date for delivery was only two weeks away, a short time for painting, firing and final glazing of all the ware that was still to be done.

To our amazement Jean and Louthian had left home very early in the morning instead of driving to the store with us as usual. "Don't worry, we'll be there on time," they said, without further explanation. The day wore on. It was noon. I sat at my worktable confronted by stacks of plates and bowls. I painted the outlines of my designs on every one of them. The assistants were to apply the colors and Gil then would glaze and fire them. The half-finished pieces piled up on the revolving top of the big round decorating table.

At four o'clock our helpers finally showed up, glowing with happiness like children at Christmas time. "We've got a new job," they sputtered.

"For God's sake get to those plates. Sit down and paint and then tell us all about it. Did this just happen suddenly, today?"

"Oh no, we've been planning it for quite some time. We are now independent. We'll earn a decent salary and we found a place to rent."

We were dumbfounded. "I can see why you are happy and I am glad for you. So when is this going to happen?"

"Now, right now. We'll just go home and get our stuff." They were almost out of the door when Gil intervened.

"Hold on a minute. Are you going to leave us in the lurch like that? We have to get this order out and we counted on your help. Stay a few more days at least so we can try and find a replacement."

"Sorry. Business is business, but we'll come and visit you sometime." And that was that. Business is business, an unholy mantra that makes me bristle every time I hear it. What comes before friendship, loyalty and plain human decency? It's *Business,* of course, you knucklehead. We felt betrayed and extremely hurt. The order got delivered two weeks late and we never heard from that San Francisco store again.

Chapter 8

Striking Out on Our Own

It was our seventh year of living together with the whole family on Occidental Boulevard. Our boys were born in that big white house. They played happily in the back yard under the gnarled Australian tea tree that spread its drooping canopy of green and silver leaves across their plastic pool and over all their laughs and squabbles.

The former garage, Uncle Ralph's and Aunt Pat's studio apartment, had its entrance along the side of the yard. The boys would go to visit off and on, would be allowed to stay a little while and then came out again smacking their lips, having received their expected *'pearing candy*, a gratuity for disappearing, for going home.

Ricky, the oldest, endlessly curious and enterprising, snuck out of the garden many times to explore the neighborhood and especially the big Catholic Church at the corner a few houses away. One day he came racing back home, out of breath and frightened to death. He had snuck into the back of the church through an unlocked rear door.

"It was so dark," he gasped, "And there was a curtain and a little bell rang and then God came out!" Rick's churchgoing days were over for the rest of his life.

He took a little revenge on the congregation, though. I looked out of my upstairs window one sunny morning and smiled, seeing a row of little uniformed Catholic schoolgirls marching by on their way to church, accompanied by two nuns, one leading them and the other following behind. Bemelmans' *Madeline* had come to life. And then I saw him.

My son Ricky, a devilish grin on his face, sat on our front-steps, aiming his water pistol and methodically shooting at each little girl as they passed by, yelling *bang, bang. You're dead*. I saw the nun from the end of the line go over to speak with him. She bent down and put her hand on his head. It seemed to me that she was talking very kindly to him and left him sitting there looking somewhat bemused at first and then breaking out into an impish smile, obviously pleased with himself. Then he raised his pistol and aimed another spray at the disappearing procession. *Bang, bang. You're dead.*

Rick must have been six at the time. A year later he aggravated my mother more then the other two boys together could have done, although they too were a constant source of complaint. It was not that she did not like them; in fact she loved them dearly. In her view it was Gil's and my lack of training and improper discipline that she could not stand.

Our housekeeping also did not pass muster as far as she was concerned. She made her views known frequently and vociferously. No doubt with the best of intentions she came upstairs to our domain when we were not at home and *made order* in our *messy rooms*. Our protests prompted outrage and no change.

"I am just trying to help," she'd say. For seven years we had lived in peace and harmony together in that beautiful home with only occasional squabbles that were quickly forgotten, but as the years progressed and the children demanded more and more attention, Mother's dominance became unbearable. She felt responsible for everybody and everything. There were fights and accusations until one fateful day in August 1952. Finding me at home, frustrated and in tears, Gil stormed downstairs to Mother's sitting room. Trembling I stood upstairs at the staircase railing and heard them yelling at each other.

And then came Gil's voice loud and clear, "We are going to move out and until we leave you are not coming upstairs unless we invite you." It was horrible. And my poor father was left in the middle of this debacle. I knew he was on our side and recognized the dilemma, but he loved his wife and understood her childish self-righteousness and lack of flexibility.

When we left the house for the last time the sound of her wailing sent us on our way. She made sure we realized that we had broken her heart. I felt awful and wished I could have spared her the pain

CHAPTER 9

A Dugout on Brandon Street, 1952

Independence! Freedom from intrusions and critiques! I had my own family just to myself. Hand in hand, Gil and I looked out the window of our new, tiny semi-subterranean living room. The window was level with the flat, graveled parking area. Beyond that a sun-dried slope rose and slowly developed into barren *Kite Hill*, so named by the neighborhood children, whose squeals and laughter we could clearly hear on the hot August wind. Their homemade kites fluttered in the sky, throwing little specks of color up into the smog-gray air. There was dust and there were bugs, but no flowers in that unlovely landscape. No Australian tea tree was in sight and no little wading pool on cool moist grass.

We were in the middle of a light-industrial section of town on Brandon Street at the corner of Glendale Boulevard. Out from under my parent's sheltering roof, we were entirely dependent on our own meager resources and they were scanty at best.

So when we found this affordable basement *dugout*, as we called it, directly across the street from our ceramic shop, we grabbed it. Since the rent was very low and since it was so conveniently located we did not hesitate for a moment and signed a one-year lease. The building housed a large lamp shop and a fishing tackle store and both fronted the boulevard, while our domain had its basement entrance to the rear, five steps down into the earth. Seven-foot ceilings spanned three little rooms, a tiny kitchen and barely adequate bath. There was an oblong screened-in space in front of the kitchen that became a play-space for the boys, whose bedroom was completely filled with a bunk bed for Rick and Ralph. It was purchased from our favorite emporium, the

Salvation Army Store. A small cot for Bruce was squeezed into the remaining space. The living room barely held a sofa, a bookshelf and a small coffee table. Our own bed shared the third room with whatever clothing and personal furnishings we had brought from the Occidental house.

A large public school was within walking distance and Ricky entered second grade. Ralph went to kindergarten and Bruce to day care in the same building. The fact that our workshop was so close to where we lived helped enormously. When school was out Gil and I spelled each other by sprinting back and forth across the busy boulevard to take care of our lively brood. And did they ever need watching.

Bruce had a little girlfriend from the neighborhood that was a year older than he was. I was relieving Gil on a Saturday afternoon and entered the house. Rick and Ralph were playing outside on the hill.

"Bruce, where are you?" I called. A duet of giggles answered me from the kitchen. There was Bruce sitting on a footstool, a tablecloth wrapped around his neck and snippets of his nice dark hair cascading down his face and over his shoulders. Little girlfriend Annie held a large pair of scissors in the air and looked at me for approval. I was too horrified to oblige her. A broad path of naked scalp ran down Bruce's head from front to back and full wild tufts of hair stood up on either side of it.

"My God, a reverse Mohawk," Gil's brother Paul exclaimed when he came to visit that same evening. "There is only one thing to do. Gil, get me your shaving kit." With squalling Bruce clamped firmly between his knees Uncle Paul finished what Annie had started, only more radically by shaving the whole head clean and naked.

Bruce looked in the mirror, refused to leave the house and tried to hide. Day care was out of the question. But we bought him a little cap with a visor on it and told him he looked just like a policeman. That did the trick. He went out again and bravely defended his hat from brother Rick's teasing assaults on the way to school.

We had a hard time at first. The money we made from selling our ware went mostly into buying more material and equipment, paying our helper and taking care of rent, phone, etc. There came a day when we literally did not know how to buy all the groceries we needed.

We returned from an errand one afternoon, having left the current employee Carol in charge.

"You've had visitors," she said, "and they left you an envelope on your desk." A gift from heaven, a gift from the best friends anyone could have had. It was a large check, signed *Bernard Garey*. Never to be forgotten.

The rift between ourselves and the parents slowly narrowed again. They must have realized that harboring hurt and resentment forever was not worth the loss of love and closeness of their family. And we, of course, were more then eager to embrace these two really wonderful people again, setting all of their quirks aside, as long as we did not have to live with them in close quarters.

They decided to sell the house on Occidental Boulevard and move to a large apartment on Cherokee Avenue. Consequently Ralph and Pat also lost their nice place and I remember feeling terribly guilty about having caused so much upheaval and unhappiness.

After their move into the new apartment my parents decided to take a long trip back to Europe. It served as a flight from sadness. They reached back to where they came from and hoped that it would help them to gain a sense of stability again. Whether or not they found what they were looking for I do not know. I think in the long run coming back to America they realized that they had made a good choice after all.

We received long letters from France, Italy, even Germany and from their very last nostalgic visit to Switzerland and their beloved St. Moritz. Later that year they traveled to Spain. Sadly, neither my brother Ralph nor I had the instinctive sense of history that my father had. He saved and treasured every family letter and we lost almost all of theirs.

Aside from filling commercial orders from various stores we developed a faithful clientele for our special one-of-a-kind pieces that I created and signed personally. People had me design plates for friend's anniversaries or large tiles as housewarming gifts.

The most challenging job came my way when the German Consul, of all people, entered the shop. Our first reaction when he identified himself was very cool and guarded, but soon we relaxed. This was no Nazi. This was a friendly, unconventional man, interested in art, music and oriental philosophies. He wanted us to make a large square tile table for the consulate's reception room. The design on the tiles should illustrate a part of a Buddhist legend about a man and his oxen that magically disappear into the sky.

He told us the story, though I can't remember it anymore. This relaxed man with his unruly hair, his pipe and his well-worn sport jacket was a German consul? Amazing! I loved the assignment he had given me and worked long hours on it, researching Chinese wash drawings and reading fairytales. Finally I called him to view and hopefully approve of my design.

He was ecstatic. "Ach nein, das ist ja ganz wunderbar!" In his excitement he lapsed into his native language. That to me was absolute proof that he liked it more than all of the words of praise that followed. "Now there is just one more thing I would like you to add," he smiled happily. "I would very much like a little red color somewhere in there."

I gulped. "Herr Konsul, that is impossible; I would have to redo the whole color-scheme, the whole painting, in fact. We'll have to start from scratch." He sat and tucked his chin in his hand. His eyes roamed all over the design.

"It is so beautiful. No, we must not change it, you are right."

Gil built the table, the tiles were painted and fired and set into their frame and the whole big job was delivered on time, received by lots of *oohs* and *ahhs* by the dutiful consulate staff, however sincere.

About a month later our Consul called. "Come and see how good your table looks in its place." We went and we saw that indeed it looked fantastic. And then we had to stifle the laughter that threatened to burst forth from both of us. Our friend had found the perfect way to implement his erstwhile wish. He had bought a bright red book and let it rest on one side of the table.

There was a prominent physician, another Dr. Steinberg, who had been our most devoted customer ever since we had opened the shop nearly two years before. On every occasion that presented itself, on holidays or birthdays or just on a whim of the moment he would come and buy a bowl or platter or order a special custom piece with an image he had in mind.

Coming into the shop, he pulled one of our bar stools over to my drawing table and fixed me with his energetic stare, one that announced that he had made up his mind.

"Gil, please come and join us," he called over his shoulder and Gil appeared from the back wiping plaster off his hands. "I need to invest some money and I am interested in helping you to succeed in your business. Your work is beautiful and very unusual, but if you continue the way you are doing now you'll never make it. Let me become your partner and we'll set up a corporation. You will move up to Beverley Hills to larger quarters, to ample workspace. We will buy a tunnel kiln so you can produce more and larger pieces and we'll get you adequate help. What do you say?"

I looked at our crowded little shop, looked through the open door out to the constant noisy traffic passing by, the vulgarity of the lighting fixture store's show windows across the street displaying black ceramic panthers and slinky mermaids tightly embracing table lamps. The customary drunk came shuffling by just then, as he did most every day.

I studied Gil's face. It was easy to read. He glowed. He reached for my hand, "All right with you?" There was no debate.

CHAPTER 10

Lapeer Drive

The modest bungalow on Lapeer Drive in Beverley Hills seemed rather incongruous, so close to the most elegant and expensive shopping area in town. Lapeer Drive was a short old street that ran parallel to Robertson Boulevard, rather like a forgotten poor cousin hiding in the shadow of his powerful relative.

We found that this small two-bedroom house had already been converted for some business use. An enormous quonset hut had been added to the back of the building and was absolutely perfect as our casting and firing area. There we placed a large tunnel-kiln that our mentor provided. It was a demanding beast, waiting to be fed and we put it to work almost continuously for nearly two years from then on.

One entered directly from the street into a good-sized room, which became part workroom and part showroom during the day and served as our living room after closing time. We put the boy's bunk beds and Bruce's cot in one of the small bedrooms in the back. There was just enough space in the second room to accommodate our own bed and my personal drawing table. The kitchen was so tiny that we could not eat in it. At dinnertime we set a folding table up in the children's room and had our meal sitting on their beds. The boys, I believe, had a good time. They had fun sitting on their beds with us, having their meals so unceremoniously.

After school and on weekends the boys went to a nearby park or were allowed to play with clay in the shop. Ralph especially loved to do that and I still have one of his masterpieces, a little man, penis and all, with polka dots on his head and green arms and legs. I also saved two painted tiles, one with a drawing of a grazing goat and the other with a wistful black and yellow clown's face.

Sometimes unavoidably one boy or another slipped into the showroom when customers were there. Most of the time they were duly admired and got their heads patted, especially Bruce, who was the youngest and very cute.

As always eight-year-old Rick was the one that supplied excitement in the family. He was playing in the park and witnessed the theft of a bicycle. When the police arrived he told them that he would recognize the man who took it and as a result he got to tour the whole neighborhood in the police car for over an hour, sitting right next to the officer while looking for the culprit. Oh Glory! I do not remember whether they had any success in finding the thief (or if there had ever been one.)

Ralph recalled that at day's end he saw his dad sitting with the officer in our showroom and was very surprised upon seeing him accept the officer's offer of a cigarette.

Why did he do that, he thought to himself. *He does not smoke.* Ralph thought that his dad was conforming unnecessarily. For one so young he already had a sense of personal integrity. He could not have been more than six years old.

Our living conditions were not much improved, but the business flourished for quite a while. My large, framed, decorative tiles were a great success. Orders came in from some of the biggest department stores and expensive gift stores in the country. We had three or four employees at a time copying my designs on bowls and trays, forms that I had sculpted and that were then made into molds and duplicated by Gil. At times we had customers in our showroom more often then we desired, because they kept us from working.

Our downfall began when the buyer from the Bullocks Wilshire Department Store urged us to produce dinnerware and gave us a huge order to start with. Lord and Taylor heard of it, as did Gump's in San Francisco. Others followed and they all wanted their own special designs.

Our lives became hell. We worked from morning to night. Sometimes there were catastrophic failures in the firing of an entire kiln load, a loss of many hours of work, not to mention the delay of delivery to the customer. Sometimes fired pieces came out of the kiln with just the tiniest flaw in the glaze that no average person would detect. The store buyer would reject it mercilessly. A day came when Gil emerged from the hot cavern of the firing shed and found me lying on my bed in the middle of the day with my eyes closed in utter exhaustion. He sat next to me, wiped the sweat off his face and looked dejected. "We've had another kiln load go wrong."

I sat up. "Gil, I can't go on. I work from morning to night, repeating the same drawings over and over again and have no time to create new ones. I am going insane. We have been driven into mass-production with all of these big orders and we cannot handle it. We have become slaves to the business with little time for our children and none for ourselves. Is this the life we want? For God's sake, let's quit."

Our partners and mentors were upset, but we did not give in. It was our life that had to be saved, not the business.

Loyal customers and friends were informed that a closing sale was going to be held in our showroom and it was a big success. Our personal friends especially came in droves and it felt good to know that some of our favorite pieces went to people we knew and liked.

CHAPTER 11

Altman Antiques and a Crucifix

In the meantime brother Ralph's *Altman Antiques* on La Cienega Boulevard was flourishing. Several newspaper articles that appeared in Beverly Hills in 1954 described the shop and its activities fairly well. Here are some excerpts from a rather lengthy article in the *The Beverly Hills Press*.

> March 18, 1954
>
> Children, museum directors, psychoanalysts, moviemakers, all visit Altman Antiques at the edge of Beverly Hills. Ralph Altman sells a particular kind of antique. Ebony African masks, carved heads from the South Seas and Pre-Columbian terracotta figures, all stare at visitors with expressions ranging from the inscrutable to the enraged. One is immediately struck with the intensely personal, active quality possessed by these primitive artists.
>
> As we stood looking at Mr. Altman's shop last week, we observed a rather worried looking carved head from New-Ireland with cocoa fiber eyebrows. "That looks rather like our editor on press day," We remarked.
>
> "Our masks often remind people of someone they know," said Mr. Altman politely. Some of the collectors in and about Beverly Hills who have bought Altman "Antiques" in the last eight years are Richard Conte, Katherine Hepburn, Vincent Price and Jane Russell, who recently purchased an Indian necklace from the Altmans.
>
> According to Mr. Altman, most of his wares are obtained from Europe—from Vienna, London, Madrid and Paris, were they where owned by collectors.

> However, some primitive objects were brought to the Altmans by missionaries from the far corners of the world.
>
> Much of Mr. Altman's work, however, is done with art museums. He has sold to, arranged exhibitions for, or lectured at the Museum of Natural History in New York, the Heard Museum in Phoenix and the San Francisco Museum, to mention a few.

Ralph groaned when he read the comments he was supposed to have made about the "child-like aspects of primitive art," and references to "wickedness and destruction," words and thoughts that were far from his mind. He regarded the art of ethnic people with the greatest respect and appreciation.

"Childlike," he grumbled, looking at the folded Beverley Hills newspaper in his left hand while extinguishing yet another cigarette on a large seashell he used for an ashtray with his right. "I never called this art *childlike*. I even hate to call it primitive. Strong, elemental, creative, yes and even sometimes quite sophisticated. Tripe." He slung the paper to the floor and lit another cigarette.

Excerpts from one of Pat's letters to the parents.

> Our Eskimo show is a glorious Succes d'Estime. We have never had so many people in for any show, nor so many admirers.
>
> But the real excitement of the moment began over a week ago when we started house hunting. It took us exactly 5 days to find THE house we want. It is 6 minutes from the shop, in Laurel Canyon—but not in an enclosed, dark and damp area. The price is fabulously low, $10,350. There is no catch to the low price; it is an estate sale. The suspense is terrible—will we get it—won't we get it?!—As you can imagine we are delirious with excitement and hope.
>
> Just a quick note about why little Ralphy came to dinner the other day. He had a very slight cold and sniffle and Fe and Gil were invited out for dinner with the other kids. So we had him at the shop for half an hour where he played his favorite African drum without stopping once, and then ate with us. He did not like my carrots, but courteously admired the totem pole and the cats. As Ralph told you, he behaved wonderfully.

Entering their gallery at any time during those years one was overwhelmed by the incredible display of ethnic art from literally all over the world, from Africa, Indochina, Japan or South America. American Indian masks and Kachina dolls were there, even a totem pole reigned imposingly next to the entrance. Everything was beautifully displayed.

Ralph and Pat acquired many friends from among those who were attracted to their shop and also certainly by their bright and winning personalities. One of their favorite champions was Vincent Price, the actor, who in contrast to his movie image as conniving villain and snarling monster was a very gentle, highly educated man, an ardent lover of art and passionate collector. Following Vincent's lead many members of the theater and movie world found their way to the store on La Cienega Boulevard and developed an interest in the beauty and variety of ethnic art.

If you were a close friend or esteemed colleague you were permitted to part the curtains at the back of the store and join Ralph and Pat and their large ever-brewing electric coffee maker. A circle of friends had developed, all people who loved art. There were museum directors, writers, physicians, lawyers and artists, like the painters Rico Lebrun and Howard Warshaw. They might bring their lunch in at noon, or just drop in for coffee at any time during the day and sit and chat for a while among the clutter of files, packing materials, unopened crates or special treasures that had just been relieved of their wrappings.

Vincent Price could be found cradling a newly purchased mask with great delight. Bob Magahee and his longtime partner George Wenham came. Bob was a costume specialist at Paramount studios and George had an antique store in Pasadena. Peter Furst, a German-Jewish emigrant, was an anthropologist and a wonderful photographer. Once at dinner he spoke about his experience serving in the American army in Germany during the war. He had a little too much to drink and the stories came pouring out almost against his will. He was among the first troops to enter the Dachau concentration camp and that account I'll never forget.

Between Peter, Ralph and me there was a certain sense of kinship that we did not share with our American friends. Peter and I used to have a lot of fun talking to each other in the most convoluted, stilted and aristocratic German we could conjure up and then we would laugh uproariously.

Ruth Mellinkoff, an art historian, was a wonderful cook and one of Pat's good friends, as was the Greek photographer Constantine Hassalevris, who had been a dancer in his youth. He prepared marvelous Greek dishes for us on special occasions. His studio and lab were only a few doors down the street, so he could frequently be found at lunchtime in the backroom at Altman Antiques, balancing his lanky frame on a little African stool, cradling a dish of his own homemade yogurt on his lap. These were more or less the regular friends that came at all hours of the day. I joined them whenever I could. Other people appeared and reappeared from time to time, gathering around the never-empty coffee pot.

I do not remember the year, but it was on a cold December afternoon. I had just dropped by the store for a quick visit and only Pat was there, no one else. Ralph had gone on some errand. On the floor of the backroom a big crate had been opened. Within, still half in its wrappings lay a very large, beautifully carved wooden figure. It was a crucified Christ, his arms were stretched out wide, and his head was tilted to the side and the glass eyes in his beautiful face shone, incredibly real. "It is very old and comes from the most southern part of Mexico," Pat said.

"I've got to have it, Pat," I sighed ecstatically. I had fallen in love. "How much would it be, do you think?"

Pat looked doubtful. "A lot. You can't afford that."

"I've got to have it," I said, pulling the figure out of its wrappings, heaving it into my arms and proceeding towards the exit.

"Wait till Ralph gets back," Pat called in distress.

"I'll call him later," as the door closed after me.

Two hours later Ralph's voice came over the telephone, "You beast. Had I been there you would not have gotten away with it. Now I am warning you, you are not going to get anything else for Christmas or your birthday next year. Let that be understood." He was the best brother in the world.

October 1943, our wedding party
Clockwise from upper left: father Gilbert, Gil, Me, brother Ralph, Pat, my father, my mother, mother Gilbert and of course Putzi in front

In our first home on Miramar Street, painting Charlie

Gil's parents

My parents buy a house for all of us

Ricky makes his appearance, 1946

The happy father

Now there are three
A Christmas present, Ricky 1946, Bruce 1949 and Ralph 1948

Twelve years later: the bright-eyed one,
the thinker and the mischief-maker

On our own in front of our shop on Glendale Boulevard

The Children's Art Workshop, Pasadena Museum

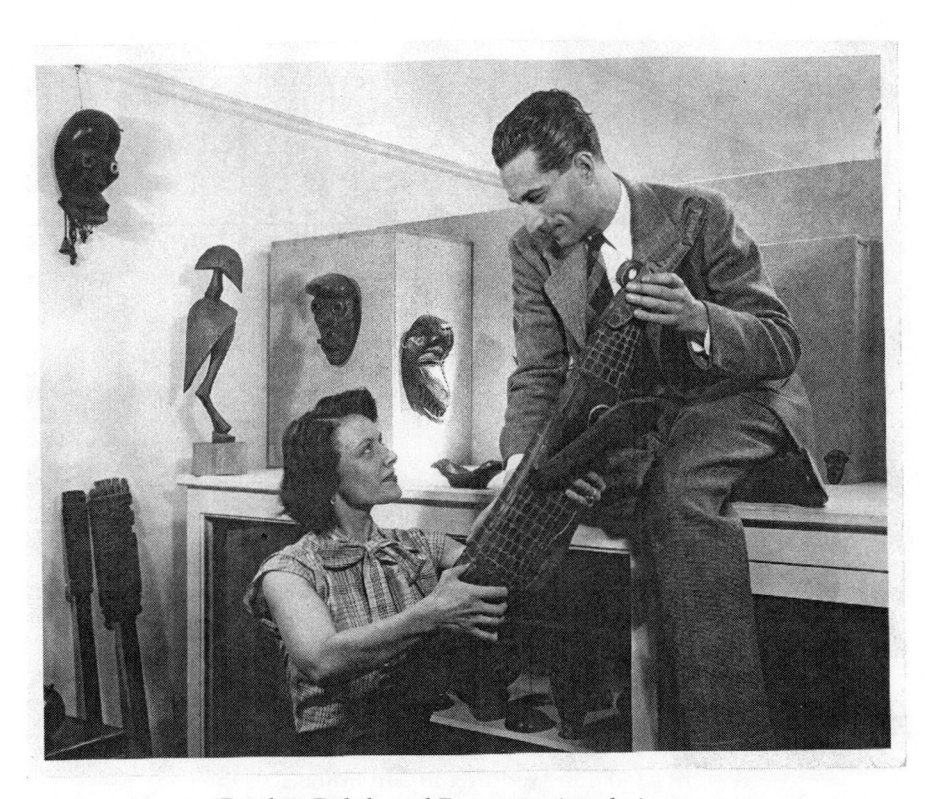

Brother Ralph and Pat arranging their store

Parent's Golden Wedding in San Fransisco, 1959

Bruce got the watermelon boat

The 3 G-notes perform

Intense communications: Scruggs

Just plain love: Heidi

Chapter 12

A Paradise with Animals
Vestal Avenue

The year was 1954 and Echo Park was still a peaceful, small neighborhood not far from downtown Los Angeles. We had heard of a house that was for rent there on Vestal Avenue and decided to have a look at it. Vestal Avenue did not really deserve the grandiose title of *Avenue*; it turned out to be a rather narrow street, like most of the roads struggling up and down the hilly terrain.

Having lived in tiny cramped quarters in the last few years, surrounded by commercial buildings, traffic and no greenery anywhere except for a few skinny trees trying to muscle their roots through the sidewalk, we entered a different world. There where lush green trees and blooming bushes nodding out of cramped little garden plots between comfortable narrow houses that stood so close together that it felt like they were holding hands to help each other climb laboriously up the hill.

A very steep driveway brought us near the top of a hill and deposited us in front of a small wrought-iron garden gate where the ground leveled. In front of a large inviting two-story house, crowned with an old fashioned gabled roof that bespoke stability, stood an enormous tree, its branches spread wide over a well-kept lawn. It was an unusual tree that looked as broad as it was high. Some of its lowest branches almost swept the ground. It had long needles like a pine tree, but I had never seen one of this size and configuration.

Away from the mowed lawn a wild, untended garden rambled over and around the hilly terrain. Little uneven dirt paths circled large loquat trees, berry bushes and a variety of rampant growth. A wooden shed stood in the back and there was a small but empty pond. Close to one side of the house there was a sharp drop to a deep ravine across which, over a burgeoning growth of eucalyptus, pine and sycamore, one could see far out to the spreading landscape below. It was a beautiful sight, but my motherly eye viewed this scene with trepidation, imagining small, smashed bodies lying at the bottom of the ravine.

Looking back at me Gil laughed, "You worry wart. I know just what you are thinking. We'll build a high fence all along that side."

Of all the moving days from the many houses that we lived in during our lifetime, the one that I will remember most vividly is the one that carried us to our new home on Vestal Avenue.

To get five-year-old Bruce out of the way of the moving men some friends of ours offered to keep him for a few hours. They were going to take him with their older children to their swimming lessons at a local high school.

Two sweating men struggled to maneuver a heavy chest of drawers up to the second floor. I stood at the foot of the staircase, worrying and holding my breath while watching them.

The phone rang. An official-sounding voice inquired, "Is this Mrs. Gilbert? This is the emergency room at County Hospital." Just at this moment the third moving man, balancing a big armchair on his back, sweat running down his face, yelled urgently from the entrance door, "Where do you want this, Madam?"

I waved him off impatiently, "Just put it down anywhere. Hello, are you there?"

The voice, sounding annoyed, then continued, "Do you have a son named Bruce?" My legs gave way and I sat down on the steps, almost dropped the phone and leaned my head against the banister.

Bruce had been entranced with the swimming pool and was allowed to paddle around in the shallow end. He watched the big children diving where the water was deep, so he decided to try this himself. He climbed out and at the edge of the pool took a stance like the big boys had done. But at his end of the pool the water was shallow and the cement at the bottom was of unforgiving hardness.

Bruce dove. Head first. At the hospital they sewed up the big gash in his scalp and checked for concussion. There was no sign of it, thank God. This was how we celebrated the first day in our new home.

Letters to the parents follow. They had gone on another lengthy trip. Mother's birthday was coming up on April 13.

April 9, 1954.
Dear ones,

I can't find pen and ink yet in the moving mess we are still in, so here are pencil birthday wishes for Mutti. I hope you have sunshine, a good dinner on the thirteenth and are peaceful and happy.

We have had a very trying time. I just did not feel like writing. We moved out of the Lapeer workshop. Legally the corporation is about to be dissolved. We sold out almost all of our leftover wares within one week, mostly to friends and former loyal customers. Only when one is deep in the dumps does one discover the real friends one has. By God, we found that we had many. Even our landlady wanted to lend us money. Max Schaffner, the Blumbergs and several others offered assistance. We did not accept any of it.

We found a large, old two-story house high up on a hill in Echo Park for $485.00 a month. Four bedrooms and a bath are upstairs. The downstairs has a large living room, an equally large dining room that will become my workroom, a den for television and books, a big kitchen and laundry room and an extra toilet. We have a big beautiful garden with giant trees, roses, hen house, green house, an arbor, rabbit hutch (for Rick's duck) and a fantastic view all around. The school is not too far and is small and friendly. It feels like being in another country, a paradise for the children. Each has a room of his own and all are very proud.

Gil needs a vacation, but after next week he will have to look for work. As soon as I get some money together I will buy a small electric kiln. There is a whole group of people who is waiting for me to produce again. Here I have plenty of space. Our living room holds the Biedermeier furniture to perfection and looks very nice. This whole environment will help us to recuperate from the years of struggle.

I have to confess that we both were at the end of our endurance. The children are overjoyed and we know that this painful defeat was for the best. Even Gil starts to recognize it little by little.

Birthday and Easter Wishes from all of us.

Gil, Fe, Ricky, Ralphy and Brucey

Gil wrote,
Dear Oma and Opa,

We have been so busy moving into our nice new home for the past weeks that there seems to be very little time to do anything else, let alone writing letters. However we are just about now getting the house in good shape and the boys have decided to get together and write you a letter for Easter and Oma's Birthday. So this letter is going to be where each boy gets to say what he wishes, and Daddy types it out for him. (The boys are 8, 6 and 5.)
The first turn is Ricky's, since he is the oldest.

We are going to get a duck this Easter. It's going to be a baby duck and we've got a special thing for it, but we cannot put it in the place until it's grown a little more because it'll be so small it will be able to get through the wire duck run. I hope you like it in Germany and I hope you have a very nice time there. You should tell me all about it in another letter. I hope you bring us a toy like you always have. Make it a toy that is very unbreakable and is very unusual. I hope you have a very nice trip home, too.
Dear Oma, now I am getting sleepy. It all occurs on if I like to write so many letters so many times and talk so much. I hope you'll like the party I am going to have set up for your welcome when you come home. Yours Truly, Ricky.

The next turn is Ralphy's, because he is the second oldest boy.

Dear Oma and Opa

I hope I can see you soon. I hope you have a nice time on the boat you loaned. When you come back be sure you bring me a birthday present. I had a nice party. The ducks have gotten lost. When you come back we might have a dog handy. It won't be Fluffy. I haven't got your birthday letter yet. It might have gotten lost. I have got a plastic sword for my birthday and a bubble-hat. I got a cowboy and Indian suit. It is not as good as the one you used to buy me, because there is a cardboard house to cut out on the box. I hope you can see my biggest present. It is a red wagon. I have a whole set of dress-up clothes. I've got lots of other things, but I can't tell you in this letter. That's all.

Best regards and wishes, Ralph.

The next turn is Brucey's, since he is the finalest boy.

I have a room all my own. I sleep in my own bed and all my toys are in the room. I am getting kind of sleepy now so I can't think of much more to say.

Brucey wants to tell you one more thing. He wants you to bring him a real horse. It can gallop around the ocean and Oma and Opa can ride on it.

Brucey signs his name. (sort of)

Ricky says Opa is too heavy for it. Ricky says he was just joking. He loves you.

Yours very truly and sincerely,
Ricky

Dear Oma and Opa,

The boys had a wonderful time, sharing this letter. Ricky is reading back the part that he wrote and he is now reading like a big boy. Fe and I are trying to rest up a little before we start getting into something else. I also think Fe plans to write and bring you more up to date on what goes with us. The boys are now ready to go up to bed and I'll help them to get there.

Best greetings, Gil

May 10, 1954
Dear Oma and Opa,

We've had the measles. Rick very light, Ralphy followed quite heavily of course, as he would, 104 degrees in the morning. Brucey was next. But now they are all on the way to recovery. Now it is I who need to recuperate. Our plans for the Easter week vacation were of course ruined. We were going to visit the circus.

My birthday passed minus any kind of celebration. Because of the measles we could neither go out nor have guests. Next week we plan to celebrate with Ralph and Pat. Many thanks for the check.

I do need shoes and a decent iron. Gil has started to look for work in earnest. The corporation proceedings are still not finished. They tried to put La Peer Drive up for rent.

I am sorry to hear that you have it so cold. Maybe Spain will be warmer. The weather here is not good either. It is cold and foggy. The house is an oasis.

Love, Fe

The huge pine tree spread the green roof of its branches like a welcoming tent over the front lawn of the house on Vestal Avenue. It was a happy house full of children and animals. Not only did three rambunctious little boys and their friends tumble about the house and garden, two dogs, a family of ducks and a rabbit added to the liveliness of our existence.

The ducks especially tended to consider themselves as part of the household. They followed my every step when I worked in the garden and frequently ended up trailing behind me into the living room when I forgot to close the screen door. It was really no problem. All I had to do was to go back out to the garden and they'd follow me in a row like a wheeled children's toy of wooden ducks on a string.

Many years later I deduced that ducks must have a special mysterious attraction to me. Wherever Gil and I traveled in Europe, whether it was in France, Italy or England, we found ducks in the country and every duck found me and trailed behind me without fail.

Ricky had a rabbit, a big white beautiful rabbit that lived in the chicken coop that was in the garden when we moved in. It was very much admired and patted. Yet this rabbit would bite your finger if you did not watch out and it had a talent for escaping.

Have you ever tried to catch a rabbit by hand? I can still see us running after him, trying to anticipate his clever side jumps and diversionary maneuvers. Neighbors came to help and at least six of us chased that cunning beast up and down the garden hills until one ingenious boy flung a blanket through the air that landed on top of our fugitive. A furry, struggling and kicking bundle was delivered back to the coop. The ducks were greatly disturbed by the commotion and the dogs, locked up in the house, barked their frustration vehemently. They wanted to be in on the chase.

I had always had dogs when I was young. When I was very small my first dog was named Rolf, a blond Belgian sheepdog. Later came Bella, the Poodle and then Putzie, a Maltese terrier. They in fact belonged to my mother, but my heart claimed ownership nevertheless.

I did not live without a dog until my stay in New York, continuing through the early days of my marriage, including our venture in the ceramics business and our move to Vestal Avenue. So I did not object when Ralph came home from kindergarten and announced that a man had come to school and offered a bunch of puppies to the children and that he, Ralph, had volunteered to take one. Mother and son went to the man's house and were shown a bunch of scrambling, tiny golden spaniels.

"Now take your time," the owner said. "Look at them slowly and carefully to see which one you'd like."

Slowly and carefully? Ralphy lunged without hesitation. "This one." He held a squirming little handful of dog aloft and was ready to go home. That's how Scampy joined the family.

Of course by that time Ricky had to have a dog too and he chose a small mutt of unrecognizable ancestry from the Humane Society. She was sleek and black and very cute and lovable. He named her Puppina, or Pina, for short.

The menagerie was not complete until an unexpected visitor ambled slowly down one of our garden paths one morning. It was a large tortoise measuring at least a foot and a half in length. She showed no concern whatsoever for the boys and their parents, who gathered around, gazing down at her in amazement. She plodded along, her small head and sleepy eyes turning slowly from side to side observing the landscape and rocking ever so slightly on her rubbery feet and lengthy claws. A tentative nudge from Scampy's wet nose on the side of her neck finally prompted her to retire into her shell and she closed the door to any further communication.

"Let's keep her," begged the boys. We found a large wooden crate that was a perfect tortoise home. Earth, sand and grass-cuttings made a bed and our new family member was installed in her new house. She poked her head out again and seemed satisfied.

"Let's not bother her too much," I warned the boys. "She likes to be alone."

"Like a hermit." Ricky had a bright idea, "I'll call her Hermie." So *Hermie* it was and whenever we found the time to be in the garden we'd put Hermie out on the lawn to sun herself and to wander about, but we watched her with eagle eyes lest she amble away again.

Gil came home nervous and exhausted from work one evening and the boys had been particularly wild and boisterous that day. They adored the tall winding staircase that rose from the middle of the living room up to the second floor and became a racetrack after dinner. They chased each other up and down, fighting, squealing, laughing and the dogs dashed after them, barking their heads off.

Almost a year had passed since Scampy, a tiny silky-haired bundle of dog, wobbled for the first time across our living room floor on unsteady legs, leaving a little brown present for us in his wake. He had grown to a sleek young pup that loved to jump and run. And little black Pina was the perfect playmate. When I had finally corralled the boys and packed them off to bed, the dogs were still wound up and merrily rolled all over each other and raced up and down the stairs with undiminished energy. That was when the master of the house, the voice of fate over our little universe, lowered the boom.

"That's enough, God damn it to hell," he thundered. "This is a madhouse. The dogs must go."

In those early days of our marriage I was still not strong enough to withstand my dear man's overwhelming temper. His word was law and when gentle argument failed there was nothing else to do but to give in. At least we came to a compromise. Only one dog had to go and it was little Puppina, being the latest addition to the family.

So it was my lot of course to deliver her back to the shelter from whence she came. I can see her in the back seat of my car, wagging her tail and looking at me with hope in her big dark eyes as if to say *are we going to have some fun?* I felt awful having to betray her. She was such a sweet dog.

Ricky was heartbroken. She had been his dog and he never forgave his dad for giving her away. I believe this was one of the first incidents in the persistent battle and emotional strife that existed between father and son throughout their lives together.

As an inexperienced young father Gil made many mistakes. It did not take much to get him angry and heaven help the boy on whom Dad's wrath descended. He never spanked any of them, but the outbursts, the vocal reprimands and thundering commands were enough to make even me quake in my boots. When everyone did well and peace reigned Gil was a very loving father. He matured and mellowed throughout the coming years and in spite of his occasional outbursts there was no question that the wellbeing and education of his sons were always uppermost among his concerns.

Anyone who met Gil saw a man with great charm, but also a man of strength and self-reliance, a born leader. I might have been the only one who knew how sensitive and easily hurt he was and how difficult it was for him to openly admit to any anxieties or frustrations. The strongman image had to be defended no matter what, until later in life when a certain wisdom and humility took over.

There were times when the boys asked, "What's eating Dad again?" as they fearfully eyed their silent and brooding father, whose heavy black eyebrows hung like storm clouds over his glum expression.

"What's wrong, Gil?" My anxious query would only elicit a gruff *Nothing*. This would sometimes persist for days, no matter that I begged to be enlightened about the reason for his unhappiness or anger. His face turned to stone and nothing could shake him out of it. Sometimes a sudden outbreak of fury engendered by a seemingly unrelated occurrence would clear the air.

Naturally I asked myself if I had hurt him somehow, or if I had done something wrong. Had something happened at work? Was he going to loose his job? Little by little I got used to these impenetrable spells and named them *Gil's Tantrums*. I came to anticipate my feelings of helplessness whenever they occurred and took them in stride. What else could I do?

As the years went by my dear husband was more and more able to open the door to troubled emotions that had been held so tightly in check. But it took a long time. I must say though that the image of the warm and loving husband and father stays uppermost in my mind. I am quite sure that our sons would agree that the good days in our family life outnumbered the occasional days of gloom and disruptive thunder.

> *Dear Parents,*
>
> *Your wedding anniversary! Are you celebrating this important event with all the dignity it deserves?*
>
> *Gil had trouble finding work for quite a while. Business here is terrible, but now we are pleased. One of Gil's old teachers at the Frank Wiggins Trade School recommended him to the Occidental*

Life Insurance Company. It is a giant business that occupies a large office building downtown. His position is called Building Engineer. That means fixing everything that needs fixing, especially furniture repair and refinishing. They told him that there is a chance for him to build up his own department and elevate his position in the long run. The salary is small, but there is the possibility to pick up cabinet jobs on the side. His hours are from 8 to 4:30, five days a week. It is a firm position with pension and medical insurance. We have $ 75.00 per week. Not much, but what a luxury to know that it's available without fail. You can't imagine what that means. At least rent and food are taken care of. If we both do some work on the side, Gil by doing cabinet jobs, framing jobs and doing house painting and I with my ceramics we should be all right.

We still feel as if we are in a dream living in this great house. Ralphy had a birthday party in the garden with ten children. He got to roast hot dogs in the barbecue all by himself. We fell heir to a big set of swings. Ricky is a proud cub scout and will get his uniform soon. Brucey goes to a very nice nursery school from 9 to 11:30 and gets constantly invited for lunch by other children. All three boys are in great shape. The upheaval was about the best thing that could have happened to us. For all of us! Even Gil has relaxed and is satisfied. No frantic rushing about, no worries. We are able to read a book in the evening or watch something on the television without feeling guilt.

I am working like crazy on my Christmas sale. Ricky and Ralphy have been home for the last week with one of those unexplained little epidemics that are going around under the vague general description of a virus. Not only we, but everybody around us is coughing and has diarrhea. Otherwise the children are blossoming. They never looked as well, even Ralphy, who is always slower in getting over a sickness. His leg seems to get stronger. He loves school. I expected that he would. The teacher believes that he will be one of the first to read. Brucy is still at home, but he will go to a day care center for the last few months before kindergarten.

It seems that a group of ten-year-old girls from the neighborhood is getting together to take ceramic lessons from me here at my home. If they collect four or five girls, I will take them on at $2.00 each per class.

Once more, Happy Anniversary! Say hello to Switzerland for me.

Fe

Chapter 13

Landing at the Boy's Club

Gil was not happy with his job at Occidental Life Insurance. It paid too little, which meant that he needed to hunt for extra work after 4.30 and on weekends. He took whatever jobs he could get, including carpentry, house painting or building fences, for which he had no expertise. Who knows how long his fences survived? He did the best he could and worked himself to a state of exhaustion. I even went to work with him at times just to lighten the load. I painted walls in people's homes and did the finicky moldings, baseboards and window frames.

It became clear to me that I had to do something to augment our family income; my limited teaching at home was just not enough. So when our friend Joe Blumberg, who was the director of the Jewish Old Age Home in Boyle Heights, offered me the position of art therapist I accepted with alacrity.

I was to work with the old people for three days per week, letting them paint, work with clay or engage in anything stimulating. This idea appealed to me and I entered the big, formidable building with the expectation of having an interesting and enjoyable time with the old people. What a disappointment awaited me. I could not communicate with most of them; they all spoke Yiddish, at least all of the ones that came to my class. They were very sweet and tried to be helpful to their teacher, an obviously not-very-intelligent young woman. Smiles and hand signals were simply not enough to affect a meaningful exchange of ideas. I lasted two weeks and as the third week was about to commence I simply stayed in bed, unable to move. Looking ahead to the long drive to Boyle Heights, then to a day of frustration and a feeling of personal inadequacy got to be too much for me. Thank God, Joe forgave me.

It was 1954 and our boys were 8, 6 and 5. Soon after this failed enterprise I landed a job heading the Arts and Crafts Department at the Times Boy's Club in the Lincoln Heights area of Los Angeles. The Boy's Club occupied a big building in this very poor and rundown neighborhood and housed not only a gym, a swimming pool, a library and many classrooms, but most importantly a large arts and crafts room that was organized into well supplied areas for woodworking, painting, printmaking, sculpture and photography.

I hired my friend, the artist Pat Cary, to help me in the painting department. Gil supervised the woodworking efforts of the older boys when he was able to join us in the late afternoon and in the evenings. He brought our own boys along and they joined in the activities with great enthusiasm. Rick was particularly drawn to the grinding machine and worked various and sundry donated plastic scraps into all kinds of small objects, circles, hearts and imaginary shapes. Maybe that foretold his later interest and talent in making and designing jewelry.

On a nice spring day I arrived for work as usual, at one o'clock, an hour before the building opened for the afternoon's activities. A few real little guys were already sitting on the front steps, waiting to be let in. Kindergarteners I presumed. There was probably nobody at home for them. Where else could they go?

"Let us in, coach?"

I could have hugged them all. "Pretty soon. In just a little while." I had to hurry to prepare my room. I poured paint into paper-cups and muffin trays, covered the tables with newspaper, got brushes out, scissors and glue, hammer and nails and pulled out the innumerable cardboard boxes with paper scraps, woodchips, shells, wire and found objects of all kinds. Dorothy Royer's Workshop experience came to good stead. The clay room needed attention: the tables were prepared and the tools were laid out.

Two o'clock came and the doors were opened. Eager little bodies scrambled in. This was the younger brigade, ages 5 through 7 or 8, to be joined later by the boisterous older bunch. There were mostly brown faces, some black faces and a few white ones. You heard them coming, noisily at first, laughing, pushing, fighting, screaming, but once inside the room their eyes started to dart from table to table, to paints, to tools and boxes and the chattering bunch broke up.

Each child was in his own world then, making his mark, choosing, forming, exploring to his heart's content. The timid were encouraged. Everyone got support and friendship. Some drifted in and out again to go swimming or play table tennis, then came back and picked up another brush or pen.

When the older boys came they just joined in. No one got pushed around. Some diplomacy, some quick intervention was sometimes necessary and confrontations were usually forestalled. Some of these children were abused at home and in the streets, badly fed, starved for affection and intellectual stimulation. Many had little family life if any.

It was obvious that Gil enjoyed the time he spent with the children when he joined us at the end of his tense and busy workday. Sometimes I watched him secretly out of the corner of my eye and was filled with admiration when I saw how skillfully he interacted with his sometimes-rowdy young charges.

One especially obstreperous thirteen-year old, Steve, was blond and blue-eyed, not Hispanic and therefore stood out among his brown and black-haired companions. He was born with a deformed left arm that ended just below the elbow. He must have gotten quite a bit of teasing from his compatriots in school and on the streets. He reacted by cutting the left sleeve off every shirt he owned to expose the naked stump even more, hitting and threatening the other boys with it, laughing uproariously to see them shrink back in revulsion. Little children fled when they saw him coming.

Great was my astonishment one weekend afternoon when I saw Gil talking to our young horror with his arm around the boy's shoulder, leading him towards the woodworking area. I tried not to make it obvious that I was following them, but succeeded in getting close enough to pick up a few sentences of what was being said.

"Now Steve, you are going to be my assistant." Gil's was the voice of authority. Aha, I thought, he is in his element and I suppressed a wifely grin. "You are bright and I know that I can count on you." Sounding kind and reassuring, he added, "I'd like you to supervise the younger boys at the carving table. Hand out the clamps and chisels, assist them with their tools and give help wherever it is needed. Also supervise the older boys at the table saw. See that they keep their hands the right distance from the blades and that they obey the safety rules. I'll show you how to do all that."

Steve's rejoinder was mumbled, so I did not hear what he said, but a remarkable change in his attitude and behavior became obvious within the next few weeks. He replaced his ratty, one-armed shirt with a clean tee shirt with sleeves that reached down to the elbows. The little kids started to loose their fear of him and the bigger ones obeyed him with renewed respect. After all, he was the assistant coach. He proudly grew into his elevated status and proved himself worthy. Gil stood unobtrusively on the sidelines observing his pupil's progress and smiled with satisfaction.

Looking back through the many years working with children of diverse backgrounds, the Hispanic ones were among the most creative. What a joy to see the outpouring of all that energy. *Look what I did, Coach.* There was an elaborately painted self portrait or a few lustily splashed globs of color, no matter. *That's just great, Carlos.*

Someone worked on a big construction on the floor using sticks, cardboard, tin cans, whatever he could find, putting it together with glue, string, hammer and nails and had been at it for three intense days.

"What is it going to be?"

"A something," he said, refusing to be interrupted. Five o'clock came and they all had to leave until seven when the doors opened again. I tidied up to get the room ready for the evening crowd. It had been hectic during the day and since most of the evening boys would be bigger I knew that the place would be jumping.

Finally things looked fairly orderly and I settled down on one of the high chairs in the clay room. With a sigh of relief I unwrapped my sandwich and opened my thermos bottle. Thirty minutes of peace and heavenly quiet lay before me. The powdery smell of clay did not bother me; I was used to it. As a matter of fact that smell and the pungent odors of paint and turpentine always seemed to evoke a sense of comfort and wellbeing in me. It meant that I was in my element. I closed my eyes for just a minute and heard a piano tinkling faintly from the music room. Someone improvised to *Chopsticks.*

Taking a sip of coffee I glanced at the shelves that ran along three walls of the sculpture area. There on plywood boards stood the clay pieces the children had done. Some had been completed and others were in progress, wrapped up in damp rags and plastic sheeting to keep them wet. I knew that their makers would be storming in this evening.

"How does it look, coach? Can I have it?" They would settle down, eager to finish and be proud of their creations.

A door banged open and crashed against the wall. "Look at all that shit," someone yelled behind me. I turned around and there stood two big boys. They must have been about 15 or 16 years old. One, baby faced, a cigarette hanging from his pouting lips, gave the impression of being even taller than his nearly 6 feet by wearing a long bright-green coat reaching down to his ankles. The other was squat, built like a bull terrier with a broad dark face and a slightly drippy nose that he tried without much success to control by sniffing audibly. Small stubble around his chin gave promise of some future maturity.

They glared at me. They looked around. They looked at each other. Babyface pulled out a nasty-looking knife and friend Bulldog followed suit. Babyface went to the nearest shelf. "What the fuck," and sliced off the head of a little clay figure. Then he said *fuck* again and cut the next piece and the next and the next, always keeping at least one eye on me. Friend Bulldog followed suit until all of the clay pieces were chopped up, sliced one by one, slowly and with relish.

Coach sat without moving. There was nothing to be done. The knives looked pretty sharp. This was early in the year. Nobody had seen these boys, either before or after their memorable visit.

When Christmas approached, the club director called me to his office. "We will conduct a tour through the facilities of the club for high officials of the city. I trust you will see to it that the entrance and assembly hall are well decorated for the holidays, Mrs. Gilbert. Tell Tony Carrillo to get a tree and he'll show you where the ornaments are that we use every year. I'll be out of town until then."

I was delighted. "The children will have so much fun doing it."

"Yes," he said, sounding a little doubtful, "But make it impressive."

We went to work with gusto, the boys and I. We taped their Christmas pictures over all of the walls. Many of them showed Madonnas and the strangest looking Babies Jesus in open garages in Lincoln Heights, instead of mangers in Bethlehem. Abstract paintings gloried in glowing colors and swirling shapes. Mobiles with birds, flowers and stars in torrents of glitter were hung from the ceiling. We constructed the strangest looking angels made of wood, silver paper, cotton and God knows what else. *Papier mâché* Santa Clauses with shining eyes and gold-flecked beards in addition to mythical beasts with Christmas stars on their heads and tails either dangled from the ceiling or climbed over the staircase and the backs of chairs. It was a truly festive display.

The director returned from his trip. We confidently expected his enthusiastic approval, yet he was quite horrified.

"This is *not* what I had in mind," he growled. His office door slammed behind him. I was told later that he had considered firing me. But the visiting dignitary's *oohs* and *ahs* caused the director to relent, though he grumbled for days.

I had planned a huge tree for the center of the entrance to be decorated by the children, of course. Why use the same old glass baubles from years past? I had purchased rolls of chicken wire to be formed into a tall cone, an armature for the tree.

I was kneeling on the floor of the large hall untying rolls of wire when I looked up and there, sauntering in nonchalantly and as innocent as can be were Babyface and Bullterrier.

A thought struck me. I slowly got up and dusted the knees of my slacks with great deliberation. "Oh, hi boys. You are just in time. I wonder if I could ask you for a great favor. You see, I want to form this wire into a cone to make a big Christmas tree, but I just don't have the strength. My hands won't do it and I am not tall enough either. You both are so big and strong. Could you possibly do it for me? I'd be so grateful!"

Babyface looked at Bullterrier and Bullterrier looked at Babyface, who snuffled furiously. "Well, OK Coach." And so they went to work and did a much better job then I could have done. And then they helped some more and Babyface became Arturo and Bullterrier became Bill and even after the holidays they kept dropping in, nosing about the workshop.

One day I found Bill with a clump of clay in his hands, squeezing it and moving it about. "Looks like a head," I said.

"Oh yeah?" He tilted his emerging creation around from one side to the other and studied it. He frowned in deep concentration and then poked two holes into the clay. "Looks like eyes, eh?"

"Sure does," I nodded happily. From then on Bill could be found in the classroom almost every night.

"Hey Coach," Arturo slowly sauntered up to me one evening, "You aren't pissed?"

"It's over," I said, "forget it." The next February I found Arturo in the workshop with a pencil behind his ear contemplating a drawing he had made. "Where is Bill?' I asked.

"Ain't comin' no more."

"Why?"

"Cops got him."

"What did he do?"

"Sold stuff," he said and touched his thumb first to one nostril and then to the other and snuffled, presuming that I knew what he meant. A runny nose was the result of a bad cold or an allergy as far as I knew. The word *cocaine* was not in my vocabulary yet.

Several years later I learned more about the temptations of contemporary youth. I learned that *everyone smokes pot, no big deal,* and that snorting cocaine makes your nose run. All of this was useful knowledge, but certainly did not concern my family. Not yet.

CHAPTER 14

A Chinese House in Pasadena

A phone call came from my friend Dorothy Royer. "The Junior Art Workshop at the Pasadena Art Museum has an opening for another teacher. I took the liberty to recommend you. Are you interested?"

At 46 North Los Robles Avenue in Pasadena the unmistakably oriental building looked like a strange intruder fronting this busy American thoroughfare. The high steep roof shone bright green, its edges jutted over the third floor windows, then reached wide and curved upwards towards the sky as if it wanted to lift into the air. At the entrance below heavy red wooden gates stood wide open and led to a large inner courtyard.

I stood transfixed. There right in the middle of the courtyard stood a huge gingko tree, splashed up to the sky like a golden crackling flame in the late September sun. Its branches reached above the roofs of the surrounding building and dappled the paving below with their shadows.

There I was to work for the next 9 years, driving the busy freeway from Los Angeles twice a week and four times during summer vacations. I also taught a special class for the museum's satellite program for two years in Fullerton. I taught at a private school for gifted children for three years at about the same time.

It felt as if I spent much of my time on the freeway just driving and driving and entering one classroom after another, facing very diverse groups of young individuals ready for action, discovering their own creative needs and capabilities through the language of art. There was so much more to it then handing out brushes and paints. There was the responsibility I felt for each child's meaningful experience, success and failure, a duty that did not rest lightly on my shoulders.

During my time teaching in Pasadena nine-year-old Bruce, the athlete of our family, came limping up the hill towards home. He was on his way back from school. "Why are you limping?" I asked, expecting a saga of fights on the playground or a stumble at football.

His answer, along with an uncharacteristic grimace of pain was, "I don't know; it just hurts." The doctor at Kaiser Hospital gave stern orders: Bruce was to get crutches and the affected leg was to be held up in a sling. No weight was to be put on that hip for the next nine months. A softening of the hip joint was the cause of the pain. No more running, no sports.

At first Bruce was devastated, but the sun broke through his firmament when Elysian Heights Elementary School refused to accept him with crutches for reasons of liability. A home teacher was assigned and Bruce was in heaven. He maintains even today that he learned more in those nine months than in years of regular school.

He was nine years old and certainly not ready to stew at home in solitude. I decided to take him along to my classes in Pasadena, though worried about his ability to maneuver the high steps to the classrooms at the museum. I need not have harbored the slightest doubt. Few children could run as fast with two legs as Bruce did on his crutches.

Two huge Chinese stone lions flanked the entrance to the museum and in the blink of an eye my plucky son had scaled one of them and waved down to me with his crutches. Passers by stared up, amazed at my young marvel. Of course Bruce had no trouble hopping on his one good leg up the steep flight of stairs that led to the classrooms on the second floor. He accompanied me to many classes and had a great time. He drew and painted and joined the other children on frequent visits to the treasures in the museum galleries.

Fifteen years later when we lived in Santa Barbara some old friends came up from Los Angeles to visit us. We were showing them the older Spanish section of our city, the real Santa Barbara, in contrast to the department store, banking, business traffic and sober concrete atmosphere of the large modern development farther up the coast. We were ambling along, peering into attractive shop windows while heading towards the colorful tourist showplace, El Paseo Restaurant. It was famous not only for it's food, but for the spectacular large removable ceiling that treated diners at daytime to a bright, mostly blue sky and at night to the stars that shone down on the tables below.

In inclement weather or when it was just too cold the ceiling rolled to a close like a blanket drawn over the people under its care.

We sat looking up at the stars, glasses of tequila in our hands and good food on the table. Suddenly someone was standing in front of me blocking my view of the mariachi band that was just about to play.

"You are Mrs. Gilbert, aren't you? Of course you are. You probably don't remember me. I'm Christian. I was in your art classes in Pasadena for a couple of years. I owe you. You made a big difference to me." I looked up at the eager face of the tall young man in front of me. Of course I could not remember him. It must have been at least twelve or fifteen years since he had been in my class and hundreds of kids had paraded through during that time. "I was shy and probably depressed. You helped me discover a lot, a way to find myself."

I was so moved that I stood up to thank him and maybe to give him a motherly hug when a group of young people hurried by, shouted, "Hurry up Chris, we'll be late," and swooped him up almost against his will. He waved goodbye and I waved back. I guess all that struggle and hard work had been worth it.

Chapter 15

Coffee at Altman Antiques and a New Job for Gil

The year 1956 came and it turned out to be another turning point in the Gilbert Saga. I was visiting in the back of Ralph's shop where a group of intimate friends had gathered as usual. I snacked on a cup of yogurt from the neighborhood grocery store, supplementing it from time to time with a fulsome sprinkling of sugar, which drove our Greek friend Constantine to despair.

"I can't stand your sugar crunching," he moaned. How strange that a silly little incident like that should be remembered after so many years in connection with an important event in our lives.

Ralph's good friend Peter Furst, a superb photographer, pushed his way through the beaded curtain to the inner sanctum, a large portfolio under his arm. He displayed his portfolio for us to admire. First came marvelous animal studies, especially several photographs of a group of proboscis monkeys whose faces could have been taken from Heironymus Bosch's *Inferno*. They had long, bulbous, pendulous noses on narrow faces with sharp eyes that stared out at you, all framed by stiff gray hair. Long grasping arms fortified the impression that these were ghostly, hellish creatures.

"You might not be interested in the next set of pictures," Peter hesitated. "I was hired to document the operation of a small company that manufactures travel trailers and is currently in the process of enlarging their enterprise. I like working for them. Nice people."

We looked at a group of about fifteen men, some in suits but most of them in overalls, standing in front of a row of low-slung buildings, smiling dutifully at the camera. A few odd looking vehicles could be seen in the background. "Those are supposed to be trailers?"

Constantine snorted derisively. "They look like blown up Bologna sausages to me."

I was reminded of a Zeppelin that I saw hovering in the sky when I was a child in Germany. A streak of sunshine in the strong contrast of the black and white photograph hit the rounded roof of one of the vehicles and it shone bright silver. "The shell is all aluminum," Peter explained. "By the way," he continued and turned to me, "I heard that Gil is not happy with his job. The Airstream people are hiring now. Maybe that would be a chance for him."

The very next day found Gil at Wally Byam's Airstream factory as a new member of the cabinet crew. This was in 1956 and he was soon promoted to foreman. Over the next 17 years he rose steadily within the organization, with its California and Ohio factories. He retired in 1973 after years as sales director of the large Airstream factory in Santa Fe Springs.

In 1956 we once again had to leave a beautiful home. We were informed that the owner's son and his family were going to take possession as soon as we could leave. "If only we had our own house where nobody could throw us out." I sat on the grass under the big pine tree. Hermie the turtle plodded thoughtfully among the blades. Absentmindedly my eyes pursued her, then gazed out at the valley beyond the trees.

"That's exactly what we'll go after. We make it happen." Gil dragged the water hose back to the spigot and turned it off. Watering and raking were his weekend occupations, punctuated by his efforts to move rocks and spread gravel. The care of plants was left to me. "Let's go," he reached his hand out and pulled me up.

"Where to?" I asked.

"House hunting, of course."

"We don't even have a down payment."

"We'll manage." The ever-optimistic go-getter would not be deterred. After days trotting over the hilly streets of Echo Park, checking one listing after another without success, we almost decided to look in another area of town.

"Let's give it one more try." I did not want to leave the peaceful small-town atmosphere of Echo Park and its nice elementary school that the children had attended for quite some time.

The next day late in the afternoon Gil and I resumed our search and walked up well-paved Cerro Gordo Street as it climbed toward Elysian

Park and it's towering eucalyptus trees. We were both dead tired and had just about decided to turn around and give up for the day when the miracle occurred. At its crest the road turned and formed a loop around a landscaped island leading back down the hill again. The last slanting beams of sunlight embraced a row of blooming marguerites and made them glow like white foam on darkening water. The air was motionless and we could see the valley below through the leafy traceries of trees that stood quietly before us. It was as if the world prepared for rest together with the departing sun. We stood for a minute feeling the peace around us. When we turned to go back down we saw it, a sign from heaven stuck to a short pole in front of a house under the drooping leaves of a young elm tree. *FOR SALE BY OWNER,* and there was a phone number.

Chapter 16

Life in a New House
Cerro Gordo Street, 1956 to 1960

It was a comfortable little house with a peaked roof and a grassy back yard, big enough to toss a ball around in, play a game of croquet or engage in a wrestling match. There was space for some garden chairs and a table for an occasional outdoor meal on weekends. Taking two steps up to the front door one directly entered a good sized living room, crossed it and reached a swinging door at the opposite end that led to a decent kitchen. Another door took you to the two very small bedrooms.

"Just too small." I was disappointed.

"Never mind; there is space in back. We'll build another room for the boys." Gil was rarely deterred from getting what he really wanted.

How we were able to buy this house and have the children's room added escapes my memory. I know that we were reluctant to accept any more money from my parents. We were determined to maintain the independence of our family and manage as best we could on our own. Maybe we got a loan from the bank or from Gil's employer, Wally Byam, who had taken quite a liking to the new young man he had hired and who showed such high ability.

With great delight we turned to the treasures of the Salvation Army and Goodwill Industries. Not only did they supply us with dishes, but also with clothes for the boys. There were well-worn jeans without our customary holes at the knee and serviceable replacements for their outgrown shirts and sweaters. We also found a comfortable sofa. We placed it against the longest wall in our living room and Gil built bookshelves around it covering the wall up to the ceiling.

"A room without books is a dead room," my father used to say and he was so right. Scampy took immediate possession of the soft pillows on the sofa and the rest of the family congregated around our huge walnut dining table for meals, schoolwork, or games.

Gil built a skylight on the roof of the narrow one-car garage that stood at the side of the house and it became my studio. I must admit that the time I was able to spend there with my easel and paints was very limited. I remember our life in the house on Cerro Gordo Street with affection. I see pictures of curving, peaceful streets in my mind and the wide view down to the valley. Towering eucalyptus trees near our house from the crest of the hill rising like a sea of flags waving in the wind, then spreading down into the ravine that ran into Elysian Park.

Enterprising Ricky climbed one of the trees and tied a rope swing onto a sturdy branch. The safety of this doubtful contraption worried me only in hindsight as I called forth a vision of the swinging rope so near the ravine. I must slightly revise the idyllic picture of that time as I see Rick coming from the park one sultry summer day. I did not see his dusty jeans, his torn shirt or the sweat dripping from his nose; all I saw was the snake he had draped across his shoulders, with the end of the tail in one hand and the head in the other.

"Look what I found, Mom!" His face shone with ecstatic delight. I held my breath. *Don't scream*, I told myself, or he'll let go of the head. A covered pail from the kitchen seemed a likely container.

I found my voice again. "Throw it in, quickly." Not used to this kind of treatment, the snake rebelled, turned back and bit Rick's hand near the thumb.

"Now Madam, calm down," answered the slow, drawling voice on the emergency line. "Just describe the snake to me. Does it have a rattle? No? Stripes? What color? Madam you have a harmless king snake. Disinfect the wound and forget about it." Obviously I still have not forgotten it.

Ricky had never gotten over the loss of his dog Puppina and Gil had a change of heart. "All-right, this next dog will have to be small and shorthaired. Scampy is shedding enough for two." So off we went to the Humane Society, just Gil and I. We did not tell the children and left them at home, knowing full well that otherwise a battle would ensue over the important choice of our new family member.

Up and down we walked, from cage to cage. We had almost made up our minds in favor of a smooth, tiny, spry terrier. Then my eyes caught a very sad sight, sitting far back in a corner of his cage. A haystack of long black tousled hair enveloped a good-sized frame and covered a face that drooped and sagged towards the floor. He was the picture of complete dejection, of one who in the near future might contemplate suicide. The saddest thing I ever saw.

Calling out and making encouraging noises in his direction, I coaxed him and he came slowly and lifted his face. I saw his big brown eyes gazing at me from behind the curtain of his hair. His long brush of a tail started to wag just a little and his whole body tensed with expectation, indicating that he could perhaps embrace life after all. Hope came to his eyes. *Are you going to take me?* Then Gil succumbed, saying only, "He is even bigger than Scampy."

We brought him home as a big surprise. The boys loved him and Ricky was ecstatic. He wrapped his arms around him and dug his hands into that great mass of hair. "I'll call him Frou-Frou."

"But Ricky," I protested, "that is a name for a dolled-up poodle, not for this rugged customer." We compromised, cutting the name in half to remove some of the fluff. We learned from the vet that Frou was a purebred Hungarian sheepdog. Without any therapy beyond a good dose of love and savory food Frou had no further thoughts of suicide. Depression was never again detected in our happy companion. From that time on Frou had only one trauma to cope with, and that one was annual: he got shorn at the height of summer to withstand the heat. On each of these occasions he was left deeply ashamed and hid in a kitchen corner for days.

It was eight o'clock and we had finished dinner. Bruce pushed his chair away from the table, still chewing his last bite of food, and announced that he would go to bed. This was a near nightly pattern that astonished every visitor that happened to hear it, especially if they knew anything about six year olds and bedtime. No protestations or hedging as far as Bruce was concerned. He climbed into bed, pulled the covers up and we did not hear from him until morning. He did not even stir when Ralph took out his clarinet to practice before breakfast, or when I walked through his room to the new addition at the back of the house.

Here the two older boys had their territory and shared it with a train set on two large plywood panels that occupied a great part of the floor. A long worktable at the end of the room was meant for homework or games, neither of which could have been pursued at Rick's end. It was covered by a wild array of tools, boxes, glue bottles, uncapped paint jars and plastic parts for ship or airplane models, with their sheets of instructions strewn everywhere.

Nothing was glued to the table more tightly than the boy himself. Food and sleep were ignored and certainly homework wasn't even considered. Rick had already graduated to some of the most complicated models that were available at the Woolworth store and nothing could drag him away from his tasks until they had been completed. In spite of an occasional scream of frustration or rage that could be heard throughout the house when a part broke or did not fit, the master builder stuck to his projects with fierce determination. We were amazed at the skill and concentration he displayed. Wild and rambunctious Ricky showed an unexpected side of his character.

The music teacher at Elysian Heights Elementary School needed a clarinetist for his orchestra. Since Ralph showed an interest, he was handed an instrument, given lessons and told that he could join the band if he applied himself and practiced. And practice he did. He became as inseparable from his instrument as Rick was from his model building.

While other boys played football Ralph would pick up his clarinet instead. It soon became clear that this boy showed considerable talent and a passion for music that needed to be supported. Gil was ecstatic. The son was going to realize his father's unfulfilled dreams; he was going to be a musician. We turned in the school instrument and bought him his own clarinet. A teacher was found and once a week Mr. Michet came to the house and gloated over his student's progress.

Next it was Bruce who caught the music bug. This was not really surprising, since the boys grew up with so much music in their home. Gil and I listened to our records whenever we had free time and felt the need for it, which was practically on a daily basis. Our friend Betts Hall, another parent from the elementary school, was a sprightly Canadian and an excellent pianist. She agreed to give Bruce piano lessons. She knew how to make it fun for him and he loved it. Now of course we had to face another difficulty. A piano had to be acquired.

Bruce marched into his room and reappeared proudly with his piggybank in hand and spilled its contents out onto the kitchen table. We all gathered around and earnestly counted the pennies, nickels and dimes, reassuring Bruce that the twenty two dollars that resulted were indeed a substantial contribution towards the purchase price of his piano. Studying the advertising pages of the Los Angeles Times we were finally able to acquire an old converted player piano that was in good shape. It was big and clumsy, but we were able to afford it, after adding rather substantially to Bruce's twenty two dollars. He was the proudest boy among his friends for *he* had bought a piano with his own money.

Of course Ricky did not want to be left behind; he wanted to become a jazz musician and play the drums. So again we scoured the ads and acquired a drum set. Ricky loved the drums, but they failed to contribute to an atmosphere of serenity and calm in our daily lives. Mr. Michet was delighted and helped the boys create our own little in-home band, soon to become known among friends and the Elysian Heights Elementary School population as *The Three G-Notes*.

"My God, how can you stand it?" asked Bluma Shuckett, as she pressed her hands tightly over her ears and scrunched her face as if she were in searing pain. This nervous little woman had come to pick up her son, who had joined our boys for the afternoon, alternating at the piano with Bruce from time to time. He was having a grand time, something he obviously was not able to do at home, judging from his mother's demeanor. Our living room walls were vibrating to the tune of *Hold That Tiger*, a favorite piece, repeated over and over, because after all it had to be rendered perfectly. Scampy was hiding under the couch. Bluma's son Ralph became a well-known musician, arranger and composer in later life.

In May 1958 my parents celebrated their golden wedding anniversary, when the boys were 12, 10 and 9. Gil loaded our car with Rick, Ralph, luggage, clarinet and drum-set and drove up to San Francisco where we were to meet Oma and Opa, who had preceded us to celebrate their special day with old friends. I had chosen to take the train with Bruce, who had never been on a train before. It was a great experience for him; he walked from car to car unceasingly, gazing at the landscape and talking to the passengers without a shred of self-consciousness.

The only time he got to sit down in all of the many hours it took to reach San Francisco was when a very large and kind African American man took a liking to him and took him on his lap. This gentleman was a professional jazz musician on his way to a performance. He talked about his children at home and laughed delightedly when Bruce told him about the *Three G Notes*.

The Golden Wedding Anniversary day arrived. All of our old friends were assembled at the home of Paul and Li Moses in San Francisco. A festive meal was served. Speeches brimmed with love and admiration for the celebrating couple and then, to top it all off, a gift was unveiled: a television-set, the first one my parents were to own. A rousing rendition of the St. Louis Blues by the *Three G-Notes* followed and Opa beamed with pride in spite of the fact that he was not much of a music lover. He was almost as pleased as if the boys had recited Shakespeare.

One of the rare personal notes in Father's diary preceded his list of the party guests, "To begin with Brucey played a prelude. Following the soup Ralphy played the clarinet and after speeches by Paul and our son, Ralph, Ricky gave a toast."

One year later, on June 15, 1959, Opa's seventy-fifth birthday party took place in a Hollywood home, where *The Three G Notes* again performed with great success in front of numerous elderly actors, writers and directors, most of whom had left behind established professions and even fame in Germany. They came to celebrate their old friend's life. There were happy faces, hugs and laughter, yet still one felt, hovering over the cheer, an unacknowledged longing among the guests for their past glories.

My three boys, proud performers all, were dressed in white shirts and ties, with hair fastidiously combed. They behaved with impeccable dignity and were received with great appreciation and rousing applause. However, when the performance was safely over the ties were loosened, shirtsleeves were rolled up and their full attention was directed to the main attraction, the sumptuous refreshment table. At the end of the evening Bruce got to keep the large hollowed-out watermelon boat with the remains of fruit and other goodies in its hold. He beamed and hugged it tightly to the shirt that had been white only a short while before.

Chapter 17

Mother's Panic Brings Family Togetherness

In October of that same year Father underwent extensive tests and had to spend a week at the hospital. Mother was alone in the apartment and she could not stand it. It was at seven o'clock in the evening, the first night of his absence, and Mother called us in a complete panic, "Come over, *please* come over. I am so scared. I hear every noise outside and think someone might break in. I just can't be alone; I know I won't sleep all night."

"Oh God, I groaned. Now what do we do? Six more days to go." At least Gil was in town that week to tend to the boys in the evening. I stacked the dinner dishes in the sink, grabbed my toothbrush and nightgown, jumped into my car and took off. Mother was a hysterical mess. I realized that she had really never been alone at night. The same scenario continued for the rest of that week. I drove to her house every night and slept with her and then had to be back home at six thirty the next morning to prepare the kids for school.

I sighed with relief when Father came home. But Gil shook his head and predicted, "This is only the beginning. Your father is vulnerable and Mother is not in such good shape either. If we don't make some arrangement now we'll face more upheavals."

"So what, for heavens sake, can be done?" I felt exhausted and at my wits end.

"There is only one thing to do: we'll live in the same house again and take care of them." Gil spread his hands, palms up, in a gesture of resignation to our fate.

My parent's delight at our suggestion was almost gratifying enough to compensate us for leaving a home in which we had lived happily for several years. *Dec. 4. Moved to 1936 N. Hoover Street*, reads the last entry in Father's coveted diary, dated 1959. It was a personal note, one of the few that seemed to be in his own voice, speaking about his life, rather than the endless accounts of travel destinations, theater conferences, restaurants in which he had eaten, and meetings with writers and theater people. His life would end three years later in this, his last home.

We considered ourselves extremely lucky to have found a handsome Spanish duplex in the Los Feliz district. Again, the parents lived downstairs and we on the upper floor, with a covered winding tile staircase connecting the two self-contained apartments, with separate entrances, doorbells and mailboxes. We were able to live our lives independently from each other. Mother had obviously learned her bitter lesson after living together with us in our first home and she rarely came upstairs without being invited. Her inevitable critical remarks were now called *suggestions* and we had learned to smile and say *yes, yes* and *do you think so?* And then put it out of our minds. That is, up to a point. Admittedly we ground our teeth off and on, but we managed to bear it.

The children were happy to cruise back and forth from our place down to their Oma and Opa's apartment, where they were always welcome. Rick was 13 at this time, Ralph 11 and Bruce 10.

These were the years when the boys were old enough to appreciate their grandparents. Their Opa seems to occupy an especially fond place in their memory. Perhaps Oma somewhat less so, particularly for Rick, because she was never able to curb her deeply ingrained habit of criticizing and interfering. Yet she loved all three boys very much and, as was true for everyone she loved, they were supposed to exist within the framework she desired for them.

When the parents asked us down for dinner it was always a special occasion. Mother's cooking skills remained shaky, since she had learned to cook after we had left Germany and then only out of necessity. Before 1933, when Hitler had made life impossible, household help was not hard to find and there were theatre obligations to keep her busy. But things changed and she had no choice but to change along with her circumstances. Mother would have started preparing her dishes in the morning, in all probability. She took herself to task with good will.

Clad in a pretty, carefully selected apron she labored, handling pots and pans, recipes, measurements, cookbooks and oven temperatures. She suffered, but suffered nobly.

We sat at the round table in their dining room on their red leather armchairs surrounded by books and masks and paintings, oriental carpets under foot. The warm glow of the crystal chandelier above the table wrapped the whole family lovingly together in its circle of light. With glints of perspiration on her nose Mother proudly brought from the kitchen a pan of veal cutlets swimming in butter, Bratkartoffeln (sliced potatoes) fried to a crisp, again in pure butter. And to top it off there was a large round earthenware dish of cauliflower that had been baked whole in a white butter and egg sauce with nutmeg and parsley covered with a thick brown crust of parmesan cheese.

I fondly recall Mother's most successful deserts and the happiness that accompanied them. There was a cheesecake that was made of pressed cottage cheese instead of cream cheese, with raisins and slivers of lemon peel. Another was a Napfkuchen (bundt cake). It was always exciting to witness the precarious liberation of that firm yellow cake from its round baking dish. She wouldn't tolerate accidents and it was not allowed to break. When it finally stood in all its glory with wavy contours and a perfect hole in the middle, snow-white powdered sugar dusted over the browned crown, my mother glowed, and not only from heat and exhaustion. Those times were intervals of peace among escalating periods of stress.

There were evenings when we gathered in Mother's sitting room in front of the television set. The boys, sprawled on the floor, were admonished not to kick each other. Mother, in her silken Chinese robe reclined on her strategically positioned chaise lounge to survey one and all, not only the screen. Her hand, elegantly raised, held a long gold and ivory cigarette holder. Slowly and deliberately she blew little puffs of smoke into the air from time to time. Was she on stage or at home? Sometimes it was hard to tell.

My father sat with his feet propped on a hassock, looking at the screen over the rim of his reading glasses. As I watched him I recalled what Erich Ebermayer, a well-known German writer and dramatist, had written about Father in his memoir after the war. "Dr. Altman was the director of the Schauspielhaus in Hannover. He wrote several books on the theater. He is one of our most knowledgeable, cultured theater men. He is a deep thinker almost to the point of being a scientist." Yet here he now sat, the deep thinker, my sweet and peaceful father, watching boxing on TV when Floyd Patterson became the heavyweight champion.

Father's special interest, though, was wrestling, because he thought it represented a kind of primitive performance, a type of theater. "Think of Shakespeare's bumbling bumpkins," he reminded us. The weird, wild-eyed and costumed muscle men fascinated him with their grunting and throwing each other about, each with his own bragging and posturing style. The boys, too, revered these abominations. Mother and Gil suffered them, but I always fled, only to return for the news reports that were so very important and exciting at that time: the student anti-segregation protests in the South were shown on the screen; the Freedom Riders were attacked. It was hard to comprehend the depth of ignorance and viciousness that reigned in the souls of many of our countrymen.

We watched when the Nazi criminal Adolf Eichmann was arrested and brought to Israel. The name of this person and all the horror that was connected to that name and all the evil it stood for could never be forgotten. No matter how it got buried and covered up in our own daily lives it could not be erased. We were too close to it. He was hanged one year later.

We were also glued to the debates between the presidential candidates Nixon and Kennedy and we opened a bottle of champagne to celebrate Kennedy's victory.

Chapter 18

A Curious Bird and a Costume Party

During our years with the Airstream Company I tried to adapt to Gil's business world, a society and culture that were completely foreign to me. I never felt like a part of it, always the outsider, ill at ease and insecure. My eager young husband sang my praises to the world, making me feel at times as if he saw me as a trophy. I cringed with embarrassment when he held forth about how much of the world I'd seen, how talented I was and on and on. Gil had a vivid imagination and I was often left to counter or evade questions from his associates following his exuberant narrations. It was all upsetting, to say the least. I dreaded the meetings and social functions I had to attend, being the good little wife, all dressed up, smiling, not knowing what on earth to say to these strangers and their wives. They also probably thought that a curious bird had flown into their midst.

In this respect things did not really change too much during Gil's working years. I did learn over time to take things more in stride and developed a suitable mask that protected me adequately from the intricacies of business and social meetings. It was not always easy.

As soon were we in our car driving to one of these functions Gil would drill me on what I was supposed to say to this salesman, that executive's wife or the boss's valued secretary. "Just mention casually how I admire his creative ideas," he would say," and, "Don't forget to be nice to Mrs. So and So and her husband."

"Oh God, I can't stand her," I muttered.

"Just try. Do it for me. It's my job. It's one of those things you have to do in business." We were whizzing along on the hot and smoggy Los Angeles freeway. I sank into my seat all sweaty in my party finery, silk stockings and high heels. No more complaints. I knew he'd just get angry, tense and nervous as he was always inclined to do on such occasions. Storm clouds would gather on his face and he'd hit the steering wheel with his fist. "God damn it, Fe, don't make a fuss. You drive me crazy."

Thinking back to those early years of our marriage I see myself as a loving and very submissive young wife, but it did not come easily to me. Little rebellions simmered under the surface, but it took several more years before they arose full-blown and they did so with energy and determination.

At one memorable and elaborate dinner party I almost stormed out of the room and I would have if Gil had not kicked me under the table just in time, anchoring me to my seat. Greeted by hilarious laughter, someone told a joke that was outrageously anti-Semitic. Had they not known that Gil was Jewish? It had just never come up.

Let it not be said that I paint everyone with the same brush. There were a few fairly nice people in the crowd. We would have been friends with none of them outside of the business world, but within it they made life tolerable. There was the short and stocky Italian, Art Costello, the powerful boss who had become Gil's champion within the company. He took an interest in the welfare of his employees. He was a shrewd businessman, but was known not to take unfair advantage of anybody. His cultural horizon was definitely limited; he enjoyed ballgames, Las Vegas entertainments and jazz. When asked why he had never joined one of the Airstream trips to Europe he replied in all sincerity, "Why would I want to go and look at all those old houses? It would bore me to death."

Art's pretty wife Caroline was quite a bit younger than he and was known to be an occasional reader. She loved clothes, shopping, parties and dancing. She piled her blond hair high in the beehive that was worn, the higher the better, by fashion-conscious women. At one big Airstream event several women appeared drawn and tired because they had spent the previous night propped up in bed to preserve their intricate hairdos.

Caroline had a sense of humor and a kernel of mischief and rebellion in her otherwise proper soul. At an elaborate conference dinner all of the executives and their wives, including Gil and me, sat on a long table on a raised platform facing the minions in the big ballroom.

Everyone waited for dinner to begin, but the speeches would not end. While I gazed dutifully at the unctuous speaker, not listening to a word he uttered, I felt a funny little touch on my hand. I looked down to see a tiny white ball rolling along the table. Caroline sat three seats away on Gil's other side. She was twirling moist bits of bread between her fingers and flipping little dough balls in my direction, hidden by a dinner menu. Her eyes skipped momentarily towards me with a sly grin and just the small tip of her tongue showed between her lips. I retaliated. Thus started the battle of the little dough balls between the top executive's wife and the ever-irreverent foreign intruder. This battle continued through many a boring dinner and had its therapeutic effect.

I'll never forget one big festive dinner and dance held in the huge ballroom of a luxurious hotel, no doubt in honor of the sales force for some very special accomplishment. Gil rarely trusted himself on the dance floor. He was convinced that he would look ridiculous and stumble over himself or me, but after a few drinks he would let go and the two of us would foxtrot happily among the crowd. We became somewhat famous for our tango performance, as the other dancers stepped aside to watch us. So it went on this special evening. We danced and I thoroughly enjoyed myself until Gil said that it was time for him to pay a little attention to some of his salesmen's wives and the office staff. So I was left to make small talk about any number of things that held no interest for me and to dance dutifully with an assortment of boring guys who smelled of cheap cologne and Brilliantine.

The evening dragged on interminably. I looked for Gil among the crowd. He was nowhere in sight. It was finally closing time and people started to leave. I stood in the foyer waiting. No Gil. I felt abandoned. Only five or six people were left and there I stood. "Where is your husband?" a man asked.

"I guess he left me," I tried to joke. "He is nowhere to be found."

"Let me drive you home," offered my savior.

When I got home I opened our bedroom door and there was Gil, comfortably ensconced in bed reading a book and looking completely unconcerned. "Where have you been?" he said. "I looked for you all over and finally left. I thought someone had taken you home. I've been here quite a while". There was no further explanation.

I'd never felt so badly shaken and abandoned before and even now I cringe at the memory of that evening. It has remained an uncomfortable mystery. There were times when my dear husband's mind and soul were quite impenetrable.

Within a few years and from a small factory near downtown Los Angeles Airstream Trailers had grown to a giant enterprise. Gil had started work there during its early years as a cabinet maker, had advanced quickly to foreman and then, when his education and leadership qualities became apparent, rose to executive status, taking over as sales director for the western region of the U.S. after an equally large factory was built in the Midwest.

Wally Byam was the founder and owner of Airstream and he promoted his aerodynamic and futuristic trailers with an ingenious travel program, known as the Wally Byam Caravan. All of his buyers were invited to sign up for an array of trips in the United States, to Central and South America, Europe, Africa and Egypt. The trailers would travel as a group, meandering in long lines and settle down by evening in wide circles reminiscent of pioneer encampments. There were often hundreds trailers. The owners were generally late middle-aged and older retirees who had adopted the travel trailer lifestyle and appropriately called themselves *Airstreamers*, wearing little black berets with the Airstream logo imprinted on them.

Some Airstreamers lived in their vehicles year round. They had all of the necessary accoutrements: double beds, dining area, kitchen, toilet and shower. There was not much space for books or art, but many had no need or interest in such possessions. For most, their travels afforded them the chance to see the world guided by a knowledgeable organization and the fellowship of a convivial group that gave rise to many friendships. It was a boon for retired and often lonely single people. An old lady and her husband had traveled with the caravans for many years and when he died everybody took care of her. She was never left alone on a trip and her fellow Airstreamers had seen to all of her needs.

Of course there were exceptions in the make up of each caravan. In the summer some younger couples with children took part during school vacations. I remember one delightful family, the Monkey Browns, as we called them. That name was conferred when we discovered that not only had they collected a bevy of exotic birds during their travels that lived with them in their trailer, but also a small monkey. This monkey happily swung from ceiling to bed to dinner table within their domicile, depositing his droppings without remorse whenever he was successful in tearing off his diapers.

His family made a fair attempt to clean up behind him, but the lingering aroma was noticeable. Dr. Brown was a physician. He had decided to take his wife and two children, a boy and a girl of about ten and twelve, around the world. He suspended his practice and took the children out of school for an entire year. That family was an inspiration for us and we envied their independent spirit. We became good friends and we loved them. The Monkey Browns were unforgettable in and of themselves, but also because they were an oasis in the desert of good old boy, hail-fellow-well-met Airstreamers. There were some other nice people, of course, but not as memorable.

I am somewhat embarrassed to admit that some of my descriptions of Airstreamers are rather arrogant. So I must add that most any fair-minded person could feel quite a bit of admiration for these enterprising older people. After all, they had the guts to travel and explore the world instead of sitting at home watching T.V. and bemoaning their loneliness.

We never got to join them on their lengthy trips abroad, but were dispatched to represent management during many of the rallies and encampments in various parts of this country. Often these rallies were held on the football fields or baseball stadiums of the towns that provided space for the rallies. We had our own trailer at that time and pulled in with all the shining silver vehicles that were circled by the hundreds around a central community meeting area. Whether the sun shone, rain streamed down or it was bitter cold, the Airstreamers showed up and invariably managed to have a good time.

It was summer vacation, the boys were not in school and we were again commandeered to rally duty. The morning started bright and early as usual, without regard to whether one wished to sleep in just a little longer. Some fervent individual marched from trailer to trailer, disgustingly cheerful, singing *rise and shine* while banging on each locked door with indisputable relish. Out came the folding card tables, the egg and cereal dishes, the coffeepots and the robed and pajama-clad humanity. Everyone settled down right in front of his or her door. Animated banter rippled across the aisles. Some stalwarts trotted off to religious services that were held at one end of the camp.

Gil and I huddled behind our drawn curtains and enjoyed a peaceful breakfast to steel us for the clamorous day ahead. The boys slipped out to look for the Monkey Brown's children, whom they knew from previous meetings. By midmorning we decided that we could not hide anymore. As soon as Gil emerged he was surrounded. *Gil, something is wrong with my toilet*, complained an old lady as she clutched his sleeve. *They assigned me the wrong space*, another complained. *Why don't you have a program printed for today?* And so it went without letup. My dear man soothed, cajoled and charmed them all. In no time he had them relaxed and loving him. *Gil, come sit with us* and *Join us for dinner tonight*.

"I've got to make the rounds, now. I'll see you later." He knew how to make his escape.

A costume party was scheduled for the afternoon, followed by an evening of dancing and a potluck dinner. I sat on a little folding chair at the perimeter of the big central meeting area that was surrounded by row upon row of the gleaming zeppelin-shaped trailers. I felt roped in by an impenetrable chain. An enormous King Kong figure, rented from the movie studios, with shameless placards on his chest and arms, towered over the festivities and proclaimed *JOIN WALLY BYAM'S AFRICAN CARAVAN*.

I was not unhappy, but was rather amused by those who rushed, hobbled, glided, sashayed proudly or strode self-consciously about in quickly invented or authentic costumes that were often acquired on previous Airstream trips abroad. There was a man in Bavarian lederhosen with an incontrovertibly authentic beer belly. A loving couple danced in bright Swedish costumes and Marius Hansen, the company's design engineer, strode about in a genuine Bedouin robe, his normally jolly, pink-cheeked Danish face smoldering in desert brown that had already begun to rub off.

My motherly heart was warmed when I discovered my own brood clambering around King Kong, waiting impatiently for the parade to begin. A prize for the best costume was to be announced. One young man was convinced that he would win, if not the first then certainly the second or third prize. He brandished an antique sword as Cyrano de Bergerac, the seventeenth century figure who had been bestowed by cruel fate with a nose of outlandish proportions. Had it not been for the fact that I had personally sculpted and applied said nose to the face of that velvet-clad young man wearing the purple Shakespearian hat, I would not have been able to guess his true identity. The Monkey Brown's little girl came up to me and whispered in my ear, "That is Ricky." I breathed a surprised *Oh!* and thanked her for the information.

Bruce was Robin Hood, with a jaunty green feathered hat, a pair of black tights rolled up at the waist and my red Navajo tunic with a sash around the waist. Painted eyebrows and a black mustache completed the picture. Ralph was a court jester, wearing something indistinct yet very floppy and constantly wrestling with his headgear. He looked positively medieval, even in the California desert. Whether or not the boys won prizes is long forgotten and the annals of history are no poorer for it.

Unforgettable, though, was the sight of all three of my boys sitting wide-eyed and open-mouthed on top of a wooden table that floated upward, lifted off the ground in the teeth of a strongman from Africa. This, for them, was the highlight of the festivities.

CHAPTER 19

A Letter from the Past

It was on one of the last days of the year 1961. There were New Years greetings and belated Christmas cards among the letters I retrieved in the mailbox and to my astonishment there was one bearing the postmark Hannover, Germany, December 17, 1961. It was addressed to my father, but it was meant for me.

> *Honorable Doctor Altman*
>
> *One of my former school friends is a secretary at the Opera House in Hannover and was able to get your address for me. May I ask you please to see that Fee gets the letter I am including in this envelope for her?*
>
> *Many Heartfelt Thanks*
> *Ursula Buehnemann, formally Zech.*

In utter amazement I held her letter in my hands. It was written on crinkly transparent airmail paper. Ursula Zech, my good old Ursel, the only one of all my school friends who had not turned her back on me when the Nazis took over our world. All the other girls in my class, when informed by our teachers that my father was a disgusting Jew, reinforced by the German world at large, determined that I was not worth their friendship and had to be avoided as if I were diseased.

Dear Ursel was there for me and suffered the taunts of all her friends. When we left Hannover so abruptly one night in 1933 I had not been able to say good-by to her. I wrote to her from my school in Switzerland. We corresponded off and on while my parents and I lived in France for some years but then lost touch when we left Europe in 1937. Soon afterwards Germany was at war. My God, that was twenty-four years ago! I had to sit down and take a deep breath before I could read her letter.

> *Dec. 17, 1961*
> *My dear Fee,*
>
> *It was last spring that I received a letter from an old school friend inviting me to a reunion of former classmates in Hannover. I went but hardly recognized anybody, although it finally turned out to be quite nice. The important thing that happened though was that I learned the address of your father in America through one former classmate who works at the Opera House in Hannover.*
> *Actually, I wanted to write immediately but then it seemed such a difficult thing to do and it is still difficult. How might you receive a communication from me today? Twenty-four years of separation and not hearing from each other over so a long time. Awful things happened in the world when we were young. I cannot make them undone, and that is the reason why I hesitated so long to send you these notes. Many years ago I read something about Christine Grauthoff in our paper and already then I thought of trying to get your address from her, but also desisted then. Now at long last I decided that my words have to reach you before this year is over.*
> *Here is a short account of my life so far. I got married in Hannover in 1940. In 1941 my first son was born and in 1942 the second. My husband was a soldier, was imprisoned in Russia and I lived with my mother in the same house that you may remember. In 1943 our house burned down and we moved to Northeim, a small city of 20,000 people. When my husband returned in 1950 we established a small printing business. My mother died in 1954. Our sons are now already 19 and 20 years old. The younger one will have to enter the army next summer, unfortunately. The older one does not have to go since he suffers from asthma. My husband and I are well. So here you have the past years in a very short account.*

> *Please write to me, Fee. Do I have to say how incredibly happy I would be to hear from you? I wish you a great Christmas holiday and a happy New Year.*
>
> *Ursula Buehnemann-Zech*

A voice from a former life, my dear friend Ursel. I had thought of her off and on throughout the years. I knew that Hannover had been greatly devastated by the war. There was also the nagging thought that she might finally have succumbed to the Nazi doctrine. Rereading her letter today, I am struck by the meager recitation of the dates of her life's experiences, mere footnotes to what really transpired, as I was to learn later.

"My husband was a soldier and I lived with my mother in the same house that you may remember." This meant that her husband was with the army in Russia and subsequently imprisoned there. Her mother's apartment I did remember well. How often we two gathered around the clumsy old living room table in their small apartment. It was mostly in the late afternoon or early evening after school. The room around us lay in shadow, especially in winter. A tasseled lampshade hung from the ceiling above us and wrapped us in a warm circle of light. We chatted, confided in each other, exchanged secrets and did homework on the side.

"Our house burned down." That meant that her whole apartment building was bombed out. She fled with her two small children and her mother to the country, finding shelter in a Quonset hut without heat or running water. Having very little money she foraged in the surrounding fields for food, raised some chickens and was helped by kind neighbors who were slightly better off than she and who shared the little they had with her small boys and ailing mother. Of course I wrote back and from then on we kept in touch and refused to lose each other again.

Chapter 20

That's When They Left Us

"You know what is coming up next week, don't you?" Father looked from one to the other at the dinner table.

"Of course," I said. "May 30, your and Mom's wedding anniversary."

And we'll have a big celebration," we all intoned in unison before he could declaim his favorite mantra.

That night our telephone rang upstairs. Gil and I were just about to go to bed but had been startled by a dull thud coming from my parent's apartment below us.

"Gil, help. George fell." Mother sounded hysterical. We found Father in his nightshirt slumped on the ground. His eyes, wide-open and staring at us in astonishment, closed only when Gil lifted him and laid him on his bed.

A few days later the blinds were raised just enough to let the sun flow gently across the bottom half of his bed, while maintaining a soothing shade around his face and slightly elevated upper body.

"Where is your mother?" I thought that was what he said. It sounded as if his tongue completely filled his mouth.

"She is next door, she'll be right back." I stroked his hand that was inert on top of the cover. It was cold and slightly clammy. Never had this hand been called upon for any labor, any test of strength other then swinging a tennis racket or wielding a walking stick in the mountains of the Swiss alps.

Again, he mumbled something and by the expression on his face it seemed to be a question. I bent close to him.

"You had a slight stroke. It'll pass. You will recover if you rest."

"Alice," he said all of a sudden. It was so clear that he called for his wife; there was no mistaking it. I got up and went to the door.

"I'll get her," I said and looked back at him. His thin arms lay stretched out on top of the cover, their flaccid skin the color of pale tea. His eyes had closed again and his mouth hung slightly open. During the next two weeks he rallied a little, gained some speech and we dared to hope cautiously.

On many an evening we sat near his bed to keep him company and he seemed to be peaceful and content, just seeing us around him. I read, Mother sewed, which was a very rare occurrence borne out of sheer boredom, and my brother Ralph looked at a newspaper.

All of a sudden Father came to life. He lifted one arm a few inches off his cover and pointed to the back of Ralph's paper. "Tickets," he said quite clearly and with unmistakable urgency. There was a large add on the back of Ralph's newspaper announcing a performance of a play by Aeschylus in the original Greek language by actors coming directly from Greece. It was to take place at the outdoor Greek Theatre in Griffith Park. Father had known about that event for quite some time and had looked forward to it with great pleasure.

Ralph got up and hugged his agitated father. "First thing tomorrow morning I shall go and get your ticket, Pappi." Father relaxed, smiled a little and closed his eyes again.

Mother motioned us outside: "You don't really mean it, do you? Those tickets are expensive and he certainly can't go. That's money thrown out."

"No matter, he'll get his ticket," Ralph would not be swayed. So the very next afternoon Father had a big white envelope on his bedside table with the imprint of the Greek Theater's tragic ancient masks on the cover and a first row ticket inside. A few days later he had a second stroke and had to be transferred to the Cedars of Lebanon hospital where he died on the ninth of June in 1962.

It was one year later, June of 1963 that I picked Mother up from the doctor's office. We had all been intensely nervous waiting to hear the results of her recent intestinal biopsy. She climbed into the back of my car while I was double parked, so I had to move on quickly.

"Well?" I looked at her in my rearview mirror. An oppressive silence that seemed interminable followed, then a deep sigh. Finally the answer came, slowly and dramatically.

"And so it is all over now." It sounded like a lament uttered just before the curtain closes. My immediate reaction was not one of shock or grief; it was anger. There she goes again, I thought, the great *tragedienne*, milking her performance for its grandest effect.

I helped her out of the car at home. She hastened to her sitting room and her favorite upholstered chaise like an animal seeking the refuge of its nest. I sat with her. I did not hold her hand. I sat in disbelief while my defenses waned and I absorbed the inevitable.

"They can't operate," she said. "It is too late." It had been exactly a year before that my father had died and now I was to lose my mother, whom I deeply loved in spite of our differences.

I aimed the wide spray of the garden hose high up into the sun, let the sparkling shower fill the air and sink back down to mist my face and hair and bathe the roses that grew in their small earthen plot in the middle of the drab, paved yard behind our large house. It was unusually hot for the end of October. The cement's heat burned upward through the thin soles of my sandals and my bare legs and arms welcomed the mist in the air. Incandescent drops of water shimmered on the roses.

I bent to smell the dripping blossoms and let my fingers gently slide over their tender leaves. I stretched my arms and took a deep breath, then looked up at the house. The room that I had just escaped lay behind a darkened window. It had become the center of our home and our lives for many months. It was my mother's dim and airless room in which she lay hovering between dreams and consciousness. I had again sat for hours keeping her company, as I had so often in the last few weeks, until the morphine took effect and she had fallen asleep.

The boys where still at school and Gil at work. A nurse watched over Mother. I was alone. I was exhausted. The horror of my mother's suffering, making attempts at keeping a steady home life for the rest of the family and trying to keep my own grief and sadness in check took all the energy I could muster.

The garage that stood at the end of the yard had been turned into a studio for me and that was my refuge. It had been weeks since I had been able to spend time there and do some of my own work. The side door stuck a little when I pulled it open as if to express its annoyance for having been neglected for so long. The atmosphere inside was stale and breathing was not easy, with the lingering aromas of linseed oil and turpentine. I opened the one small window that allowed in a bit of air and with it a delighted party of flies that buzzed along a streak of dust and sunlight.

I had no plan, no thought, except to forget my grief and exhaustion and to do something else, to escape. A large, narrow celotex panel leaned against the back wall. Without having any plan for it I had primed it quite some time before with a coat of gesso. It was nearly six feet tall and two feet wide. I placed it on the easel, grabbed a large charcoal stick and attacked its brightness and rough surface in one continuous gesture, swinging slowly into its plane, from top to bottom, crossing and wandering from side to side without ever breaking the line's path. I felt like a blind person entering an unfamiliar room, moving from wall to wall, exploring the space and making it my own.

And then I stopped. It was a natural and intuitive moment of completion. I did not think or reason, but stared at the shapes that had been created by the crossing and swirling paths of my line, shapes that advanced and retreated and made that plane come to life. I spread my colors on the palette: umber, ultramarine blue and a large amount of white, mixing them into multiple shades of gray. And then I took full possession of the world of shapes I had created, attacking the painting with my brushes and knives, pulling some spaces out and pushing others back. I worked as if in a dream; it was not I who did this.

My mother's scream pierced the walls and the silence of the studio. I ran and held her until the nurse's syringe did its comforting work.

The next day was the fourth of November and a very important day for our son Ralph, who was then 14 years old. He played the clarinet in a trio with two other young musicians, the pianist Mona Golabeck and the cellist Jeffrey Solow, who both went on to careers in classical music. The group had worked hard for months, coached by the violinist Manuel Compinsky, in order to take part in the Coleman Auditions in Pasadena. The eminent judges were to be the cellist Gregor Piatigorsky, the violist William Primrose and the pianist Leonard Pennario. We were to leave the house shortly for the drive to Pasadena.

That morning Mother's suffering was again unbearable and again I called Dr. Abraham. Soon he stood before me, a very small man with a gray and wrinkled face whose eyes, peering over his glasses with obvious concern, searched mine.

"You must know," he said, "If I give her even more morphine now she won't survive it." The room was still and the little gray man dissolved in the gray November morning.

"So do it." I whispered. He came out of her room, offered a short nod and left, the door closing behind him for the last time.

I sat for a long time, unable to move, then I went in to look at her. She lay on her side, her face half covered by the blanket she had frantically pulled over herself. Her mottled gray hair was still in curlers, since she had insisted on having it done at night in order to look pretty for the daytime. Swatches of orange-blond dye still clung to the ends of some of the escaped strands against the dead whiteness of her scalp.

I thought of the plucky little girl of her childhood, the beautiful, scintillating young actress, later the famous diva at the height of her career. A rasping breath now, not a golden voice.

I stood and closed my eyes. *How I had cuddled up with you when I was little, creeping under your light woolen shawl. It was white with roses woven into it. I rubbed my face against the inside of your arm. You had me in your nest and oh, you smelled so good.*

A hand fell on my shoulder. "You have to go, Mrs. Gilbert. They are waiting for you." It was the nurse to call me back to consciousness.

"I can't. I can't leave her."

"She does not know us anymore. She does not feel any pain. Go, your son needs you now."

I do not recall how I survived the day. I do remember seeing Ralph and his trio on stage and hearing their beautiful playing, which allowed me some relief for just a few moments from the emotion-numbing control that had possessed me all day.

The auditions were over and the young people, their coaches and their parents milled about with great excitement. The tension seemed almost unbearable when the room turned suddenly quiet and the judges appeared on the stage. There was tall impressive Gregor Piatigorsky, the cellist. There was the violist Primrose and the pianist Leonard Pennario. A most impressive assemblage. The announcement came. It was not our group that won. Jubilation and embraces came for the glowing winners, but also a few mutterings and grumbling could be heard among the other guests.

The cellist Gabor Reijto came rushing up to us. "This is outrageous. You were by far the best. You were the winners."

Other voices could be heard confirming his judgment. And still others muttered something like, "Of course they were bound to prefer the group with the young Daniel Heifetz. Could they judge otherwise?"

On the long drive home the car was overloaded with the young musicians, two other mothers, the big cello, plus the constant whining of spoiled and immature cellist Jeffrey Solow. He wanted to stop for ice cream and drove us all crazy. Even his indulgent mother gave way to nervous strain and told him to shut up.

The nurse received me at the door. "It's all over, Honey. She never woke up again and went peacefully. Your brother came already and arranged everything. They took her away. I cleaned up. You go rest now."

I fled to my studio. There was the painting on the easel. I looked and then I saw her, a figure weaving in the mist among the pulsing shapes, a faceless apparition from another world. My mother's embodiment? My mother's soul? Finally I wept.

A decision had to be made. Will we stay in this house?

"If so, then we'll need to rent the downstairs apartment." Gil was right of course. I walked down the curved staircase as I had so many times in past years and opened the door to my parent's apartment. They should have been there to greet me. I stood in the middle of the living room, closed my eyes and felt their presence surrounding me. Father would be sitting in his big armchair at this time, skillfully manipulating the ever-present cigar in one hand while holding the evening newspaper open, looking at me over the top of his glasses. I thought I could hear Mother moving about in the kitchen getting her afternoon cup of coffee. I opened my eyes. I must not cry again.

I leaned against Father's big oak desk with its silver framed family pictures and the large agate ashtray that looked like a deep blue pool of water. It was highly prized by my children, especially Rick. A fat Waterman fountain pen rested on a stack of papers by a sizable open notebook. Even my fanatically orderly Mama had not disturbed it after he died. The walls were lined with books from floor to ceiling, interspersed by ethnic masks and theater memorabilia. I glanced toward the open door to Mother's room and caught a last glimpse of the waning sun, which seemed to tremble as it crossed the carpet to the foot of the beloved chaise lounge on which she died.

I could not go there. I could not enter. Yet I then knew what we had to do. We had to move, find another house. I could not live there any longer with those memories.

We were faced with a big problem: what should we do with the parent's furniture and other belongings? A mountain of painful decisions followed. The Biedermeier furniture had to go. There would no be space in a new home. The sofa, the armchairs, my desk. The delicate little chairs had already been demolished by the boys through the years and the wood of the big armchairs was so brittle that an upholsterer had refused to work on them. I kept the big old grandfather clock that had chimed throughout my childhood, the tall corner cabinet, the round birch table and the smaller sewing table with its four little drawers that I had always investigated for hidden treasures. Father's oak table with the inlaid turquoise Grecian tiles, his library steps and his revolving advocate's bookstand were so intimately connected to his memory that I could not possibly give them away. Neither could I relinquish Mother's beloved teacup collection and her porcelain figures of the Russian ballet. The K.P.M. dinnerware was distributed between us and my brother Ralph and his wife Pat, as was all of the silverware. The library of thousands of theater and related art and history books went to the University of California at Los Angeles, as were Father's papers, which are now housed in the library's special collections.

I found myself in a confused state at that time. Even at 45, clearly middle aged, my parent's deaths seemed to mark the end of my youth and to bring to conclusion a great part of my existence. Yet at the same time a sense of rebirth and a new creative life stirred in me.

Shortly thereafter I had a dream that somehow shook me deeply. Driving on a city street that sloped slightly downward towards the ocean, I was aware of a faceless male companion sitting next to me. He was pointing to a tall reddish brown building on my left side. It was heavy and dark, with cornices and turrets. As I looked, more buildings arose behind it as out of the ground, forming layers and layers of ever taller, darker, browner protrusions, walls, towers and veritable battlements growing up towards the sky. And yet my car was gliding slowly on, moving, but not leaving the sight behind. The air was clear, the street broad and free on my right and I looked on, amazed but untroubled

I awoke and wondered whether these were images that in their strange way portrayed life as it confronted me at that time. Was it a completion of some kind? I saw the heavy battlements, the masses, the built up heaviness. But the air was clear and the road on the right broad, free and uncluttered. The car moved, but did not leave, did not run away.

After I awoke I wrote down this dream and added a note to myself. *So maybe then it is time to look at the buildings, to enter the doors, peek into the chambers, climb the turrets. I have no plan, no road map. I will not start at the top or at the bottom. I'll wander up the stairs and down, open this door and that, curious about what I find. If the going gets a little rough here and there I will climb one of the towers, stick my head out of the window and look at the sky.*

I had another dream at that time and I recalled it by writing a poem.

>*A boat in the sky*
>*So bright the day*
>*So clear and beautiful the sky*
>*And in it high above me in the glassy globe of air*
>*There sits a boat*
>*Young people rock in it and sing*
>*And stretch their arms toward the ocean*
>*So far from them, far, far below.*
>
>*And then the boat descends in one majestic arc*
>*And sinks its load into the waves*
>*Like altar offerings to the universe*
>*And silence reigns.*

Father dies and this is how I remember him

Mother dies in 1963

We lose brother Ralph, 1967

Rick and Dorit and the wedding cake, 1968

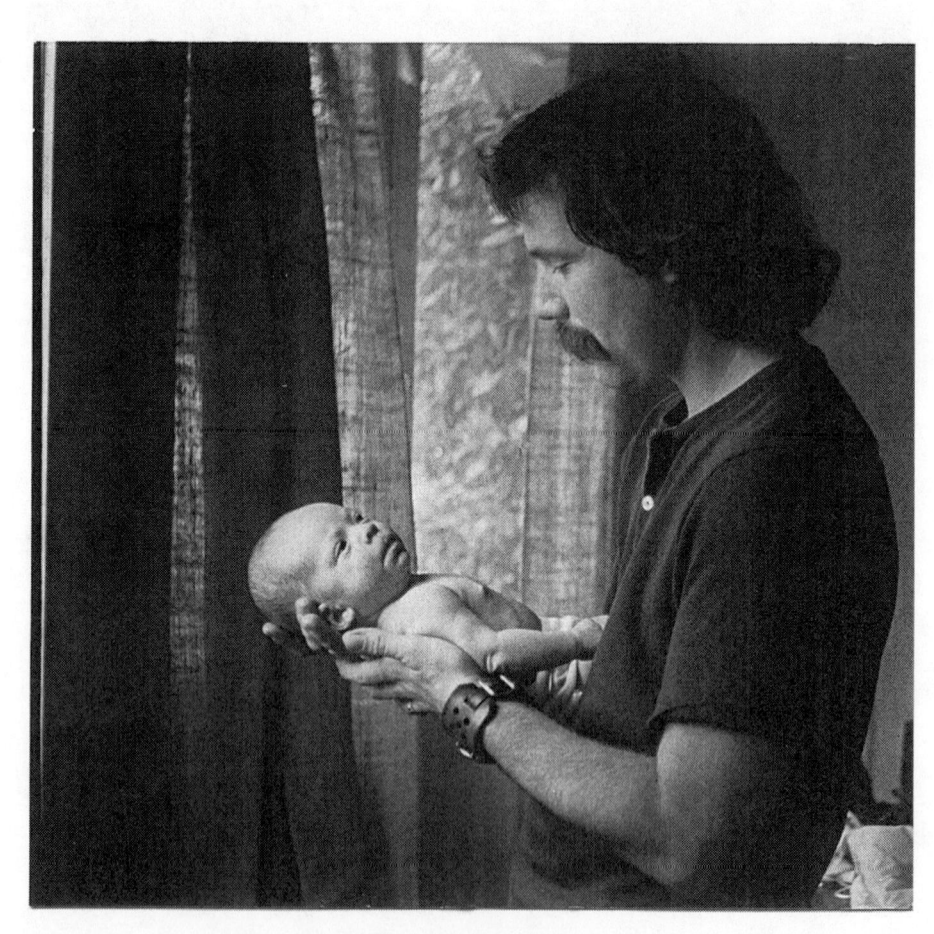

Noah is born, 1974

Rick and Noah some years later

Bruce at his wedding feast at Synanon,
a proud father looks on

Triumphant Bruce, Rhonda and Zac, 1975

Ralph with tiny bundle Isabelle, 1978

Isabelle with mother, Valerie

Isabelle already looking down upon Grandma, 1992

Santa Barbara, 1972 to 1999, the house on Olive Mill Road

The garden and fountain we built

The garden and the small Japanese teahouse

The master builders Jim and Gil, around 1985

Chapter 21

At The House of the Giant Hibiscus
Tracy Street, 1963-1966

House hunting. Moving. It seemed to me that I had experienced these upheavals so many times that they should have been routine by now. But each time proved to be a new adventure, another chapter in the story of our wanderings. From adolescence, young womanhood and into married life each time my family moved, traveled and moved again life was fraught with apprehension and excitement. I have written about many houses in my previous book and all of the roofs that sheltered us in later years, so many of which were important and brought changes to our lives.

We climbed the steps up the steep incline that led to a tall house on Tracy Street. A giant white and pink flowering hibiscus flanked the entrance door and was almost high enough to reach above the windows of the first story. It was like a festive wreath of flowers that welcomed us. We knew that this was to be our home when we first saw it and entered the living room, presided over by a tall arched window under a high-beamed ceiling.

We were devastated when we learned the price, which was way beyond our reach. When we found out that it had been on the market for quite some time, dear Gil, who was never one to give up easily, returned to the broker and managed to bargain and bring the price down almost to our level. Luck was with us.

Ralph and Pat came to inspect our new home. I took my brother by the arm and pulled him into the high-ceilinged living room. "You see, this is the reason we bought this house," I laughed. "Isn't this the perfect place for him?" I pointed to the bright white wall that rose upwards fronting the staircase that led from the living room to the second floor.

There reigned the majestic wooden crucifix that I had abducted from his store some years before. It seemed to hover above us as if it had interrupted its upward flight for just a moment. The overwhelming sense of past history and the strong emotion the artist had brought to his work still transfixed us.

The crucifix looked down on our family from morning to night and stretched his gnarled wooden arms to bless us, unmindful of our indifference to religion. It looked down upon the boys clattering in and out of the house, coming and going with their dogs and their friends from school. It looked down upon our grown friends who gathered in the living room. Most of them were parents whose children went with ours to Elysian Heights Elementary School in Echo Park when we lived on Vestal Avenue. We had become a close-knit group of friends and remained that way for a long time. On the last Friday of each month we got together to read to each other and share ideas, continuing until we moved to Santa Barbara. Even then we kept in touch for many years.

Our group was not a typical book club and there was no obligation to read an assigned book ahead of time for later discussion. Rather, each one of us brought whatever he or she had been impressed by in their personal reading, from fiction to interesting newspaper or magazine articles to poems that we loved. Harper Lee's *To Kill a Mockingbird* had recently come out and so had James Baldwin's *Another Country*. Minette King, the actress in our midst, read poems by Ferlinghetti; Alex Kritcheff, the sculptor, inundated us with the writings of Franz Kafka, until the entire group rebelled.

Those were pleasant evenings among our little circle of friends. Though it might sound as if we lived in a peaceful time at home and in history, there was unrest in our family as well as in the world at large. These were the times of the civil rights demonstrations in Birmingham and Selma, Martin Luther King's arrest and the Freedom March on Washington. The war in Vietnam was beginning and then the horrendous day that had us watching the indelible assassination of President Kennedy on TV.

On the home front it was always my dear son Ricky who was the source of worry for Gil and me. He graduated from High School, but barely, not for any lack of brains, he had plenty of those, but because he found homework a nuisance; it just did not interest him in the least. Instead he read independently. He was entranced by Nikos Kazantzakis' *Zorba the Greek* and *The Report to Greco* and then discovered his love for science fiction, especially for Ray Bradbury's *Martian Chronicles*. Otherwise his passion was concentrated first on cars, then girls and last, but not least by any means, on marijuana.

The use of *pot*, as it was lovingly called, as if one spoke of a dear but slightly eccentric uncle, was strictly against the law. Consequently, the allure for our youth was not only for its euphoric effect, but also for the delicious feeling of doing something forbidden. Whether Gil and I were naïve or just too busy to realize the impact of pot on the young, including Rick and Bruce, I do not know. Ralph, the thoughtful individualist, was never tempted.

Liberal-thinking people and, of course, Rick assured us that smoking pot was really quite harmless and that everyone did it. The law, went the opinion, was ridiculous. Nevertheless a narcotics squad, the *narcs*, as the kids called them, started to show up wherever young people congregated, near schools, on playgrounds and at parties. We heard from time to time that this or that boy from Rick's high school, or even Bruce's junior high, had been picked up and sent to Juvenile Hall.

So when Ralph came to me out of breath and pulled me to the window, I panicked. "Mom, look. See that car parked across the street? I think those may be narcs. What if they are looking for Rick? Quick, let's search his room. If he has anything hidden there we must throw it out."

Franticly we turned Rick's room upside down, wading through his layered mess, the clothes on the floor, shoes on the bed, LP records strewn and intermingled with car magazines and leftover snacks from God knows how many evenings past. We found nothing. Looking out the window again we saw two men in black suits get out of their car. I held my breath. They did not turn toward us, but went across the street, rang the doorbell and when there was no answer got back into their car and left. This encounter sounded a warning bell for me. Was it that serious? Three years later I was to become thoroughly enlightened.

Ricky in his teens was like a young fighting cock ready to lash out when anything like conventional behavior was expected of him. He rebelled against every authority, especially that of his father. In 1964, not too long before his high school graduation, Gil berated Rick for something. It might have been for getting another citation to appear in court either for a driving violation or for yet again amassing a slew of unpaid parking tickets. An argument ensued and Rick stormed out of the house screaming, "I'll never come back." He dashed out into dark and streaming rain.

I was crushed. My son, my child was running away from us to an unknown fate. I cried and it was not the last time I cried about one of my children.

A week or so later he reappeared. We were sitting at dinner. The door opened and there he stood, dirty, cold and hungry, looking very sheepish and unsure of how he would be received.

All Gil said was: "Sit down; we are just starting." He was a good father, no matter that he made many mistakes in the early years. Subsequently we learned that our son had broken into the basement of our former house on Hoover Street, still unsold but with a sale pending. How he had managed to live there without a bed, heat and light at night I cannot imagine.

The memory of another incident in the Ricky Saga brings me to the Emergency Ward at County Hospital. There he sat, bloody, pale and shaken on the examination table. "You have a lucky young man here," said the doctor, applying the last bandage. "With that crash he could have lost his life. His young friend is worse off."

Rick had raced his sports car on Mullholland Drive, a narrow ridge at the top of a mountain with steep drops down slopes on either side. Zooming along at top speed, my son lost control of his car, rolled over and careened downhill, coming to rest against a stout tree preventing the last, surely fatal descent to the bottom. Rick was hurt and terrified, thinking that he had killed his friend David, who was unconscious, half under the car. Able to claw his way up the hill Rick flagged down a passing car and asked for help. David recovered and Rick was relatively unscathed, though at least somewhat chastened for a while.

I think back now to all of the emergency wards I have graced, with a girl from our house who had attempted suicide, to three-year-old Ralph eating an entire bottle of Baby Aspirin and at the age of four having his stomach pumped out after swallowing a stack of pennies. Years later, twelve year-old Bruce had a violent reaction to an injection of penicillin. To my horror his whole face turned into a tightly blown up balloon and his eyes swelled shut.

While I soothed Bruce at the hospital the episode was enhanced by a phone call from Ralph. "Mom, we just had a big rattlesnake in the garden. Rick did not see it at first and jumped over it, but don't worry;

it did not bite him. We killed it with a rock." That surely relieved my mind; or did it?

Harassing Bruce was one of Rick's favorite occupations. This began in early childhood when little Bruce was quite defenseless. As the years went by Bruce, now quite a bit taller than Rick, became an athlete and would be bullied no more. Some nasty, scary fights ensued and Gil and I found our family in frequent turmoil. Where, we thought, did all this aggression come from? How could Rick, who could be so warm and loving at times, be so reckless and rebellious as well? He loved nature and was great with small children and animals.

I always believed that Rick's troubles began in early childhood, when Ralph and I had polio and the house was in quarantine. To keep Rick safe from infection he was sent away to Gil's parents, the grandparents he hardly knew. He was miserable there and did not understand what was happening to him. When he was finally allowed back home there was a gruff nurse who kept him from seeing me whenever she could. I was still in bed and a lock was installed high up on my door to keep him from entering. Already resourceful at four, he managed to pull a heavy chair to the door, add a few big books, climb up and shove the bolt aside.

Ralph, then only a few months old, was the object of great care and concern. So Rick battled for attention and fought for his individuality. His fury against an intruder should logically have been directed towards Ralph, but instead it landed on Bruce.

We sought the help of Al Freeman, a psychologist in Beverly Hills. He worked with Rick and also with our family. I believe Gil and I profited more from these sessions than did the boys. We learned much about ourselves and our relationships with each other and our children.

1963 was a memorable year. It was the year my mother died. Gil rose steadily in the ranks of Airtstream management and did not have to travel quite so often. He was liked, admired and fawned over at the plant, especially by the female contingent, which often made me slightly wary when one of his admirers was a young and pretty secretary. Sometimes he must have felt my uneasiness and made a point of being loving and reassuring. He was my tall and handsome husband and I could easily imagine that any woman could fall in love with him. As a matter of fact several did pine for him at that time and, throughout the years of our marriage, there were always women who looked at me with jaundiced eyes, wishing to replace me.

I never quite lost my faint and nagging insecurity. I never saw myself as particularly pretty and felt uncomfortable and awkward in situations where I was presented to a group of Gil's business associates and expected to make casual conversation. For that matter in most social occasions I felt ill at ease and frequently just shut up, convinced that everybody found me to be boring. I probably was.

On the other hand, before a large audience of parents and others at the museum auditorium I was able to give a more or less extemporaneous lecture on art and my work with young people without any hesitation.

At the end of 1963 my teaching job at the Pasadena Museum of Art came to an end. It had lasted for nine years. A huge new modern art museum was being erected at another location and it did not include a children's workshop. The old building closed for a while and then reopened, showing Asian art exclusively. I suppose that was it's original purpose; judging from the style of the building it really belonged more to a city in China then on Los Robles Avenue in Pasadena, California. The giant gingko tree that stood in the middle of the courtyard soared up to the sky and fanned the air with its delicate leaves, fresh green in spring and gloriously gold in autumn. Gingkos became my favorite tree. Many years later when we bought a home in Santa Barbara with a big garden I planted a gingko tree on the day we moved in.

1964 at Tracy Street. Summer vacation had just begun. I slowly realized that I had no more need to commute on the freeway in the heat. Every year summer had been my most strenuous season of work, teaching mornings and afternoons five days a week at the museum. I was relieved that it had ended. The workshop was closed and it felt strange to be able to sit at home with Gil on a hot morning instead of driving to work.

"Well, I guess I'll look for another job." My elbows on the breakfast table and my head in my hands, I must not have looked particularly enterprising. "I miss the museum and the kids, but not the long drive to Pasadena." I closed my eyes for just a moment and sighed in utter fatigue. Gil put his newspaper aside and reached for another helping of his favorite Wheaties.

"Has it occurred to you by any chance that you could stop working? I think we can manage on my salary now if we are very careful." This was such a new thought that it drove me out of my chair and over to the window that looked out to the still-neglected back yard.

The giant agave plants, some as much as five feet high, were still threatening with fat green spiked fronds like weapons lunging into the air. The whole yard had been festooned with them when we moved in. My dear brother wanted to be helpful, rolled up his sleeves and attacked the beasts with a machete. The executed warrior plants retaliated by drooling their vicious juice on him and poor Ralph broke out in huge blisters over his hands and forearms. He was not soon helpful with gardening again.

Absently, I gazed at the untended mess and tried to let Gil's revolutionary idea filter through my tired brain. No job? No rushing about to do justice to work, to home and to family? I could sleep, paint and even read some of the many books that had been patiently awaiting my attention. If I had expected real leisure I would have been sorely disappointed, but after a week of rest I found that I was too eager to get back into my own creative endeavors.

I signed up for classes at the Otis Art Institute. I rounded up some artist friends to form a drawing group that met in the spacious family room in our basement once a week. We hired models and shared not only the cost but also friendship and the stimulation of common interests.

I don't recall how we located the models that posed for us. I may have snitched their names from a list at Otis that was not carefully guarded. The shortage of professional models for classes at the universities, colleges and the various art schools in town resulted in closely guarded lists of names and addresses that were not given freely to outsiders.

A colorful parade came through the basement of our house on Tracy Street. There were handsome young women, displaying their bodies with pride, challenging us to do them justice. During rest period they might wander among us, appraising their likenesses on our drawing boards, registering approval or hiding their displeasure rather unsuccessfully. Some of them dreamed eternally of Hollywood and cleaned houses on the side.

There were also shopworn ladies who shed their flimsy robes with careless disdain and fell into tired poses that were their stock in trade, used in all the art schools night after night. There was LaLa, an older woman, quite thin and bony, with sagging breasts and belly. Her red-dyed locks were held by an arrangement of paper flowers tied with a gold ribbon, sabotaging the dignity of her nakedness.

Men also posed for us. There was a young studious fellow who brought a book. He seemed embarrassed to take down his pants, so we let him keep them on. He sat on a chair reading his book while he posed. He was pathetically grateful and the portraits that emerged on our drawing boards exuded a sense of peace and contemplation. The drawing I made of him hangs prominently in the home of a teacher of literature who declared the image of the reading boy a symbol of his profession.

The mood of peace and contemplation that seemed to float through our studio evaporated one evening like a morning fog when the sun brakes through the clouds. The new model was late and we had already resigned ourselves to drawing each other. But all of a sudden the door opened and we found ourselves confronted by a majestic apparition.

Long black hair framed his broad, brown face and fell down to his muscled, bare chest. He wore a roughly woven cloth of many colors slung over one shoulder. He was tall and stern and not much given to chatter. His name was Joaquin and he came from South America, so he said. That was about all he let us know. Hastily, fresh paper was pinned to drawing boards, pens scratched, brushes danced black ink across white sheets of paper and charcoal sticks broke, the result of excessive fervor. We resolved to hire him for several evenings during the weeks to come. After the first concentrated and tense work session I burst into the upstairs living room where Gil was reading peacefully, having shooed the boys to bed at last. I was still exited and quite exhausted.

"The next time he comes you have to see this guy. He is a wild and primitive man from a jungle in South America. I can just see him paddling down the Amazon in a dugout canoe or raft or whatever they paddle in down there. I am making a very large drawing and I think it'll be good."

Gil smiled his very pleased smile. "I am so glad you are enjoying it," he said, and I knew that he meant it.

During one of the last sessions, the drawings almost finished, our "primitive" friend finally opened up and started to talk. He was a pediatrician with a degree from the University of Mexico. He had practiced for several years and finally decided that it was not what he wanted out of life. He came to Hollywood hoping to get into the movies, doing some modeling on the side. My romantic dreams fell by the wayside and left me slightly shamefaced. The Amazon, indeed! My drawing of Joaquin hangs today in my son Bruce's living room, a handsome and permanent companion for Bruce and Lex, his wife.

There was one job from which I could not escape: I was the family chauffeur. Weekly I drove Ralph to either his saxophone teacher, Russell Cheever, or to Louella Howard, who gave him flute lessons. I transported Bruce, who had discovered his love for the saxophone, to Harvey Pittel for beginner's lessons. I went to art school, did my housework, chased the fleas in Scampy's fur and once in a while Gil would call me on his way either to or from work.

"I am stuck; the car won't start. You have to come and push."

So I would dash off to give Gil's old car a push with my old car, hoping we would get it started. All that kept me both on my toes and constantly behind the wheel.

In 1964 Lyndon Johnson became president and the Vietnam War started in earnest and escalated rapidly. Young men were being drafted. Rick had turned eighteen and was supposed to join the army.

"I'll register as conscientious objector or I'll go to Canada. I hate this war," he screamed. Al Freeman came to the rescue. Rick presented himself to the draft board with a letter from his psychologist that convinced the authorities without a doubt that this young man would not be an asset to the United States armed forces.

Ralph, at 16, would be pronounced unfit when the time came and would not be eligible to serve in the army. This was the one reason to be grateful that he had contracted polio. What kind of world was this that a mother was grateful for a son's physical impairment?

Bruce was 15 and also still too young. We hoped that the fighting would be over before he turned eighteen. What we did not know was that the escalating war would rage on for many more years and could have claimed Bruce if fate did not have other plans for him.

January 15, 1965

"Is Dad going to be here for my graduation from junior high?" It was a very important event in Bruce's life and Gil seemed to be more on the road then at home.

"You know perfectly well he would not miss it for anything. As a matter of fact he'll be here tomorrow." We were having dinner, the boys and I. The chair at the head of the table been empty for two weeks and Gil's absence was felt acutely, both because of Bruce's impending graduation and also because of Ricky's approaching birthday.

"It's tough to go from junior high to high school," explained Rick, the experienced older brother, addressing Bruce with grave concern. "You'll find some really rough guys. If anybody bothers you, tell me and I'll beat them up." Rick clenched his fists in pleasant anticipation.

"I'll take care of myself." Bruce shoved his plate aside and left the table.

I knew that Gil had a meeting in Denver and was due to come home the next day. That night I had a dream. I saw Gil walking along a city street. It seemed to be early in the morning. He passed a men's clothing store and the door was open. He went in. A *Sale* sign stood on a table and there among other things was a turquoise bathrobe. Gil liked it and picked it up, thinking *it is very good looking, but I know I'll never wear it,* and then put it back down.

I woke up and shook my head. What a silly dream, I thought and laughed for a second or two before heading to the bathroom. Then I looked at the time. It was already nine o'clock. I had slept late, but it was Saturday and I could afford it. Towards evening my dear husband returned, looking a little rumpled and tired.

"It was a rat race today." He threw his briefcase on the nearest chair. "I am hungry."

"I expected that you would be." I brought him a big bowl of chicken noodle soup, the cure-all for whatever ails you, as my Jewish half firmly believed. I watched him eat while I reported on the boy's doings.

"And what about you?" he asked.

"Oh, I must tell you about a ridicules dream I had last night," and I related the whole episode. Gil dropped his spoon.

"My God," He stammered, "That's exactly what happened. I walked the streets in the morning. It was eight o'clock, too early for my first appointment." Point by point he described the whole scene as it had happened in my dream, turquoise bathrobe and all. "It was about eight when I was there," he said, "that would be nine o'clock here."

"Yes, I know," I nodded. How does one explain such an occurrence? What were the currents that ran mysteriously between Gil and me? Am I clairvoyant? Hamlet was right when he said, "There are more things in heaven and earth, Horatio, than are dreamt of in your little philosophy" Will another Einstein be born some day and figure it all out? We won't know in our lifetime.

Three days later, on January 18th, I waited on the telephone for Granny Gilbert, Gil's mom, to answer my call. I waited and waited, yet no response. That was unusual. She rarely went out. I started to worry, got into my car and drove across town to her little house. No answer to my ringing and pounding at the door. I tried the backdoor. It was locked. Finally after rattling several windows I succeeded to pry open the one that led to the kitchen and after several attempts managed to climb in.

"Hey Granny, still asleep?" She was in bed, the covers pulled over her head. No answer. And then I knew. I pulled the blanket off her face and shoulders and touched her cheek. It was ice cold. Her fingers were stiff. Her bad heart had finally given out. I held my breath and finally let it out and sank into the chair right next to her bed. I knew I should call someone, but I could not move for a while.

I gazed at her face. A few wispy strands of her thin gray hair lay across her nose and cheek. Her body, short and sturdy when she was up and about, now looked small and vulnerable, curled up in bed. I got up again, gently brushed the hair back from her face and gazed at her for quite a while. It felt like we were communicating for both the first time and the last. I recalled my own mother's death, the way I had stood next to her couch, looking down at her with love, pity and regret just as I gazed now at Gil's mother in her bed.

Had anybody really known her? She grew up in Poland, a neglected Jewish orphan who could neither read nor write, because nobody ever took the trouble to teach her. Was she starved for love and affection? Maybe that's why she had been so belligerent. She hated her husband and blamed him for the pain the birth of his children had caused her. She ruled her boys with an iron hand and the spanking rod was never far away.

On rare occasions she was able to laugh uproariously and then her broad face became even broader and she squeezed her eyes together so that they almost disappeared above her high cheekbones. She and I had a good relationship and she was on her best behavior when I was around. She did not scold or complain. She seemed to have a strange respect for me and always treated me carefully and with as much warmth as she could muster. I knew she liked me in spite of the fact that I was part shiksa, only half Jewish. She had forgiven me for that.

I don't remember much of the rest of that morning. I think I called 911. A policeman came and then a physician who verified that *yes, the lady is dead*, in a very matter of fact way. He had me sign papers as if it were a business deal and left. An ambulance came and the sorry little bundle was taken away. I called Gil at work.

"Go home," he said, "I'll be there as soon as I can." I stepped outside. The litter carrier's boots had left their mark; Granny's much loved and carefully nursed Calla lilies lay trampled in the dirt all around the entryway. I locked the door behind me.

Chapter 22

Going in New Directions

On January 29, 1965, Bruce proudly graduated from Thomas Starr King Jr. High School and subsequently entered John Marshall High without trepidation and with no intention of calling on big brother Rick for protection. Bruce was big and strong and had been Athlete of the Year at King.

Ralph, already in his second year at Marshall, was inseparable from his clarinet and saxophone, even in school.

Dorit, a former classmate of Bruce's told me, "We all admired him and his musicianship. Ralph could do no wrong. The music teacher often literally begged him to sit in at orchestra rehearsals to fire the kids on." Ralph's school orchestra experience and the encouragement he received from his teachers led him to audition first for the Los Angeles Junior Philharmonic Orchestra and then for the prestigious Meremblum Symphony, with little hope and then astonishment and pride when he was accepted.

Early one evening Ralph left to join the orchestra for a concert and we were to follow later. He was fourteen or fifteen years old and felt himself to be nearly grown up. He was dressed up and seemed a little nervous, which was unusual for him. I, in contrast, was very nervous, which was completely usual when anything important was impending for my children.

"Now Mom, for heaven's sake, don't wave to me when I come out on the stage."

"It would not have entered my mind." I suppressed a smile and stopped myself just in time before reaching out to straighten his tie. Here he was, feeling very grown up in all of his fourteen years, ready to play his first concert with the famous Meremblum Orchestra. Understandably, this was all very important to him.

We were a little late in arriving and when we entered the large hall there were rows and rows of seats and almost every one was taken. We managed to find seats and craned our necks to see the stage. The musicians were already assembled and tuning their instruments. We looked at the program and there it was, the first selection on the program, the L'Arlesienne Suite by Bizet, Alto Saxophone Soloist, Ralph Gilbert.

So *that* was why he seemed so unusually agitated. When he had played with the orchestra as a clarinetist on other occasions or performed by himself he always appeared as cool as a cucumber, having no apparent stage fright. As usual, he had not alerted us to the fact that this was going to be a big night for him. Maybe he did not regard it as such, but for doting parents it certainly was. Ralph was a very private boy. Perhaps because there always was so much commotion and upheaval around Rick and Bruce Ralph tended to retreat and lead a life on his own.

The tuning stopped. Conductor Peter Meremblum mounted the podium, raised his baton, the music swelled around us and then the saxophone joined in, rising out of the multitude of sounds singing it's own melody, beautifully nuanced and passionate. Right in the middle of the piece, using the briefest of intervals while keeping his hands and baton moving, old Meremblum turned just slightly back towards the audience and called out with strong emphasis and in his best Russian accent, "Fourteen years old!" and continued to conduct.

A rousing ovation followed and there we saw our son, well-composed and looking almost grown up, bowing to the audience, his hand shaken by the conductor and leaving the stage with Meremblum's arm around his shoulder. We were very proud. No, I did not wave to him.

Another crucial date, an early morning in March of 1965. Bruce had finished eating his big bowl of cereal and chomped on a huge sandwich he had made for himself. It consisted of ham, cheese, a cut up hotdog, pickles and tomatoes on rye bread. Oh, I think a little leftover turkey was also included. He saw the helpless amazement on my face when I discovered his creation.

"I am just plain hungry, Mom." He grabbed his lunch box with one hand and his book bag with the other. A swift kick sent the heavy entrance door back against the outside wall. "Goodbye." Still chewing, he clumped down the long set of steps to the street on his way to school. I looked after that tall, broad-shouldered boy. Gil stood next to me and laughed.

"He is fifteen and captain of the football team. What do you expect? He needs nourishment and lots of it. By the way, where is Ralph? He hasn't eaten breakfast yet." I went upstairs and peeked around the door to his room.

"Ralph, it's getting late." He was still comfortably ensconced in bed, leaning against bunched-up pillows, his crossed arms supporting his head, a picture of complete leisure. "Hey, what goes? Are you sick?" I went in and felt his head, which was completely cool. "Is there no school today? This is not a holiday, is it?"

"No, it isn't," he said, "I just decided that I won't go to school anymore. I do my assignments and then sit in class, watching the clock on the wall while the teacher goes over the same material we studied all week because so many of the students didn't get it or did not complete their homework. I am so bored there, Mom. I just can't stand it."

I rejoined Gil in the kitchen and reported Ralph's rebellion.

"So now what are we going to do with this boy?" Already standing to leave for work, having swallowed the last drop of coffee in his cup, my dear husband, rarely at a loss for answers, sank back down in his chair and just stared at me for a few seconds. He knew as well as I that this son of ours, once he had made up his mind, would not budge from his decision.

"So what, indeed, are we going to do?" Just for once he sounded helpless. "He has to finish school. Private school then? Christ, how can we afford that?"

I took a deep breath. "There is only one way. I've got to get back to work, find another teaching job. Let's figure that I had two years of vacation. How many people are that lucky?"

"What about your own studies, your classes at Otis? I hate for you to give all that up again." Gil shook his head in utter frustration. He knew that his son was bright and gifted. How could we deprive him of the education that he needed?

On the first of April in 1965 Ralph entered the Rexford School in Beverley Hills and I found a job as art teacher at the private Oakwood

School in the San Fernando Valley, beginning on the twenty-sixth of April. In September of that year Bruce followed Ralph to Rexford. We heard such glowing reports about his classes from Ralph that we felt that Bruce should have the same opportunity.

I received a call from Nancy Watts, my former colleague from the Pasadena Museum. She had been made director of a Children's Workshop at the new Los Angeles County Art Museum of Art on Wilshire Blvd. "Come join us," she said. "We really need you."

On the ninth of October I began teaching at the Los Angeles County Museum of Art. Nancy had a staff of four teachers and from semester to semester we had a waiting list of children from the ages of five to the early teens who where clamoring to join our classes. It really was a great success until we had not the rug, but our eventually well-worn linoleum pulled out from under our feet. It was the wealthy businessman and art collector Norton Simon, a most influential major donor to the museum, who made the idiotic pronouncement that *children have no business in a museum.*

If you, Mr. Simon, plan to deprive children of an education that opens their eyes to a richer world of art and creative discovery, who will visit your exclusive museum when this generation grows up? Should we just let them watch TV? In 1970, just five years after our happy and bustling classes commenced the doors were shut and the bright and spacious rooms were closed off, curtained and chopped into small business offices.

In contrast to Ralph, Bruce did not do too well at his new school. He joined a group of boys from very prosperous families who had money in their pockets and very little, if any, supervision at home. We suspected pot smoking, but that did not worry us too much. It still seemed to be a rather minor social peccadillo at the time.

We had serious talks with our son, though, especially on mornings following his weekend band engagements on the Sunset Strip. He frequently had trouble getting up and going off to school, looking very pale and drowsy. Of course that was from all of the exertion of performing so late at night, we reasoned. Or maybe?

"You guys don't drink, do you?"

"Oh Mom, of course not. Honest!"

It was sometime in July of that year. Gil and I were sitting in our living room enjoying a peaceful Sunday. We were both reading and the hot midday sun was trying unsuccessfully to squeeze its rays through the slats of the lowered blinds. I do not know what I was reading. It may have been the just-released book by Truman Capote, *In Cold Blood*, or maybe the more enjoyable *A Movable Feast* by Hemingway that had come out a few months before.

Gil was buried in the massive Sunday edition of the New York Times and not even the top of his head could be seen above the first page. It was so quiet. Very little traffic in the street below. Rick and Ralph where both away in San Francisco, Ralph in college and Rick—who knew what he did, except carting trays to patients and washing dishes at Mount Zion Hospital and otherwise having a good time in Haight Ashbury. Only Bruce was left with us and he was out rehearsing with his guitar, his saxophone and the members of his band.

Heavenly peace. Even the dogs seemed to be resting. Gil's paper rustled. He turned a page and suddenly a black projectile shot across the room. A wild leap and Scruggs, our big dachshund, landed on Gil's lap, scrunching the Times under his paws and looking up at his master with love in his eyes. This was a rare occasion. Only once in a long while had our roughneck, suddenly overcome by love, show such a need for affection. Gil grabbed dog and paper in a warm embrace and laughed heartily.

The reading spell was broken, but still we did not talk. The living room looked lonely and the big table in the raised dining area at the far end was empty; there was no life around it. There should have been boys in sneakers tromping up the staircase to the second floor and giggling young girls ringing the doorbell asking for their company.

"House getting too big, isn't it?" Gil knew what I was thinking, as usual. "Miss the boys?" I nodded. "Might we feel better in a smaller house?"

Chapter 23

A Small Cottage, A Panther in the Tree
Elrita Drive, 1966 to 1974

Brother Ralph and Pat had had lived in Laurel Canyon for many years. We loved the area and had always enjoyed visiting them, driving the narrow winding roads that curved their way up the hilly terrain, flanked by old established homes. These homes had to fight high and precipitous shoulders of earth that tended to rob them of living space.

"Well, all I have in Laurel Canyon right now is one small cottage on Elrita Drive. You can call it unconventional if you want to be charitable. So far I have not found a buyer. Nobody wants it. I'm not even inclined to show it to you." The realtor scratched his head and continued leafing through his papers.

"Now here is an elegant home right smack in Hollywood on a nice street that could be had at a reasonable price." He looked up and nodded at us with hope in his eyes. We disappointed him.

"Let's look at that cottage first." Gil spoke my mind exactly. Leaving noisy Hollywood Boulevard behind, we were driven up Laurel Canyon Boulevard and turned off onto short, partially paved Elrita Drive, that accommodated just a few homes on only one side of the street. It finished its short run at a dead end and that was where the house stood. I called it *our* house right away, because we loved it at first glance. It was a white one-story country cottage slightly elevated from the street, hugged by a friendly little picket fence. It did look a little run down and the garden was quite neglected, but as far as we could see there was nothing irreparable. Beyond the house reigned the rocky canyon wilderness, with bushes that spread and climbed the hilly terrain towards the canyon rim. There were laurel and other trees, some cactus and scrubby growth, a multitude of birds, and even a snake or two slithering among the rocks.

"Now do come and look at that fine residence in Hollywood, a truly respectable abode for people like you. And the price is right. Not too much more than this." I thought he'd almost said *this disreputable shack*, or something equally degrading. We ignored our exasperated realtor friend's efforts to lead us to more *respectable domiciles*. We signed the papers and after a relatively short escrow period the house on Elrita Drive was ours.

A few weeks later when we spent the first night in our new home we found that coyotes howled not far from our bedroom window and a resident owl had her favorite perch high up in the branches of the eucalyptus tree in our garden. This house was certainly unconventional. It must have been just a bungalow to start with and then several different owners had built onto it, a room here, a room there and helter-skelter passageways connecting them.

Which way do we turn to get to the bedrooms? Oh no, that's the bathroom. Turn left. One entered the house from the garden straight into the fairly small, but adequate living room. There was just enough space to gather a half circle of chairs in front of the sofa and around the coffee table to accommodate friends for our monthly reading group.

Following the turns in the narrow hallway we finally located the two bedrooms without landing in the kitchen. One of these rooms was going to become Gil's and mine, of course, and the other one was meant for Bruce, the only boy left with us. From his room a steep, narrow staircase led up to a tiny cubbyhole of a room that we called *the crow's nest*. It could just hold a single bed and a chair, enough space to house a visiting son on occasion.

We went for a final inspection of our empty Tracy Street house. We discovered a few articles of clothing in a closet and some dishes on the top shelf in the kitchen, gathered them up and locked the front door behind us for the last time. Descending the long steps to the street, we turned once more to look back at the house that held many memories for us. The white hibiscus was still in full bloom.

Next we stopped at the Rosen's, our nice young neighbors, to say goodbye and there almost stumbled over their running and shrieking little boys.

"Stop it! She is not a toy." Their mother Ruth dove into the turmoil and extracted a tiny shivering dachshund from under the sofa. "We just can't keep her. She is too young and delicate and the boys are too rough. How would you like to take her? Her name is Heidi and she already answers to that name."

"Heavens no. We have three dogs already." Gil raised his hands in protest.

We drove off with Heidi cuddled firmly in my arms. Arriving at our new house there were Scampy, Frou, and Scruggs awaiting us. They stared down in utter amazement at this tiny red-brown creature scampering up the garden path between them, tail up in the air, seeming to say *Well, here I am and I plan to stay*. And so she did for nearly sixteen years. The procession of dogs led the way into their new home (and ours, needles to say) and we followed.

Here I need to say a few words about our dogs, our four-footed family members who, after all, were so closely connected to us and to the homes in which we lived.

Scampy came to us many years before when Ralph was in kindergarten and claimed him as his own. He was a venerable thirteen year old gentleman in 1966 when we moved to the Elrita house and, sadly, died one year later.

I have described Frou's acquisition earlier. Once settled at Elrita he lived for several more years, looking peacefully and sedately at the world through a cascade of long black puli hair. Frou never got used to the indignity of being shorn nearly naked in the heat of summer.

Then there was Scruggs. A friend of my brother Ralph, an archeologist, was going on an expedition overseas and would be away for a year. He had a problem: what to do with his dog in the meantime. Would we keep his dachshund while he was gone? So we were expected to live with the dog for a whole year, fall in love with him and then give him back? Impossible! "If we take him he will be ours for good." The archeologist agreed and we had a new family member.

Scruggs was a big, sturdy, black dachshund, a tough, enterprising roustabout who had been used to canvassing all the neighboring houses in the canyon area where he had lived and had made himself welcome in many of them. He was an independent character, not the sweet little lapdog that I had hoped for. He became most decidedly Gil's special soul mate. It was two weeks later that I took Heidi in my arms.

There was one room at the back of our house that must have been an open veranda, but had since been enclosed. There stood my easel with a broad north-facing window that looked out to the wilderness and provided just the right light for painting.

Scruggy was barking and yelping outside in front of my window one day. The grasses and weeds were almost three feet high and though at first I could not see him I knew he was there, because the tall blades were waving back and forth. Then all of a sudden his black head and tail popped up for just a second, went under again and reappeared several times in staccato rhythm, bounding towards the big oak tree that stood right in front of my window.

And then I clapped my hands over my mouth and stared with unbelieving eyes as a large black shape suddenly shot up the trunk of the tree, turned and settled down in the crook of two big branches. It was a giant cat. No, not a cat. It was a panther, a panther whose long tail swung slowly back and forth, his strong shoulders hunched, his face turned down and his slanted eyes glaring at the puny little creature that barked and skipped about down below, wanting to follow him up the tree.

Oh God, Scruggy, he'll come down and kill you. I carefully opened the backdoor just a little, the box with dog biscuits in hand, shaking it vigorously and yelling for Scruggs to come in. At other times the rattling of the biscuit box would have had an immediate result. But now I had thrown poor Scruggs into a terrible quandary. He took two jumps in my direction, turned back to the tree, returned towards me, but then decided that he just could not risk loosing his prey and biscuits could not compete.

All I could think of was to call 911, the general emergency phone number. "Call the police," they said.

"You have *what* in your tree?" The policeman sounded censorious enough to do justice to his profession. "You mean a cat."

"Have you ever seen a cat who is about four feet long?" By that time I was shaking with excitement and fear for my dog.

"Lady, what did you have to drink?" He hung up on me. Next I called Animal Control and they were calm, much too calm.

"Yes, yes, we'll come out. We'll have a look." Nobody ever came. Trembling, I rushed back to see whether I still had a dog. The panther was gone and Scruggs came in panting, clearly asking *where is my biscuit?*

All those to whom I told this story repaid me with the strangest looks and giggles. *A panther in Laurel Canyon? What did you have to drink?* Yet a year later I was vindicated. A ranger knocked on our door one day. "Madam, I just want to warn you. We are putting traps with meat around this area back here to get rid of some of the pesky coyotes. Do not let your dogs out of your garden for a few weeks." I thanked him, we talked a little and I told him about my adventure with the panther and how everybody kidded me.

His eyes widened in astonishment. "Oh no! He is still around? Well, let me tell you that three years ago there were some Barnum and Bailey circus wagons crawling up these narrow roads to visit Roy Rogers, who lives on top of that hill. Two wagons overturned on a steep curve and a mother panther with two babies escaped. They found mama and one of the little ones, but the other young one was never found."

So there! *Who* had been drinking?

Since I am on the subject of Scruggs, the indestructible, I will add that in addition to attacking a live panther, his adventures included getting his head stuck in a barbed-wire fence and, on another messy occasion, consuming a large package of licorice that had been left on the coffee table. He ate it all, except the paper. When obvious signs alerted me to the problem, I quickly grabbed a kitchen towel, wrapped it around his behind, trying to stem the black ooze and transported him to the vet. After three days the gusher finally stopped.

And then there was the occasion on which he came prancing up to me in the garden shaking his head violently. I could not see what the matter was until I grabbed him by the neck to steady him and discovered a small snake with its length wrapped around his snout and its fangs embedded in his nose. One last shake and he dislodged it and it slithered away. Scruggs' nose began to grow immediately and at an alarming rate before of my very eyes.

"We have to keep him under sedation for several days." Our vet was very worried and he put Scruggs out with an injection immediately. "We must not allow him to regain consciousness. If he moves he distributes the poison even more. He has to be watched for several days and nights and as soon as he shows signs of waking he has to get another shot."

"Doctor, it's your Sabbath tomorrow. Isn't your practice closed?"

"I'll take him home with me. My wife, my teenage kids and I will watch over him. This dog has to be saved."

So, by the grace of a wonderful vet our Scruggs lived for many more years and was able to look forward to as many adventures and as much mischief as could possibly fit into one small dog's life history. And a final ensuing example comes to my mind: Scruggs ate half of Gil's leather wallet, contents and all.

"Enough. I've had it," my not-always-patient husband screamed. He tucked the dog under his arm and headed for the car.

"Where are you going with him?" I was alarmed.

"To the Humane Society," he called back and roared away.

It was the custom with us that a dog was always allowed to sit next to the driver when no one else required the seat. So there sat Scruggs next to Gil with his head on Gil's lap. Gil looked down at him. Scruggs raised his eyes full of love and trust and returned Gil's gaze. The car slowed down a little and a little more, stopped at the side of the road for a minute or two and then turned back. Scruggs was soon bounding happily back up the garden path on Elrita Drive.

"Just couldn't do it." With a little shamefaced, apologetic grin Gil went to the living room and turned on the radio and within minutes Mozart's Requiem enveloped us. The antithesis to Scruggs's exiting triumph.

My father used to say, "A house without books is not a home." He was so right and I like to add that a house without a dog is not a home. (Apologies to my cat-loving friends. I'll be magnanimous: a cat is OK too.)

Chapter 24

Losing My Brother

A late autumn evening in 1966, a few months after we had moved in. Unexpectedly Pat appeared at our door and stood stock still in the middle of the living room. She tried to speak. Her mouth opened and closed a few times. Shimmering moisture glinted in her eyes, but she did not permit the tears to flow.

"Pat, speak. What is it?"

"Ralph has lung cancer." The words flowed slowly from Pat's lips then drop by drop into my mind.

The year 1967 came. It was a fateful year. Time went on and my brother's strength was leaving him little by little. Some loyal students picked him up from home and took him to class in a wheelchair. Courageously he continued to lecture for quite a while. The gray hair above his temples had acquired a distinctly yellow hue from the incessant cigarette smoke that drifted upwards from morning to night and it was slowly falling out, the result of radiation.

In March we were beset by another upset, in addition to the worry about my brother. We learned to our horror that Bruce was being expelled from Rexford for being a disturbance to other students.

We did not understand. What was happening to our boy who had always been so friendly and considerate? His behavior had changed. He was always with his band, rarely at home and when he joined us he was grumpy, looked tired, pale and sloppy. He locked himself in his room and did not communicate with us at all. We thought that maybe his teen years were responsible for all that sleeping in the daytime and carousing at night.

"Let's make him quit his band," Gil looked determined.

"You'll get some screaming objections. Prepare yourself." I was worried, but I agreed.

Fate relieved us from certain unpleasantness, but only for the moment. At the beginning of June, Bruce came down with a whopping case of hepatitis that kept him in bed for almost two months. Since it was summer vacation we did not have to make an immediate decision as to his further schooling. He had lots of visitors, mostly female. Little dachshund Heidi was pleased to have someone in a bed during the daytime, someone to nudge and curl up with.

And then when August came brother Ralph did not go to the university any more. Wrapped in a blanket he crouched in his favorite chair. The hot summer air was coming through the open living room windows and he complained of being cold. He hardly ever talked, except to mutter once in a while, coming from deep within, "Damn it. God damn it." A moan of despair.

August 14, 1967. I'll never forget that day. A phone call came from Pat, "I have to go to the market and to the bank. Can you come and sit with him?"

We lived so close. It took only five minutes to drive to their house. As usual he sat in his favorite chair, bundled up in this August heat as if it where the middle of winter. He stared at me without a glimmer of recognition.

"There is your little sister." Pat tried to rouse him from his stupor without success. "He does not want to eat. Maybe you can get him to take a little tapioca pudding. That's the only thing he ever accepts now."

I settled on the sofa close to his chair and stroked his hand. Did he know that I was there? I was not sure. My adored brother, my love. The protector, the friend. He was too young to go, having just turned fifty-nine the month before. He had been a strong and energetic man, bright and creative, loved and admired by students and friends. I could hear our mother's voice from long ago, "Ralph don't smoke so much. It's bad for your health."

I closed my eyes. My hand kept resting on his. I remembered, oh yes, I remembered and saw it as if it happened yesterday. I am seventeen. I am lying on my bed, crying my eyes out. Another fight with my mother and a deep depression caused by emigration and teenage growing pains has thrown me into a pool of desperation. And there in the darkened room I hear my brother's voice. He comes and sits beside me, the friend, the helper, the one that pulled me up so many times.

A soft swishing sound made me come back to the room. One of their three cats had jumped up on Ralph's lap and now nested in the folds of his blanket. I was about to remove her, but unexpectedly my brother raised his hand and dropped it on her furry back.

Pat returned. "Did he eat something?"

"No, he just slept, I think."

"I'll put him to bed." This sentence came out with a deep sigh and Pat put her bundles down.

I started to fix dinner at home, but I could not concentrate. I leaned on the rim of the kitchen sink and looked out of the window at the virtual tent of trees that covered the backyard. An old gnarled grapevine sent its tentacles up some of their trunks and in all directions. Its twisted branches crept along the wire fence that was meant to keep the wilderness from encroaching upon our property, but weighed on it so heavily that it was bent in places like a mishandled construction toy. At one point its heaviest branches formed a jungle gym, winding upward around each other in swooping open curves, building platforms and roadways for Heidi and Scruggs to climb while forever chasing an unreachable squirrel.

My brother. Nothing else was on my mind. Pictures appeared again, as in a book that one leafed through slowly, page by page. I could see him in Nice at the French Riviera where we stayed for some years after leaving Germany. In swimwear we are at the oceanfront. His well-muscled young body is brown and slim. We are lying on towels on the heavily pebbled beach and my dear brother attracts girls from all around, of course, while I sit by, shy and quiet, but happy to have him home. He laughs and jokes and I am so proud of my big brother.

I could see him in Switzerland, a passionate mountain climber, as he trudges down a road with heavy boots, a coiled rope over one shoulder and climbing gear in an enormous backpack on his way to join a group that will climb one of the highest peaks in St. Moritz, the Piz Palue. He'll scale rock walls and walk over glaciers past steep ravines and my parents and I will be terribly worried until we have him back in our embrace and marvel at his sunburned nose.

The shrill telephone pierced my thoughts.

"Come help. He fell out of bed."

He was not heavy; he was so thin. We lifted him back up to his bed and from there on I do not have much recollection of the rest of the day. I know that Pat washed the floor of blood and excrement, the sign that life had ended. They carried him away towards evening. I stayed with Pat that night. We did not cry, holding our tears in check with stoic restraint, not wanting to break down for each other's sake. We were so much alike. Today I know that we should have given in and shared our grief. Days later I wept in Gil's arms. Poor Pat. Who held her?

Chapter 25

Meeting Up With Synanon

Bruce worried us more and more. He did not seem to have an interest in anything. Even his band was not as important as it had been previously. His hair grew long, partially falling over his face as if he wanted to hide from something. He had few friends by this time and they all looked as sloppy as he did.

"What on earth is bugging him? What is wrong?" Gil shook his head and looked at me as if I had the answer. "We've got to get him into counseling. Let's tackle it right after the holidays."

November, 1967, a day before Thanksgiving. Gil was out of town again and Rick and Ralph were living in San Francisco. It was ten o'clock on a nasty, wet and windy night. I was sitting in the living room reading, absent-mindedly scratching Scampy's neck. As usual he had squeezed in next to me on my recliner, firmly planting his head in my lap, doing his best to nudge an annoying book to the side.

Bruce had a few friends over and the door to his room was shut. Yet I could tell that something was going on. I heard footsteps going down the hall and the bathroom door was slowly and quietly shut so as not to make noise. But then I could hear a clicking sound, perhaps where a glass touched the rim of the washbowl, followed by a small clatter like small metal objects being scattered about. A minute or so of silence and then the footsteps returned to Bruce's room, not so quietly or gingerly as before.

Why, for heaven's sake, do they have to go to the bathroom so often? I shook my head and listened when another trip was undertaken down the hall and then yet again in intervals of several minutes. The same clicking noises, the same stealthy footsteps.

Scampy started to growl tentatively, *sotto voce*. He too did not quite like the situation. I decided to investigate. The rim of the bathroom sink was strewn with burnt matches with a bent spoon teetering in the midst of it, a still-life puzzle for the uninitiated. I went straight for Bruce's door and entered without knocking.

"No Mom, you can't come in," he said urgently, with his palms thrust towards my face, wide eyes glaring in horror. Was this a ghost or my son? The room was only half lit, the shade of a floor-lamp hovering dimly over his friend Eddy's head and arm, a small syringe poised in his hand ready to pierce an arm held tightly against his lap.

"No! Stop that. No!" Two long jumps and I grabbed the needle just in time.

"Party is over. Out. All of you." They rose from the sofa, the floor and seemingly even the walls, a tangle of pale faces and scared eyes, wild locks, torn T-shirts and frayed jeans. They slipped out into the night and rain, leaving the smell of smoke and great upset behind them. Just Bruce and I were left.

"I'm sorry, Mom." A low little croak, almost inaudible.

"Tomorrow . . ."

I waved him off and stumbled from the room. The toilet managed to swallow the syringe.

A sleepless night followed by a cold, gray morning found me sitting up in bed holding my head in both hands. How could this have happened? Why were we so blind? Didn't I see his pale face, the unkempt long hair falling over his eyes, the refusal to wear short-sleeved shirts even on hot summer days? What to do now? *Gil, I need you; I need you right this moment, not just later this afternoon when your plane comes in.* We were to join his brother Nat's family, but how could we face them at a Thanksgiving dinner?

Quite some time before I had heard of a drug treatment organization called Synanon that was supposed to be very successful. It took some searching, but I found a telephone number. The man who answered my anxious call sounded calm and reassuring.

"Bring him over to see us on Monday and we'll talk to both of you." I'll get expert advice on how to handle the situation, I thought. Thank God! I breathed a little easier. Gil arrived back home in the late afternoon, quite horrified at learning about his youngest son's state of affairs.

"Bruce, how long has this been going on?"

"Since the last New Year's party."

"So that is for almost a year?" He leaned against a wall in front of us, head hanging down toward his chest, a picture of complete misery. "How did you get into that?"

"From Mitch and his band at Rexford. They used it."

I looked at Gil and he groaned. So when the director of the school had summand us in May before summer vacation to inform us that Rexford did not wish to enroll Bruce and hinted that there might be a serious problem, Gil had exploded in a furious outburst against the poor man. *His* son was a good boy, no problems, certainly not with drugs like other hoodlums. So when Bruce came down with hepatitis a month or so later, we were still none the wiser.

Years later we learned that on a night when I thought that Bruce was just staying overnight with a friend, he almost overdosed and the other boys had to drag him to school the next day. He fell asleep in class and was so drowsy and incoherent that they sent him home. That was the reason he was expelled.

That Thanksgiving was anything but joyous. We did not want to let Bruce out of our sight, so we made him accompany us in spite of his protestations. Once we arrived at his uncle's house he disappeared into a bedroom and did not show himself for dinner or for the rest of the evening.

November 27, 1967

Monday's early traffic slowed us down until we reached the road to Santa Monica. The sea air found its way through our open window and dark, gray clouds moved overhead, drifting slow and heavy as if to mirror our mood. I looked at Bruce who sat beside me, eyes closed and lying back in his seat. I broke the silence.

"Bruce, we have to get you out of this. You cannot squander your life on drugs."

"I know, Mom, I know. I want to stop. I tried, but I can't." It was a mumbled reply, but it gave me hope. He was willing. That seemed to be a first step.

"We'll see these Synanon people now and maybe they can tell us what to do."

Gil had left his factory and was already waiting for us at the expansive entrance to the large, imposing brick building that stood five stories high at the oceanfront, only a broad sandy beach separating it from the water. We entered a large hall that looked more like a hotel foyer than the lobby of a drug rehabilitation establishment. As a matter of fact, we learned later that it had once been the elegant Del Mar Hotel and Beach Club.

"Would you please wait? We'll to talk to your son first." Two well-dressed young men escorted us to a small waiting room, offered us some coffee and left with Bruce, who looked back over his shoulder at us as if pleading for protection. We sat together silently, choked by fear and worry. I sank into the red plush sofa but could take no comfort in it or anything else. Gil walked up and down. No rest for him either. We gazed at the clock on the wall. It ticked and ticked but did not seem to advance. The room was dark, as was the sky outside. I kept checking my watch. Half an hour passed, forty-five minutes, one hour and finally the door opened. Our son was ushered in by the young men. One of them had his arm around Bruce's shoulder.

"Bruce has decided that he wants to stay with us," declared the taller of the young men and the other nodded in affirmation. There was something very official and undeniable about this statement.

"Bruce?" We both looked at our son for an answer that would determine the course of his life for many years to come. Little did we realize the importance of this moment.

"Yes, I do." A few seconds of silence and Gil and I looked at each other, puzzled and shocked.

"How long might it take until he can come home?"

"Maybe a year or more. It's hard to tell"

Oh God, that long, I thought. I clenched my hands and tried to sound composed and reasonable. "So when shall I bring him? We'll need to pack his clothes and . . ."

"Sorry, there is no going home," the young man interrupted me brusquely.

"He stays right here now. You can bring whatever you wish another time."

We then discussed a few details and paid a fee to cover his expenses until Bruce could participate in community life and pull his own weight. I was in such a daze from the suddenness of the situation that I only heard part of what was said. But the young men delivered a very clear edict that we were not to communicate with our son under any circumstances for three months. No visits, no phone calls, no letters, period.

Outside the black clouds had joined forces and now poured wind-driven streams of water against our faces. "I have to hurry back to the plant. I never thought I'd be away this long. I'll call you." Gil's car door slammed. I sloshed to the far end of the lot where I had parked, water dripping off my hair and shoulders. I hunched over the stirring wheel and stared out to the ocean. Through a curtain of streaming rain I saw white-crested waves rising angrily and rolling to the shore as if they were trying to catch the seagulls in their swooping flight. I wept and felt like floating out into the watery turmoil, only to disintegrate and fade away. Three months ago I had lost my brother and at that moment it felt like I lost my child. It was as if parts of me had been taken away, torn off, leaving an empty hole.

It took twenty-two years for Bruce to leave Synanon and fully reenter our lives. I asked Bruce recently to write a short description of the community that was Synanon. I knew that he would do it better then I could.

> *Synanon was a revolutionary live-in drug rehabilitation program founded in 1958 in Santa Monica, California. Using intense peer pressure plus a unique brand of brutally honest group therapy called "The Game," Synanon exploded the popular myth that heroin addiction was incurable. In it's heyday Synanon was wildly successful and attracted drug addicts as well as non-drug users who where captivated by the Synanon lifestyle and pursuit of inner peace. Over time Synanon evolved into a peculiar and highly controversial utopian society and grew to over 2000 live-in residents and countless thousands of non-resident members.*
>
> *Most old-timers in Synanon were profoundly committed to the vision and control of the charismatic founder and monolithic leader, Chuck Dederich. Synanon dissolved in 1989 after a much-troubled final decade. The internet is a rich source of conflicting opinions about Synanon's contribution to American culture. These opinions aside, Synanon saved my life.*

Synanon gave us to understand that parents were expected to contribute some volunteer work on a regular basis. So there I stood behind the desk of the receptionist, a stern-looking schoolteacher type, where I was assigned to be her assistant, to shuffle papers and check files. There was constant movement throughout the large lobby behind me. Men and women, mostly young ones but also middle aged and quite a few older ones went forever up and down a broad staircase. They all wore blue denim overalls, men and women alike. They disappeared and returned through various doors and all looked very intent, as if each had an important task that had to be taken care of without delay.

I kept stealing glances over my shoulder hoping to spot my boy in his strange new environment.

"You remember, of course, that you may not acknowledge your son in any way if you happen to see him. No eye contact, no waving. Turn away and ignore him completely." The tall, skinny receptionist, a determined woman, fixed her gaze at me over the rim of her glasses.

If I disobey she'd put me in jail, I scoffed to myself, realizing that she must have been directed to watch me and to control my behavior. Helpless anger arose in me. Again I glanced furtively over my shoulder. And then I saw him. He came down the staircase, obviously as intent on his task as was everyone else around him. I almost did not recognize him. His beautiful black hair was gone. His head was shaved and the baggy overalls he wore were the uniform of the group to which he belonged. I do not think he saw me. He would not have expected me to be there. The instinct to get up and run to hug him, to tell him that I loved him almost overwhelmed me.

"It hurts, doesn't it?" my guardian dragon whispered. It was more of a statement then a question. So she was human, after all.

Every Wednesday night Gil and I drove out to Santa Monica to take part in sessions called *The Mama's and Papa's Group*. Those meetings were called *Games* and as far as I was concerned they were far from constructive therapy for non-addicted parents. Under the leadership of a long-time Synanon member a group of upset people sat around in a circle while being urged to criticize and harass each other. This was the way the *Game* was conducted for the recovering residents. The goal was to tear down their defenses and to build up new and positive character and personality. This notion was completely unsuitable for the poor parents who had suffered enough, grieving for their disturbed children.

There was a woman who had been depressed and in tears at several sessions during the previous weeks. She appeared one evening with a much happier face and declared that she was finally coming to terms with what had happened to her son and looked forward to having him home again one day.

"What the hell do you have to be so pleased about? Who got your son to turn to drugs in the first place? You must have been a rotten mother." The whole room turned against her after the leader signaled the attack. Her face fell and she rushed out in tears.

I once made the mistake of mentioning that we always had to rush to get to Santa Monica at night. It was a long drive from home at the end of a hectic workday for both of us. There had not been time for dinner.

"So you must be starved," someone said.

"Oh no. I brought a dish and a spoon along and fed my husband while he drove." I thought this was pretty clever.

"What, you fed him like a baby? You are the typical mother-tyrant, keeping the whole family under her thumb, making babies of them all. No wonder your son turned to drugs to escape you."

I weathered this and other assaults from January until the end of July when I had finally had enough.

For weeks the group had pestered me about my long hair. "You are too old to wear your hair like a young woman. Look at all your wrinkles. You *must* cut your hair." (I had hardly any wrinkles.) I was forty-nine and sometimes wore my hair loose, but mostly pinned up.

Every week the same heckling. *Cut you hair, cut your hair*. They did their best to wear me down. After months of stoic resistance I just got up one night and walked out.

Gil, who had been assigned to another group, followed suit. We did not miss the long drives to the ocean and Santa Monica for the games and my weekend volunteering.

At the end of July when we were finally allowed to visit our son we could see the beneficial influence the group had on Bruce. We were able to visit him every few weeks and over time saw his behavior and appearance change; he ceased to be a pitiful, muddle-headed kid and again became a clear-thinking, normal young man. The lines of communication were open again between us, but still there existed an indefinable strain, a lack of ease in our relationship. Bruce now belonged to this strange new group, this self-sufficient society that had its own rules and regulations, so unlike the way we lived.

Synanon was a community in which everybody looked out for the good of other members and shared equally in the maintenance of their property. People were assigned to man the kitchen, cook and serve the crowd that was assembled in the vast room where once elegant guests of the former beach club had dined. All shared in the work of general housekeeping and laundry. The business office was staffed by more experienced people. Everybody was considered equal and everybody had various tasks to perform on a rotating basis, except for one man, Chuck Dederich, the founder of Synanon, the unassailable leader. Every word that came from his lips was sacred, every pronouncement became law. He was the king.

Almost a year after Bruce entered Synanon he was allowed to invite us to a party that was in full swing when we arrived. We were led to a raised platform that ran along the full length of the former ballroom. There we sat and gazed in awe at the mass of people below us. All of them were dancing, but not with each other. Each stayed in his or her assigned place within one of the long lines that moved wavelike forward, back and forward again to the rhythm of the music.

"You see," said the young woman who had escorted us, "We invented this dance with a philosophy behind it. We all use the same basic steps, but then improvise upon them in any way we like. We are a group together, but also remain our own selves. This is the Synanon dance. We call it the Hoopla."

"That sounds quite admirable," I whispered to Gil, scanning the stomping and gyrating figures below. Little did we realize how the powerful group influence over time swallowed the individual personhood of its members. They followed the leader without question. Scanning the intense faces of the enthusiastic dancers we saw brown, white, black and a few Asian men and women, young and old, even a grandparent or two.

After absorbing this remarkable scene we paid attention to the musicians. There stood Bruce, leading the band with his saxophone, blowing his horn with enthusiasm and having a great time. I reached over to take Gil's hand. He nodded and sighed a deep breath of relief.

It was at about that time that Bruce started to communicate with us by mail. Here are just a few excerpts.

6/28/68

> *I am now residing in Tomales Bay and am a part of Chuck's research and development program. It is the most fascinating experience of my life. Tomales Bay is fantastic. I am a landscaper. I am learning about gardening and landscaping, flowers and trees,*

soil and peat moss, trenches and ditches for planting and all sorts of stuff like that. Some of the other jobs that I hope to work on are construction, the barn and automotive. I will learn about sheet metal work, carpentry and welding. At the barn they are learning about horses, cows and chickens. The interesting thing about this kind of learning is that it all applies to my life directly and is very visible and tangible. I love being here.

8/8/68

I am now in a printmaking class which is taught by Oscar Camagno, who is a nine-year Synanon resident and who studied under Rico Lebrun, of all people. I am having a great time in his class.
By the way, Emerson is the basis of the Synanon philosophy.
Please don't be offended if I do not write more often. The reason I do not is because I have tremendous attacks of homesickness when I do.

9/12/68

I now play in four musical groups: a Gospel choir, a choral group that is doing Bach and stuff like that and a Jug band, in which I play guitar and sing. I also play piano.

Reading his letters, how could we not rejoice that our son was alive and in full health and apparent wellbeing? From deepest fog back into the light.

Chapter 26

A Wedding and an Earthquake

A few years before Bruce became addicted and entered Synanon, he and his friend Eddy Sony were star football players at Marshall High School in the Los Feliz district of Los Angeles, admired and courted by female classmates. It must have been around 1965.

It was not quite dark on a hot August evening and the rain poured down as if it would never end. I opened the door in response to a rather consistent and urgent doorbell. I was not too surprised to be faced with three teenage girls, giggling and dripping wet. All were barefoot and wearing jeans that were not considered lady-like by many at that time and were not allowed in school. Umbrellas? Heaven forbid; they were strictly out of style.

Two girls were blond and one had long, shiny black hair that released rivulets of water down her face, her neck and down to her toes. She had large black eyes, very pale skin and strikingly handsome features. She could have been a gypsy, a girl from Spain or the inhabitant of a tent in the Moroccan desert. As a matter of fact she was Jewish and her name was Dorit, an Israeli name.

"Is Bruce at home?"

"No, I am very sorry. He went out some time ago."

"Awe—"

Three long drawn-out sighs of disappointment met my smiling face as I tried to transmit a little empathy without expressing it verbally. Little did I know that Dorit, the black-haired beauty before me, was going to be my first daughter-in-law. It was not Bruce but Rick who fell in love with her and she responded with enthusiasm. She was only sixteen and her parents were scandalized.

The shrill voice accosting me through the receiver of the telephone, that I now held inches away from my ear, sizzled with indignation. "Are you aware that your son is pursuing my daughter?"

"I know that the two of them like each other and have gone out quite a bit, but I do not think that pursuing is quite the right expression as far as my son is concerned. Your daughter seems to enjoy his company as well."

"You must talk to him. I do not wish to see him with my daughter under any circumstances from now on."

"I'll give him of your message, but that is all I can do. Be assured, they are really just friends." I started to get annoyed.

"Don't you have any influence over your son? What kind of a mother are you? Forbid him to see her. Just forbid it!"

I had had enough of her screaming. Forbid something to a nineteen-year-old boy? I mumbled an excuse and said goodbye. I am sure she did not hear me above her screams. I hung up.

It took no more than a week or two before Dorit was shipped off to relatives in Israel to escape the threat of an unsuitable alliance. This happened in 1966. Six months later she returned in protest and escaped with Rick to San Francisco. She was sixteen and Rick nineteen. They were so young, but irrefutably determined to share their lives from then on.

Two years later in 1968 Dorit turned eighteen and parental permission was no longer required. The wedding was planned and Judy, her mother, although defeated, took the reigns in hand, planning elaborate festivities to be held at an elegant hotel. She ignored the stated wishes of the young couple to be married at the top of a mountain preferably barefoot with flowers in their hair surrounded only by family and their closest friends.

"So your parents want to mess things up again." Rick was bristling. "We'll do it our way, not theirs."

Poor Dorit was torn between her furious husband-to-be and the desire not to hurt her parents. "Look Rick, I've caused them much pain already; let them have this last pleasure and then we are on our own."

August 9, 1968. The large entrance hall of the Townhouse Hotel. Crystal chandeliers, gold and glitter wherever you looked. People in summer party attire moved about or stopped momentarily for a quick chat and then proceeded towards open double doors that lead to a formal garden. Many rows of chairs were set facing a lavishly flower-decorated pergola.

"Now where would Rick's wedding be?" We looked around and were completely puzzled.

"*Hello* darlings! What a great occasion." Our friend Minette rushed up to us and threw her arms around us. "Everything is just so beautiful." Here too were our friends Betts and Michael Hall.

"Now where do we go for the wedding? Have you found it yet"? We asked, starting to feel a little anxious.

"This is it, kiddo. Her parents went all out, that's for sure. We saved you seats in the front row." In amazement we gazed at the strange crowd and looked for familiar faces.

"Who are all these people?"

"I've already figured it out." Mischievous Betts, pleased with her snooping talent, grinned at us triumphantly. "They are mostly business acquaintances and customers from Dorit's parent's store. A few of their relatives and personal friends are probably also here."

So this was Rick's intimate little wedding, not much more than an inspired business promotion. At least Dorit had won one skirmish with her mother. She had refused to wear the wedding dress picked out for her and proceeded to crochet her own, a fitting symbol of her budding independence. It turned out to be a great success and she looked lovely in her homemade gown.

Our son, her young husband to be, had always shown disdain for customary formal attire for any occasion, but this time he gave in to Dorit's urging. He had to wear a suit for the wedding. When they were still living on their own in San Francisco he and Dorit visited a clothing store that catered mostly to rock musicians and other performers. There he purchased a double-breasted light beige knobby linen suit. The jacket's wide lapels were each split in two sections giving the impression of wings at rest just before takeoff. Rick looked fresh and happy, sporting a new well-kept moustache.

Just before sitting at my reserved seat in the front row I let my eyes search for faces of family and friends among the strangers. And then I saw our party. They had all somehow found each other and clustered together, chatting and laughing happily, waiting for the young couple to appear.

There were young people, Rick and Dorit's acquaintances, and then the older generation, our friends. Most of our reading group was present and then there were Bernard and Ethel Garey, Gil's old school chums, Ruth and Larry Rosen, the former parents of our little dog Heidi.

"Hello! Congratulations!" Someone stepped out from behind me and put an arm around my shoulders.

"Dr. Steinberg, how wonderful that you could come. We invited you with little hope that you would be able to get away from your office."

"I would not miss a wedding of one of my children if I could help it. It happens rarely enough that I am free." Dr. Steinberg had helped all three of our boys enter this world with great care and we felt that he was our special friend. His German Jewish upbringing could be discerned quite easily just by looking at him, even without his strongly accented speech. He held himself erect and tended to be a little formal at times with people he did not know well. He always wore a tie even at a garden party and probably at dinner at home. His voice was gentle and calm and behind his serious eyes flickers of merriment could appear from time to time just short of downright laughter. He was a wonderful man and Gil and I were very fond of him.

Another special person I discovered in one of the last rows was Mildred Jackson, who had cleaned my parent's home for many years and had also helped me from time to time. All our boys were fond of her and she was invited as a matter of course. I waved and motioned to her to sit in front with us but she signaled *No* and stayed where she was. This was so typical for her. Even at home she would never sit down for a meal with us in spite of being invited. She was part black and part Cherokee Indian, too used to sitting in the back-row. Oh, what a shame.

The guests were getting restless. It was over an hour before the bride appeared. It had taken her so long because her mother had insisted at the last minute to have her daughter's long hair styled at the beauty parlor, an endless procedure. Finally after a long wait the bride walked down the flower-strewn walkway to the pavilion on the arm of her father, towards the Rabbi and the happy, almost teary eyed but smiling young husband. Each set of parents stood behind its own offspring to witness the event. Ralph was Rick's best man, well dressed and sedate, but obviously pleased. Dorit had a favorite girlfriend at her side and little Tammy, her sister, was the flower girl.

The rabbi intoned the blessing, the rings were exchanged and Rick performed the last ritual act required by Jewish custom, the breaking of the ceremonial goblet. I doubt that many grooms performed this symbolic act with as much vigor and obvious relish as our Rick did by stomping and smashing the glass on the ground, the grand finale to the ceremony. Seeing the happy faces of our young people sealing their marriage vows with a fervent kiss, surrounded by family and friends, made us forget how the ostentatious and impersonal affair had annoyed us so recently.

A large adjacent hall had been arranged for the reception, with dishes and platters of elaborate, festive food. In the middle of that array a silver fountain bubbled champagne. The obligatory receiving line formed. The whole family had to keep smiling and shaking innumerable well-wishing hands while Rick and Dorit waited, no doubt, to run off by themselves.

Judy, Dorit's mother, the omnipotent hostess, fluttered by smiling broadly while nodding and greeting everybody, sparkling as if the whole affair took place in her honor. I quickly stopped her for a second, trying to be friendly. After all, our families were to be related from then on.

"Our kids are so happy. I trust they will have a good marriage."

Her response was a piercing, disdainful smile, showing all of her front teeth as if she were ready to bite. She raised her hand in a quick dismissive gesture towards the whole world. "I don't trust anybody," she said and set off to regale the crowd. As she left me I shuddered.

(I am sitting in front of my computer reading some of what I have written and contemplating the many years and experiences that are still to be written, to be relived and shared, no less then forty years worth. Impossible. Quite, quite impossible. I am afraid that I will not have that much time left. I am 94. I would still like to see this second part of my memoir finished. So now, as I travel back through my life I will only lightly glance at the landscapes that I pass on the way to the destinations that remain most vivid and clear in my mind.)

Rick and Dorit lived in San Francisco for a year and then in the fall of 1969 they went on their delayed honeymoon to Europe. They bought a used V.W. bus in Germany and traveled all over France, Italy, Germany, Austria and Greece for six harrowing months, coping with a shortage of money and battling constant car trouble. Their letters abounded with mishaps and dire pleadings for money, but also of glowing descriptions of things they saw and experienced.

When they returned home Dorit's father gave them a vacant space to open a gift store in a commercial building in the San Fernando Valley. Rick and Dorit's shop opened on a late November afternoon in 1970. I stood in the middle of the room, looked around and marveled at the artful arrangement of pottery, weavings and ceramics. Small sculptures and decorative items were displayed on shelves and tables. It all looked great, but for me seeing the excited faces of the young couple was the highlight of the display. People were milling around, family and friends admiring, laughing and chatting, celebrating this happy event.

And then there was Judy. Since she was neither the instigator nor the star of the show she was almost subdued. We greeted each other. We were cool and polite, exchanged a few words and separated again. After a while I glanced at her from across the room. She was self-consciously poised as the reigning mother of all, accepting congratulations for her daughter's success with a slight smile on her face, appropriate for the occasion. Nevertheless there was a vague defensive air about her. I did not know where it came from, but all of a sudden I felt sorry for her. There was something so lonely and needy about her. This was not a happy woman.

Most prominent and impressive was a glass case in the middle of the room entirely filled with Rick's own gold and silver jewelry. I have never understood how Rick acquired the skill and knowledge he needed to become an expert jeweler without formal schooling in that field. Ten years later in 1980 he won first prize for one of his gold rings at a competition sponsored by the illustrious DeBeers Diamond Company.

Eight months had passed since the store opened with great hopes for a successful future. In July of 1971, in the early hours of the morning, Gil and I sat straight up in bed holding on to each other for dear life. The bed was careening from one wall to the other and we tumbled along with it trying to stay upright. The floor rolled, the ceiling shook and pictures jumped off the walls. It felt as if we were sitting in a big open truck that was racing over bolder-strewn terrain at top speed, ready to crash. It probably only took a few minutes, but it felt like it would never stop.

Rarely had I been that frightened. It was the big earthquake that hit Los Angeles in 1971 and caused much damage and loss of life. It also spilled into the San Fernando Valley where the contents of poor Rick and Dorit's shop were crushed and broken, bespattered and shattered. Nothing could be saved. It was miraculous that our house did not sustain any damage. We learned later that our immediate area was built on rock, which had saved the house.

A year later in1972 our first grandson Noah was born. In the years to come he lived with us on and off, sometimes for months. It almost felt as if we had produced another child of our own and we loved him as if we had. Rick and Dorit were busy at a retail space they occupied in the Whole Earth Marketplace that housed a conglomeration of gift and craft stores on State Street in Santa Barbara. Their business was quite successful, especially with Rick's jewelry, but unfortunately the marriage was not. They divorced some years later. I am pleased to say that I have remained friends with Dorit.

Chapter 27

Gil Retires

Every few months at the close of a pleasant weekend at home, not looking forward to a busy Monday at work, my dear husband would turn to me, raise his index finger in a gesture calling me and the whole world to attention and make the inevitable pronouncement, "I will retire at 59." February 14, 1973 was Gil's 59th birthday. It was his big day and he had not forsaken his goal. One year before had he informed Airstream of his plans.

Gil had spent time pondering what he would do with himself when he retired. He had always loved woodworking and the feel and texture of wood. *I'll try my hand at woodcarving,* he thought, and then tried to explain that to the to the upper echelon of his company, to those who would try their utmost to convince him to remain.

Art Costello, an energetic Italian American, was the big man at Airstream, the owner of the company. But aside from the big shadow he cast in the company and his superior position, of which he was most aware, Art was really quite small and square, though admittedly robust. He did not want to loose his successful sales director.

"If that's what you want to do, we'll give you a room in back of the office and you can sit there with your wood and whittle whenever time allows." Of course it was not whittling that was on Gil's mind. He saw himself carving figures, animals and abstract forms. He was going to read, get his bicycle out again, go to concerts and, above all, we were to travel to Europe.

My son Ralph attended the University of California at Santa Barbara at that time and his advice was well taken. "The only way to convince them that you are really going to leave is to buy a house in Santa Barbara and move away from Los Angeles."

But Art Costello was not impressed. "So we pay your plane ticket to Los Angeles a few times a week, you join us in a consultant capacity and we raise your salary." This turned out to be such a tempting offer that Gil could not refuse it. Once we were established in Santa Barbara he drove for over two hours to the Santa Fe Springs factory every Monday morning and returned home on Thursday evening. He preferred to drive and they reimbursed the cost of gasoline and automobile use instead of the plane ticket.

Of course, at times there were unforeseen emergencies at the plant or at one of the dealerships and we had to do without our boss at home for more days then expected. Through it all Art Costello did his best to hold on to his valuable man.

A number of friends and associates agreed that Gil was a born salesman. Yes he was, but he was so much more. He was a good man who could not stand to see anyone hurt or suffer injustice. I do not ever recall his taking advantage of anybody, sometimes even acting to his own detriment in favor of another's benefit. And he loved his life, his family and his home. Music was his passion. He admired and appreciated art in many forms and he was a tireless reader. So it was not surprising that his desire to shake off the burden of his job in order to enjoy all of the things that really mattered to him became so intense.

We decided that I would go house hunting by myself at first. Gil could not stay away from the plant for an extended time, so I drove on the busy freeway from smog-shrouded Los Angeles to Santa Barbara, where it felt like I had entered another world. The sun shone brightly, the sky spread a dome of incredible blue over the city and the fresh air that blew in from the ocean seemed to shimmer over houses, streets and people.

I stayed with Ralph in his Montecito apartment. For several days I drove all over the landscape of Santa Barbara looking for just the right house for us without success. Finally I went back home and returned the next week for more house hunting. This time I was driven by Mrs. Palumbo, a small, bustling woman who was a very nice and knowledgeable realtor. The July sun was hot and we were both very tired.

"Just one more house to see and we'll call it a day." She fanned herself with her little black notebook but did not seem to get much relief. We turned right off Olive Mill Road in Montecito and drove down a narrow unpaved path, flanked by wild, untended greenery. Tall eucalyptus trees and oaks formed a canopy overhead, while vines climbed up their trunks and wild bushes cushioned both sides of the *bumpity road*, as little granddaughter Isabelle named it years later.

We came to a one-story home of whitewashed adobe. A good-sized chimney announced the presence of a fireplace. A large two-car garage with doors hanging by their hinges stood unattached and flanked a graveled parking area in front of the house.

"It looks quite Spanish, doesn't it? It is unoccupied but I do not have the key. Let's look through the windows." We walked around to the side of the house. My forehead pressed against one of three adjacent sliding glass doors while my hands were cupped around my eyes to avoid the glare of the sun. I peered into an unusually large, bright room. On the left I could see an open kitchen with a long counter separating it from the rest of the living space. A good-sized fireplace occupied the opposite wall to my right, still full of ashes and charred remnants of wood. It was faced with diagonally laid adobe brick, stretching the entire length of the living room wall, climbing toward the ceiling, capped by an odd saw-toothed edge.

As my eyes wandered deeper, passing an entrance hall, I found myself peering into another room, as generous in its way as the room through which I was gazing. This house had obviously stood empty for quite some time. Various little beasties crawled or slithered across the thick, soiled carpet. Spider webs decorated a lonely chandelier. Obviously, children had lived there; rainbow colors of crayon drawings, squiggles and smudges danced on one white wall and muddy prints of small children's hands told the story.

Mrs. Palumbo shook her head. "Well, I would call this a fixer upper. The price will have to go down considerably, no doubt." We walked around to the back of the house. "It seems you'd have quite a bit of land here."

Some magnificent oak trees extended their branches possessively over the large expanse of ground that appeared once to have been covered by manicured lawn. Wherever one looked there were weeds and clumps of strange grasses with tough stalks that grew four or five feet high. Here and there some thirsty camellia bushes bravely produced a few tired blossoms. A forgotten lawn chair lay upside down against the side of the house, attesting that someone had once lived there.

Turning around the next corner we found two long brick planter boxes that still contained earth, rotting stems and leaves. They stood parallel to and about five feet removed from the wall of the house. Beyond that line, with orange and apple trees at the end of it, was another large piece of land that stretched as far as a neighbor's house.

"I think these bricks mark the end of the property." Mrs. Palumbo rooted around in her voluminous briefcase. "I don't seem to have the plan of the grounds."

I had an idea. "Why don't I go and ask the neighbors? They will know where their land begins and this ends." And off I went across the stubbly turf.

A nice lady opened the door. "Oh no. None of that land is ours. We end on our side of the fruit trees. If you bought the house those trees would be yours. You'd have a lot of work to do there, wouldn't you?"

I was amazed. That much land! Could we handle that? It turned out to be an acre and a half. I called Gil in L. A.

"Come. There are two or three houses I want you to see. All are nice and would work for us, but I want to know which one you'd like. I know which one I want, but we must decide together."

Gil came and, as was true so often, our tastes proved to be the same. He loved the house on Olive Mill Road and realized all its possibilities. With some renovation we could turn it into a special home, fashioned to our taste and style of living. The papers were signed on July 22nd and escrow closed at the end of August in 1971.

CHAPTER 28

The Olive Mill House Was Ours

Fumigation was ordered and completed. Now the serious work could begin. Ralph and I comprised the cleanup crew. Gil, as usual, had to be away on a lengthy business trip just at that time. Pat came up from Los Angeles to join us for an unforgettable weekend. With bug-spray, vacuum, brooms, mops and buckets we attacked the delinquent house. Its rehabilitation had begun. We worked hard, but had a lot of fun. We joked and laughed, a happy beginning for a new chapter in our lives.

Arriving home from a nearby coffee shop on the first evening we discovered that the electricity had not yet been turned on. We were too exhausted to care and soon fell asleep with blankets on the floor, hoping that we had cleaned the carpet thoroughly enough. I awoke in the middle of the night to find the room lit by a gentle glow that seemed to come from within the walls. But it was the moon on it's eternal path on this cloudless night that graced us with the gentle power of it's light.

The strange, tumbling brick pattern above the fireplace seemed to careen in a broad swath towards the three great glass doors that led to the garden. I followed, though feeling stiff and achy; the floor was no featherbed. A bit of air breathed through the grass and bushes that surrounded the faded lawn. Here the moon shone in its full glory, transforming the earth to a world of mysterious light and fleeting shadows. Nothing was quite real, as in a dream. I did not dare to venture on. What might lurk behind or under the dense foliage in that wilderness? I stayed by the door, peering out at the landscape, trying to imagine what we could do to make it our own.

In anticipation I spied little hillocks, dips and hollows that held fine promise for our garden, yet to be designed. What would we find once the wild growth was shaved? How wonderful to look forward to future discoveries. If, at that time of newness and possibility, someone had told me that this was to be our last home and that we would live there for twenty-seven more years, that would have been beyond my grasp.

From August of 1971, when we took possession of our home, another year passed before we moved in. Gil found it difficult to divest himself of his job at Airstream. In the meantime we rented the house to a group of appreciative and reliable university students who took good care of it. On one of their last days in residence two of them invited us to their wedding, held in our garden. It was a festive and delightful party and we thought it to be a great omen and a blessing for our new life at Olive Mill. One week later we moved in, on August 10, 1972.

For twenty-seven years we lived in that house and loved it. Above all it was the garden that gave us never-ending pleasure. Year by year we made it change and grow until it became our own creation. Gil worked especially hard on it, tireless and passionate. When in the passing years some well-meaning friend suggested that it might be time to move to smaller quarters and make life easier, Gil would have none of it. Even when he got increasingly tired due to age he kept digging and moving rocks. I knew that no one could drag him away from his garden.

We found a strong and determined man, sun-browned, pony-tailed and shirtless most of the time. He wore cut-off jeans and leather sandals on his feet. We could easily believe him when he told us that he was a mountain man and had no need for earthly goods. But even nature boys and mountain men have to eat. So he allowed us to hire him to get rid of the most stubborn of the wilderness impeding us. Riding a small rented tractor he went on the attack in a cloud of dust. Shrubs and shredded branches piled up in his wake and small twigs and little stones flew into the air as he lumbered up and down the uneven terrain, screeching and rattling.

"You sure have a lot of poison oak." He held a long vine with innocent-looking leaves in his bare hands and waved it at us. We thought he was insane and were horrified. "Don't worry, I am immune." There was a little condescension in his grin as he looked down at us from his high seat. "I know an Indian recipe and I use it every year. As soon as the first few poison oak leaves appear in the spring I pick one off the stalk and take just a tiny bite from it, chew and swallow it. I do this every day for several months and every day the bite becomes a little bigger. There is no reaction and I am immune for the rest of the season. It's too late for you now, but try it next year."

Needless to say we were never inclined to try this miracle cure in the next or any of the succeeding years. In the seasons that followed our garden kept growing and changing. By dragging a sturdy stick or rake handle over the earth I designed winding paths that we built by light digging, spreading gravel and bordering with rocks.

We brought the lawn back to life as a lush green sheet edged by camellias and other flowering bushes. We planted a grove of birch trees and a variety of creeping groundcover here and there. One area floated gently up to a higher plateau where tall leafy trees admitted sparse swatches of sunlight through their crowns. Here was my cactus and succulent collection, carefully arranged among rocks and sea shells that Gil and I had collected on our excursions. Near the neighbor's house, close to the existing orange trees and the lone apple tree, we planted an apricot and a fig tree. Both of them became very large in the ensuing years and we relished filling baskets with fruit in spite of a constant good-natured war with marauding birds.

Years later Rick and Gil built a good-sized pond and Rick, as our fish-expert, stocked it with magnificent Japanese Koi that he obtained by trading his jewelry.

Our house was close to the beach and we could walk down Olive Mill Road to the water and the boardwalk in about ten minutes. Gil and I dragged treasured driftwood up from the beach. We found the most intriguing pieces of sculpture in many shapes and sizes, sanded and polished by the waves. We found a twisted and convoluted tree trunk that was almost six feet tall when we stood it upright in our garden. It had a human shape, with full sumptuous curves and arms that hugged its own body. The small oblong protrusion at the top had a face that was slightly bent back as if to look into the distance. I named it the Venus of Olive Mill Road.

When a giant root rolled up onto the sand Gil and three helpful young sunbathers carried that beast up the steep sandy stairs to the street and our waiting car. We set our trophy on a large old tree stump in front of a half circle of bushes in our garden. It was a black and brown crouching beast with tentacles and two long, wicked claws reaching into the landscape. We installed smaller, artful pieces of driftwood in strategic spots throughout our domain.

Way back beyond the level lawn the ground rose and a flimsy wire fence denoted the end of our property, separating us from uninterrupted wilderness and a running stream in a shallow ravine below. A narrow trench scooped its way from under the fence down to our garden and leveled near a row of nandinas, further pointing towards the lawn. It must once have contained a small brook or drain for runoff from the stream. I fashioned it as a dry creek bed lined with various kinds of stones, letting bigger rocks and small plants mark its banks at pleasing intervals.

That was when Gil rediscovered his love for wood and recalled the skills gained when, many years before, he had attended a furniture making and woodworking course at the Frank Wiggins Trade School in Los Angeles. "Don't you think there should be a bridge to cross the creek?" He was quite sure of my approval and he was right.

The first Japanese design element sprung up in our Montecito garden. Gil's small arched bridge should have spanned a lilly pond instead of a dry creek bed. We planted a group of young Japanese maple trees near by. It was a delight to see their delicate light green leaves turn red when autumn came.

I do not recall whose idea it was, but we decided to renovate the garage and turn it into a guesthouse. It was understood that Ralph was going to occupy it as long as he studied at the University of California at Santa Barbara. "I know exactly who can help us with it," he said. And that was how Jim Colley came into our lives.

Jim was in charge of installing exhibitions in the art galleries at the university. We never knew where or how Jim was trained, but he was a wonderful designer and practically an architect. He had built houses for friends and designed and refurbished many a home and workplace. He was the proverbial *Jack-of-all-Trades*. A stoppage in the kitchen sink? Jim will fix it. Special lighting for our art collection? Jim will install it beautifully. He was an expert in everything that might need to be done and he let us know it with unrestrained pride.

The first meeting between Gil and Jim could have ended most unpleasantly if Jim had not been such a good psychologist, taking the incident in stride. Gil and I stood in front of our house surveying the position and structure of Ralph's future domicile when Ralph drove up with Jim Colley and introduced him to us. After a fairly formal greeting Gil proceeded to elaborate on his ideas for the renovation of the garage without first asking for Jim's impression of the project. Gil could have been giving instructions to a hired hand.

I had to go inside. From the kitchen window I looked out at the three men standing at the front of the house. I saw Gil gesturing by sweeping his arm in a wide circle encompassing the whole landscape before him. I could not hear what he was saying, but it was evidently forceful and determined. Neither Jim nor Ralph said a word, although Ralph obviously tried a few times to interrupt. When Gil had his say he got into his car and drove off to the Airstream factory without saying goodbye. He simply left us all behind, confused and irritated. He must have been upset about something that morning, because it was not like him to be so rude. Jim had listened quietly to Gil's performance and now turned to Ralph with a smile on his face.

"Now let's look at the situation and see what we can do with it." In addition to his other gifts Jim was tolerant. He soon recognized that Gil's occasional outbursts were not malicious and that even I, his wife, had no idea what brought them on. In time these two men, as different as they were, became close friends and stayed so until the end of their lives. (They met in 1972 and both died in 1999, just a few months apart.) Jim must have been about Gil's age and was almost Gil's height. He was slim, wiry and moved with energy. When the need arose he could instantly speed into action. His narrow face held a short, carefully tended beard and a rather substantial nose. A light grey toupee, carelessly perched on the crown of his head, tried but failed to give him an aura of dignity, especially when he giggled like a schoolboy, amused by one of his funny but questionable stories.

Oh yes, did he ever tell stories! He had fought and was wounded in the war. His bravery in combat and his recovery at the Veteran's Hospital in Los Angeles were big subjects. As a matter of course, every doctor, every nurse and every patient as well as the staff he worked with at the University had a part in Jim's stories, which could be sad or funny, outrageous or pitiful. More often then not they were sarcastic and occasionally unkind, but so skillfully told that you could not keep yourself from laughing, against your better judgment.

But as time went on and we got older and Jim got older, listening to these stories became an ordeal. Nevertheless we were and continued to be fond of him and overlooked his various quirks. Gil and I, though, passed muster as far as Jim was concerned. He loved us. Whatever we needed or asked of him he was right there. I always knew that he had a magic wand hidden somewhere on his person. He waved it over our dilapidated garage and with the help of just two hired men, doing most of the work himself, he turned it into a very livable cottage with a tiny bathroom and a small kitchen.

Ralph lived in the cottage for quite a while, even after graduation from U.C.S.B. He was then hired to teach at Santa Barbara City College and at the University, with an additional night class at Adult Education, where he had the dubious honor to have his own mother as student. That mother had a great time and experienced what a good teacher her son was.

When Ralph left the cottage and moved back to Los Angeles Rick moved in with his dogs, photography equipment and jeweler's tools.

Gil and Jim became bosom pals. Jim had lived in Japan for several years. I saw the two men in the shade of a big oak tree pouring over drawings and blueprints of Japanese architecture, spread out on the large redwood table in the garden. Off and on they pointed to various sights in the landscape. That was when our garden took on more of the Japanese character that started with Gil's bridge.

Their first project was a small teahouse on a rise at the creek that led to Gil's bridge. Then months later they began work on a large Japanese pavilion near my cactus and succulent plantings. It was the perfect project for Gil's final retirement and he was completely absorbed and loved it. Gil and Jim searched through building and wrecking yards for special fine woods, bamboo panels and decorative materials. The two friends labored without extra help.

"Come, let's see if you approve," was a frequent summons to view their creations. They had embarked on a lengthy undertaking and it made them and me very happy; I gained free time and there was peace in our household. Moreover, it was exciting to see it take shape and the results were spectacular. The teahouse was slightly elevated on piers and several broad steps led to the open front that was protected by large movable shoji screens. It became a perfect performance stage and party house. We outfitted it with a very low round table, some bamboo stools and a wooden chest that contained a Japanese traveling tea set that we had found at an estate sale. I had brought a long rice paper scroll depicting cranes, floating clouds and lotus leaves from China and we hung it in a ceremonial alcove. I could not have known what a good home it would find.

I had taken up writing on my memoir again and was quite reluctant to spend time weeding or doing any type of outdoor work. So Gil devised a surefire way to get me to come out to the garden. All he had to do was to snap his big pruning shears as hard as he could, close to my window where I was sure to hear him. He knew that I would come running to keep him from butchering bushes that he had decided needed trimming. The finer points of gardening eluded him and without my intervention he would snip away with zeal and catastrophic results.

It was Scruggs, my black dachshund, who was responsible for introducing us to several of our neighbors. "Where is that dog?" I called and called him without success.

Our large garden was fenced. A tall adobe wall started at the front of the house and embraced part of the yard before giving way to a low run-down wire fence that continued around the rest of the property, which is where I found the answer to my question. There I found a little tunnel dug under the fence near the cactus plants through which Scruggs slid neatly into the neighbor's small yard.

"I've got him!" A strong voice called out to me and sounded unmistakably victorious, as if a big fight had been won. There in her yard beyond the fence stood a tall old woman with a firm hold on our escape artist's collar. "He drank my cat's milk." It was not said in anger, but rather with a mixture of amusement and complaint. She bent down and shoved his milky nose back through his tunnel and gave his behind a resolute push, sending him head over heels into my cactus patch. Next she fetched one of her numerous rickety garden chairs that were lying around and propped it up against the offending hole. There was a mass of old lumber, empty flowerpots, paint cans and sundry debris surrounding her, but she stood majestically erect amidst this disarray. A mantle of snow-white hair fell below her waist and a long brightly colored caftan gave assurance that this indeed was a regal personality. Large earrings framed her wrinkled face and bright intelligent eyes belied the fact that she was really a very old woman.

"I am Helga Hansen." She lifted her hand now to shield her eyes from the sun. There were large glittering rings on almost every finger. Strings of multi-colored beads hung around her neck. "Join me for a cup of coffee," she smiled invitingly.

There was no way for me to scale the fence, so I walked out of our garden, circled back down the road and found a little path that led to her door. I had not noticed her house before. It was half hidden from the road by tall trees and bushes, ivy and kudzu vines that spilled over the ground, climbing up the trunks of sycamores and oaks and doing their bit to shield her home from view. It was a low-slung redwood house that must have been comfortable and nice looking once, but was neglected and badly in need of repair. The creaky screen door brought me straight into a tiny kitchen that had just enough space for one person to barely turn around. From there I entered a large room that was dominated by a slanted skylight looking down from a high ceiling. From one wall a broad sofa jutted out into the room and was spread with a faded oriental rug, piled high with mountains of big, small, round and square pillows in a multitude of colors and designs. I discovered later that this was Helga's bed at night. The walls were covered with paintings.

"You've heard of my husband, the painter Einar Hansen? He was a wonderful man and very well known. All of these are his paintings."

With a wide sweep of her hand she gestured toward the walls, at her husband's work and her treasure, like a proud museum guide before an admiring audience. One large painting stood out among the others. It showed a tall, handsome young woman clad in white holding roses in her lap and looking straight out at the painter, almost piercing the canvas with her wide, adoring eyes. "That's how he painted me when I was young and we fell in love. But about that I'll tell you another time. Now I'll make us some coffee. You just look around a bit."

I watched her out of the corner of my eye, puttering in her kitchen, digging out a pot from somewhere under the stove, dumping in the ground coffee without a measuring spoon and adding water from the kitchen faucet turned on full blast. It could have been three or four or six cups worth, it was hard to tell and I don't think she cared. She set the uncovered pot on the open flame of the gas stove. Shaking her hair back from her face seemed to indicate that the job was done and that she was pleased. Looking back at me she saw that I had been watching. "That's how they do it in Denmark," She explained.

She showed me the rest of her home. "Einar built this big room first. It was his studio. That was all he thought about. What could be more important? These two little rooms in the back he added when I quietly reminded him that we'd need a bedroom and a place for our son to sleep." She chuckled as if this were part of a very happy memory. In spite of her mirth I had my suspicions that wonderful, self-centered Einar did not always make life easy.

Helga and I became friends and remained so for many years. To make our visits easier we installed a little gate between our gardens where Scruggs had prepared the way. I learned that she had been married before Einar. It had been a good marriage, solid and uneventful she told me, but "Oh, so boring."

We sat opposite each other near the window looking out at a golden blooming mimosa tree that rose triumphantly out of the wilderness in back of our properties. A table stood between us that was heaped with magazines, notebooks and sheets of paper that were covered with reams of writing in black and red ink. Helga pushed it all aside to make room for our coffee, no matter how her papers might be mistreated.

"I was very young when I got married. I was not in love, but I wanted to get away from home." She gazed pensively into the ominously black brew in her cup. "John was a dentist and aside from his profession there were not many things that interested him. It was in the fifth year of our marriage. I sat in my dreary kitchen trying to think of a present that he might enjoy for his approaching birthday, an almost impossible task. There was not much that he cared for except his tiny daughter and maybe also his wife. A great idea struck me. How about having my portrait painted for him."

Elbows on the table, her coffee cup held tightly between both hands, she fixed her eyes on me. Was she challenging me to show some sign of disapproval? She did not get what she was looking for. "Can you guess how the story continues?"

"Of course, the poor man did not get his painting," I said.

Then, laughing uproariously, she completed my sentence, "And I married the painter." There were laugh lines in her wrinkled face and her white hair, red lipstick, lacquered fingernails and dancing blue eyes showed a font of youthful spirit in spite of age and stiffening joints, of sore feet and shortness of breath.

I did not join her laughter. I smiled a little but thought about her husband and child left behind so abruptly from one day to another without looking back, without a care. No matter how much I admired her independent spirit and enjoyed her company I remained aware of her inherent selfishness. Helga was Number One. Helga needed to be admired. She was bright, interested in many things, read voraciously, wrote poetry and had a lot to say. Her poems I do not remember, except for some reason the very last words of one of them that linger in my mind. It was a funny and quirky poem about being taken to a nudist colony by friends. She was ashamed of her old body and hid behind some bushes. Referring to herself, she ended her poem with these few words, "So much to give and nothing to see."

I have a vivid mental picture of Helga, presiding from her big armchair, looking down on several young people that had somehow found their way to her door. They were sitting on the floor at her feet listening intently to every word she said. They were mostly high school seniors and a few from the university. She read her poems to them and also listened to their stories and concerns. She gave them attention and advice. After all, they were not her children so she could be magnanimous.

Helga's daughter, who by this time must have been grown up, was never mentioned and perhaps not even thought of. She had a son by Einar whom she adored. Jorgen, an artist like his father, was a nice and gifted but very troubled man, volatile and moody. For years he had taught at a large art school in northern California, but had eventually lost his job. He reappeared at his mother's doorstep and moved in with her. Once settled, Jorgen resumed teaching, this time in the Adult Education program of Santa Barbara City College. I enrolled in his classes and he proved to be a good teacher.

Soon there was strife between mother and son. Their screams and accusations were clearly heard in our peaceful garden. Away from Mama, Jorgen was a different man. He became our friend, especially with Gil, who seemed to have a calming influence on him. It was not always convenient when he dropped in on us unexpectedly during the day for a little visit and conversation, but we hated to hurt his feelings.

And then one day Jorgen appeared looking disheveled and more upset then usual. "Gil, they'll turn our lights off if I don't pay the bill today. I don't have the money. Can you lend me some, just to the end of the month? I'll get paid then." From that time on this entreaty was repeated frequently, but let it be said that he returned the money promptly every time just as he said he would. Finally we discovered that his money problems stemmed from his hopes for a winning streak at the races. He was sure that the horses were going to be his salvation. Only when he came to see us with shuffling gate, his hair in wild disarray and his complexion grayer then usual did we know that he had lost again.

The big stone home across the lane from us was the original olive mill where years before the growers of the region brought their olive crops to be ground to extract oil. One day we opened the pages of our local Montecito paper to see a big fat headline announcing *Singer Lena Horne buys Olive Mill*. There was quite some excitement in Montecito over this occurrence. The famous Lena Horne was going to be in our neighborhood. In general people seemed pleased, but mutterings of disapproval could also be heard.

Ralph was washing his car in front of our house when Walter, the old man who lived at the end of our lane, came ambling by. He stopped, pushed his hat back from his sweating forehead and nodded. "Well, what do you think about the niggers moving in? I'll be damned if I let any little pickaninnies cross the bridge to my place."

Ralph didn't even pause in his labors before answering, "Well, Walter, I'd rather have them as my neighbors than you." At this Walter turned beet red in fury, pulled his hat back down over his forehead and stomped down the lane cursing and muttering words that were muffled, but conveying meaning that was quite clear. To offset any of the negativity that brewed in the community I wrote a letter welcoming Miss Horne and offering assistance in whatever she might need.

A few days later I was in our side garden when I heard a strong melodious voice coming from behind the high wooden fence that shielded the back entrance of the big house across the lane. "Get your black ass back over there where you belong!" Scruggs, our black dachshund, appeared, sliding flat on his stomach out of a very narrow gap at the bottom of her fence. So here again he became the initiator of a wonderful friendship. It was not a famous diva that emerged from the wooden enclosure but a tomboy with tousled hair and flashing white teeth, with mud-specked blue jeans rolled up to her knees.

"I can't shake hands, forgive me. I am digging up a flowerbed. Such fun! I've never had a garden of my own." Lena asked me in to see the house and showed me how she was going to undo the monstrous renovations undertaken by the former owners, insults to this venerable old mansion. "Can you believe a stainless steel wet-bar in the middle of this grand old living-room? This is the first thing that has to go. Now we will have to strip the walls of this awful white paint. We scraped some off already. Look at the beautiful wood hiding underneath."

Lena was wound up, excited and happy. Here she could create her life in her own environment instead of only on film or the stage where it was fleeting and constantly changing. She also showed me the large attic and a remnant of its history. A huge wooden vat occupied most of the floor. It must have been used for the production of olive oil and been built right where it stood. Nobody could have transported this giant through the house and up the stairs, so it was equally impossible to remove it. "It's history. We are kind of proud of it. Lets go down. What would you like to drink?"

We sat in her kitchen, chatted and a friendship was born. She was not at home very often, coming only when she was not performing and the road, but when she was at home we visited often.

On the forth of July a festival traditionally took place in front of the big Mission in Santa Barbara. There were fireworks, nighttime dances and during the day a blessing of animals. An elaborate marketplace was set up with booths of not only fruit and vegetables, but of art objects, fancy clothing, toys, jewelry and trinkets of all kinds.

Lena wanted to go. She donned dark glasses and a hat with a very broad brim that she pulled down over her face, hoping to avoid gawkers and autograph hunters. We took off, Lena and I, accompanied by Gordon towering over both of us. Gordon was bodyguard, secretary, manager and chauffeur and I do not know what else. In any case he was easy company, a handsome and friendly man.

The stones of the Mission shone creamy pink. The sun was hot and hundreds of scantily clothed people floated among the festive aisles that were decorated with banners, flags and flowers. And Lena bought. Lena bought shawls, jewelry, necklaces, and a plant or two until Gordon's arms finally gave out. He had no capacity left for even one small package. Then we sat on the Mission steps, snow cones in hand, having a great time gazing at the throng passing by. Lena's dark glasses and floppy hat did their job and we were left in peace.

A small tableaux comes to my mind: Lena weeding in her garden. She is kneeling and digging out little tufts of grass. One by one she examines what she has in her hand and turns to Gordon showing him what she has discovered. He stands there with a small silver tray in his hand. "Look at this sweet little plant. Its too pretty to throw out." That said, she deposits the weed onto the silver tray held by patient Gordon and continues her horticultural pursuit. Unforgettable.

As I wrote these lines I looked for the exact date of the festival and was aghast, July 4, 1977. Lena and I, having been born in the same year, were both fifty-nine years old. It is hard to believe; in my mind's eye we were at least ten years younger. Of course beautiful Lena with her impeccably smooth skin and flawlessly slim figure would never look her age. She looked so young and swore to me that she never had a facelift. I believed her.

It took only two years or so before Lena sold her beloved house and garden and moved away. She gave a gala solo performance in Los Angeles and Gil and I drove down to attend. It was a fabulous show. All of a sudden during the intermission there was Gordon tugging at our sleeves. "We thought you might be here. The lady sent me to bring you backstage. She wants to see you."

Lena gave us an enthusiastic reception and we hugged and talked for a few minutes before she had to go back on stage. That was our last meeting. For Christmas that year she sent me an old-fashioned toy, a wooden rocking horse with candy in a detachable saddle and that was the last we heard from her. I sent a few letters but never got an answer.

Chapter 29

The Wedding at Tomales Bay and Zachary is Born

We had just moved into our new house and were in the midst of unpacking the last of the crates when the phone rang. I climbed over boxes and wrapping paraphernalia to answer the insistent ringing. No matter who the caller was I planned to make it a very quick conversation, short of being impolite. Yet the voice on the line captured my full attention.

"Hi, Mom. I can't talk too long, but I have news for you. I am getting married on the 10th of October and I want you and Dad to come up. You'll like your new daughter-in-law and her family. I can't talk much longer, so say you'll come." This was the nicest hurried conversation I could have imagined.

"Isn't it wonderful?" We had not even known that Bruce had a girlfriend. It was a complete surprise. Gil pulled me into his arms and gave me a hug, his face bright with happiness.

"Now if they would only move to Santa Barbara and live near us."

"You are greedy," I laughed. "He is safe, healthy and happy. How much more could we want?"

"Just a *little* more." He nodded affirmatively.

The car swung up a gentle hill and dipped down again on the other side only to tackle the next rise and the next, one after the other. It felt like a continuous slide in an amusement park. This narrow country road had no intention of landing anywhere. The bright October sun embraced the treeless landscape and we marveled at the expanse of it and at the fields, still mostly green, that surrounded us as far as we could see. Last summer's heat had not done too much damage to the land.

Our goal was Marshall, a small town at Tomales Bay. Near Marshall, occupying acres of farmland and nestled up in the hills, a group of modern, low-slung structures clustered around older buildings. This was another Synanon settlement, with Bruce in residence. We were happily on our way to attend his wedding.

We found a sturdy old house in the village that had been converted to a bed and breakfast inn. We looked out at the bay from the window of a cozy, old-fashioned room with a large four-poster bed, two upholstered rocking chairs and an imposing gold-framed mirror that loomed over a timid Victorian dresser. There were oil paintings on the walls, lovingly but inexpertly executed with obvious verve and pleasure, unlike the horrors one finds on the walls of many hotels, produced on an assembly line by tired and bored copyists.

Our room was on the second floor and we looked down at the water from just a few feet above the foundation of the house. We spent two nights in this room and never tired of watching the animal life on the water, the occasional fish jumping up to snap at an insect and water birds circling to catch those very fish as they broke the surface of their watery world. A great variety of birds appeared at early evening's descent and in the morning, just before the sun announced its arrival, throwing hazy golden light on the gray water.

"Mom and Dad, I want you to meet Ronda." He sounded a bit formal, but looking at my son's face I knew that the formality was going to be of short duration. He looked so happy and exited as he introduced us to our second daughter-in-law, a tall handsome young woman with shoulder length brown hair and an eager smile. She, like Bruce, had been addicted to drugs and had lived in hippy squalor in San Francisco's Haight Ashbury district. When her parents found her they brought her to Synanon where she had been saved, as had our son. We now saw a healthy radiant young woman before us.

I am sorry that we never really got to know Rhonda very well. Synanon was a world apart from ours. Parents were not the most desirable visitors and were presumed to be the most likely cause of their offspring's drug habits. We were just seen as a bad influence. This was the attitude of the organization's management, the old guard. The young people, on the other hand, were very friendly and made us feel welcome. The few times we visited through the years, whether at the ranch at Marshall or later at Badger, the woodsy campus high up in the foothills of the Sierras, we were tourists on a one night stop.

Yet the joy of seeing our son made up for any unease we might have felt. He was so proud to show us the living quarters of the settlement, the farm animals, the orchards and the fields at Marshall; and later, in the woods, the lake and the recreation facilities at Badger.

Driving up to the ranch we did not realize what an unusual experience awaited us. Had we really thought that any of our boys would have nice traditional weddings? Rick had come the closest, but it had been an overblown and complicated affair. Two years later, accidentally finding an announcement in the newspaper, we learned that Ralph and Valerie St. Jean had gotten married. We subsequently hosted a festive party for them in our Olive Mill Road garden that healed our hurt feelings.

Now it was Bruce's wedding and we were startled with a spectacle of most unusual dimensions. The sun shone brightly over all that transpired. A festive mood was in the air throughout the day, shared by the many people within and around the large community hall. I was astonished by the wedding ceremony and marveled at the many loving couples that were lined up in rows in front of a podium. There, dispensing blessings and proclaiming one and all to be husbands and wives, was Chuck Dederich, the uncontested head of the clan, the king, so to speak.

We were informed that the legal formalities had previously taken place at city hall. There must have been thirty couples or more, the women dressed in festive dresses, while the men all wore overalls, their everyday uniforms, but enhanced for this special day by bright white dress shirts shining under blue denims that were spotlessly clean and ironed to perfection.

Later I learned that more than a few of these couplings were ordered by Dederich, the indisputable boss. Others, like Bruce and Ronda's, were decided by love and free choice.

The wedding was followed by a very good dinner, during which we got to know Ronda's parents, whom we liked immediately. Since we had gone through the same heartaches with our children there was a bond that was keenly felt. Our day ended after the meal and in celebration, savoring a stroll through the hills and fields with several of us walking arm in arm.

From then on we visited maybe once or twice a year. January 3, 1973 was the highpoint of those visits, when we met our second grandson, Zachary, a sturdy, strapping bundle of boy. In the years to come Zac grew to be an exuberant little three, four and five-year-old who lived with a group of children his own age at Synanon in a special house set apart from the adult population. His parents were able to visit him when they were not busy or if they wished to have him for an overnight stay. It was an arrangement similar to a kibbutz in Israel.

When we visited during those years Zac would see us approaching and burst out of the swarm of junior Synanoners screaming *Grandma, Grandpa*, and throw himself into our arms.

When he was four and a half his parents separated. Ronda left Synanon to find her own way with Zac in tow.

Some years later Bruce found a new love and this time it was for life. We met Lex at Marshall. She was an attractive, bright and capable young woman who had never been addicted to drugs or alcohol, but had moved into Synanon because communal living appealed to her. There were quite a few people, idealists like her, who were drawn to Synanon and were called *lifestylers*. Lex became very close to Gil and me during the ensuing years and when Mary, Ralph's second wife, joined the family four yeas later I felt that I had gained the daughters I had always wanted.

Ralph and Mary's wedding festivities were held years later in their home in Atlanta and it was a celebration without stress or reservation. I remember Mary's father giving a wonderful speech full of love and wisdom, noble and touching. All of Mary's 8 siblings with their spouses and children came up for the wedding, the majority of them from New Orleans. That alone made for a full house, but was enhanced by many friends from Atlanta who helped to create a party worthy of the happy occasion. In a vague way I remember lots of color, hugs and kisses, animated talk and laughter churning and bubbling throughout the room. Rick, weaving his way among all the lively bodies with his camera, ducked and turned to create pictures for the family archive.

Bruce and Lex

Ralph and Mary

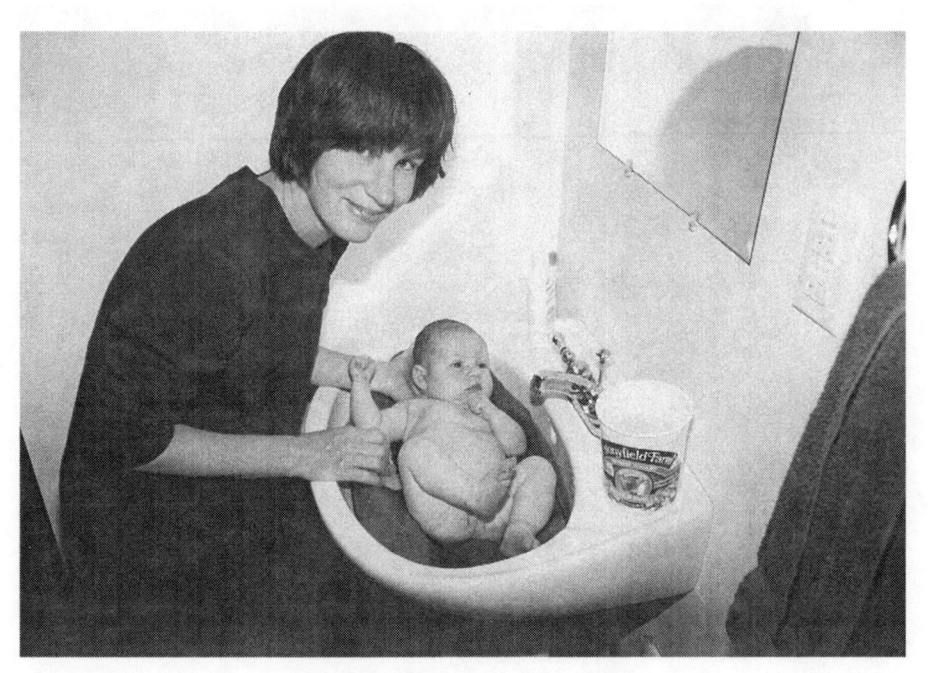

And here is Leah Clare, 1997

A dedicated grandpa, 1998

He listened to music, a final picture, 1999

Thanksgiving in Atlanta, 1999
Standing left to right: Noah, Lex, Zac, Isabelle, Mary, Leah
and Ralph Bruce and I are seated

Ralph and Mary wed, loving the two daughters

Leah bakes a cake for my 84th birthday

Settled in with Leah and Freddy for support

Chapter 30

Never a Dull Moment in Retirement

When Gil made his dramatic speech about retiring at age fifty-nine and traveling to Europe I knew that he meant it and that it would come to pass. We made three extensive trips to Europe, two to the continent in 1977 and 1979 and one to England in1982, each lasting for several months. When we made our first trip and reached Germany we inevitably headed for the home of my friend Ursel in Hannover. That was in 1977, sixteen years after I received her first letter.

Our Volkswagen camper pulled up in front of Ursel's house and there she was with outstretched arms, glowing with happiness. Our eyes met and we saw the young girls we had been, unchanged and as close as ever. The last time we had seen each other we were sixteen years old and now we were both sixty-year old grandmothers with wrinkles and slightly graying hair. We both had doting husbands standing behind us watching the scene, bemused and smiling.

For two days and two nights we stayed with Ursel and Lothar, her husband. Neither of our hosts spoke English, so the three of us chattered away in German while poor Gil searched for understanding by way of the few Yiddish words that he remembered from his mother's extensive vocabulary. While some Yiddish words sounded German they really were no help to him at all. So I tried to translate off and on, but then forgot again in the course of the animated conversation. I must say that he was sweet, patient and quite amused just watching us.

We ate at the kitchen table, warmed by the pungent aroma of beef stew and dumplings that reminded me of my parent's home and my Nanny Seusa's cooking. In that setting the past came back to me as I remembered my childhood and my early adolescent years. Even the giant larch tree we saw through the window recalled the garden were my imagined fairytales and games had grown in peaceful solitude.

Ursel's husband Lothar was a smallish, stocky man who, while trying to gloss over the fact that he had served in the German Wehrmacht, still held himself as erect as he could in spite of his frail health. His imprisonment in Russia and some serious combat injury or shellshock left him emotionally incapable of outside employment, with a tendency to withdraw from social activities. He worked from home and traded in rare coins for collectors. His *Ursula*, as he formally called her, swore that he had never been a Nazi sympathizer. Of course most every German made similar claims, but how many deserved to do so? I would have liked to believe that Lothar was not involved in the Nazi *Weltanschauung*, but all I can say is that he could not have been a more welcoming or friendly host.

Ursel was completely devoted to Lothar, helped with his business correspondence and kept house impeccably. I suspected that the compulsive activities of cooking and canning and scrubbing floors and washing curtains and windows and supplying fresh flowers for the dinner table compensated for her loneliness and seclusion. Her sons lived elsewhere and she saw them rarely. She read voraciously, was much interested in art and deserved a happier life, especially after the hardships she had endured during the war. At least once a year during the summer months Lothar roused himself and took his Ursula to some peaceful village in Switzerland or Italy for two weeks. They took long walks, enjoyed their unaccustomed surroundings and breathed fresh air that had to last them for another year. It was not easy to say goodbye when Gil and I left after two so very nice and peaceful days, filled as they were with remembrances of the past and warm expressions of close friendship in the present.

In April of 1991, fourteen years later, I received a note from Ursel accepting the most recent of my many invitations to visit us in Santa Barbara. I was overjoyed. I knew that for her this trip was going to be a momentous occasion. So on the 6th of May 1991, Gil and I left Santa Barbara at the ungodly hour of 6:30 AM. We drove to the Los Angeles airport, and then waited for two hours at the gate before seeing her ecstatic face as she emerged from the crowd. Dropping all her baggage she literally fell into our arms.

We two friends spent an unforgettable month together that summer. Ursel was overwhelmed by all she saw. A few months later she sent me a copy of the journal she kept during her visit, in which she wrote, "Never could I have imagined such a beautiful place that awaited me when I arrived at their home in Montecito. The garden I named the Garden of Eden as soon as I set foot in it. Wonderful large trees. Many of them I saw for the first time. Flowering bushes, a goldfish pond, a fantastic cactus collection. It was so large I almost lost my way the first few days."

Every day we went sightseeing all over Montecito and old-town Santa Barbara. I introduced her to some of my friends and everybody loved her for her indomitably joyful spirit and she, in turn, loved everybody and everything she experienced.

Before her trip Ursel had taken English lessons, but still supported her communications with energetic hand gestures, along with some stammering and helpless giggling. She became great friends with Rick, whose German, still hobbled in its own funny way, was better then her English. Listening to those two in conversation was a never-ending source of amusement for Gil and me. Ursel loved our dogs and especially took Rick's dog Gracie to heart. So as far as Rick was concerned my friend Ursula could do no wrong, she was perfect.

I did not permit Ursel to join in cleaning or cooking in spite of her desire to help. This was going to be her time away from drudgery and housework. I did let her expend some of her energy in the garden. She adored pruning the plants here and there and above all weeding, getting her hands smudged with earth and the knees of her slacks stained green.

I think the high point of our visit came when Rick took us on a trip to San Francisco where he had a business appointment. It was the month of May but still quite cool and windy and the drive along the rugged and beautiful coast was unforgettable. White foamy waves gushed over flat black rocks, the sky was bright blue and the gulls were swooping with the wind, screaming as if the whole sea belonged to them. It was hard to keep driving with all that beauty running past. We stopped a few times, went down to the water's edge, climbed on the incredible rock formations and picked up some special shells for Ursel to take home as souvenirs.

After spending a night in a hotel at the center of town, Rick left the two of us to explore on foot, by cable car and bus. Away from downtown, Ursel was astounded at the rows and rows of narrow houses that climbed the hilly streets, while we climbed along with them, breathing hard and feeling our legs rebel. We looked down at the bay and the Golden Gate Bridge, the cable cars that looked like toys and the broad expanse of water shimmering in the sun. It was our good luck that the fog took a vacation.

As we sat on a low garden wall for a while I thought of the years I spent in this great city, the people I had known, the friends. There were the doctors Ostwald, the Groppers, Werner Philipp, the painter, and Elisabeth, his wife and then Doctor Paul and Li Moses. Paul had a very special place in the storehouse of my memories. Was it admiration of his intelligence, was it trust and affection, or had it even been love? Where was the demarcation, the dividing line? I didn't know.

"Let's go on. I've rested enough." Ursel stood before me, eager for more adventure. Another note from her journal read, "I am having such a wonderful time. I feel so good being with Fe and Gil. He said the other day, 'You are not a visitor. You belong to the family.'" Ursel also wrote of concerts we attended, of seeing the Missions, museums, of great dinners in restaurants and again and again how happy she was. I was so glad we were able to give her this special time.

Years later I received a letter from Lothar. "Ursula does not react to the outside world any more. She just sits at her window and stares out without moving. She does not even know who I am."

During all the years of Gil's retirement in Santa Barbara our lives were never dull. We went to many concerts. We took classes at the wonderful Adult Education Center where we met many interesting people and developed a great circle of friends. Gil became involved in the Santa Barbara Night Counseling Center that was staffed by psychiatrists, psychologists and social workers, all of them contributing their time to provide free services to needy people. Gil contributed his skills to raise funds and manage operations.

I taught children's classes at the Art Museum for quite awhile, did my writing and enjoyed my grandchildren. Noah, Rick's son, lived close by in Santa Barbara. We visited Isabelle, Ralph's eldest daughter, in Los Angeles and were overjoyed by the birth of his second daughter, Leah, to whom Mary gave birth in 1996. I also attended drawing and painting classes, especially those given by Howard Warshaw at the University.

We led a good life. Our spirits even withstood the awful flood of January 1995 that washed us clear out of our house. Following torrential rains the creek that ran behind our house felt obliged to disgorge it's ever-rising waters, letting them rush into our garden and into the house and over the entire adjacent neighborhood. It even transformed Olive Mill Road into a shallow stream that splashed over sidewalks and ran down to the sea. A car or two, prompted cautiously by their courageous drivers, traveled slowly along the road, carried as much by flowing water as by turning wheels.

All of this transpired early one morning when Rick drummed me out of my bed. "We've got to get out," he screamed. At first I thought he was joking, but realized quickly that he was not. He called Nancy Bradford, a close friend who arrived in record time with her big station wagon. She got to work with determination and a clear head, more then could be said of any of us at that point. First she dashed to my bookcases and dragged my big treasured photo albums, all twenty eight of them, off the bottom shelves and piled them on my large drawing table, out of harm's and water's way; she knew how much they meant to our whole family.

By that time we had gotten over our initial shock and set to work in earnest. We filled our three cars with indispensable things like clothes, jewelry and important documents. Nancy said that she had space in her house to store many of our art objects and stuffed her wagon with African sculptures, paintings and our various treasures from around the world. What would we have done without her? Nancy, we are forever grateful!

For three months we stayed with generous friends. And we had no choice; water stood three feet high throughout our home. Much had to be repaired and refurbished. I must say that after the initial shock we both held up well. We went on with our jobs and favorite pursuits in good spirits. Our reading group gave us much pleasure.

During the following year shadows began to gather. Gil's brother Paul, of whom we were all so very fond, died on January 18, 1996 and on the same day Gil endured the first of several surgeries. To everyone's amazement, following two weeks rest after that ordeal, he declared himself recovered. He ambled around in his beloved garden, puttered a bit among the plants, but did not move any rocks. I suspect, though, that he tried.

In March of that year Gil underwent a second surgery and then, oh joy, in September after monthly checkups his doctors released him from their care. We were all disappointed two years later, on June 9 1998 when another surgery was required. Yet another followed in September and on November 17th Gil underwent the worst of his procedures, the removal of his bladder.

Up until that time he had recuperated to a degree after each assault on his body and spirit. He had gone back to Mark Ferrer's Shakespeare classes, attended board meetings at the Counseling Center and met with friends, frequently dragging himself out in spite of fatigue and some pain. He wanted to live each day to the fullest. I never tried to stop him but I watched him with deep anxiety in every nerve of my body.

The period that followed the bladder surgery did not see him bounce back. He was not ambulatory and was connected to machines and monitors even at home. Nurses came twice a week to check on him and help him bathe. After some time he seemed to rally somewhat and we tried to look for hopeful signs. The nurses left and he walked about the house on his own.

Chapter 31

Respite at Hedgebrook

Mary's friend Melanie put her coffee cup down and leaned her elbows on the table, looking at me with concern in her eyes. "Look at you. You are one nervous and exhausted mess. When will you get back to your writing again? You should look into Hedgebrook. It's a not-for-profit residency for women writers on Whidbey Island on Puget Sound, across from Seattle. It is not easy to get accepted. You send your application and a sample of your writing and hope they'll have a place for you. I applied several times, was refused twice and accepted the third time. I had a cottage all to myself where I could write, sleep, read, dream or do whatever I wanted all day, undisturbed by anyone or anything. Meals were provided and the company of other writers enjoyed in the evening after dinner. It was heaven. I was finally able to finish my novel."

So without much hope for acceptance and to please Melanie, as I tried to convince myself, I sent in my application in August of 1998, asking for a stay in the spring of the next year. Then I forgot about it. It was a pipedream anyway.

The takeoff had been smooth and I was on my way to a new adventure, a six-week residency at Hedgebrook, the Foundation for Women Writers on Whidbey Island. I had received this incredible news just before Christmas. What was I feeling? I did not know. Was I right to leave Gil for such a long time? I had asked Dr, Koper for his prognosis.

"He is well into a remission," he told me. "Don't worry, you can go. Enjoy" Still I felt uneasy. But by then I had a clear mental image that claimed my attention: a little wooden cottage in the forest that was there just for me and for writing. No household duties, no cooking, no shopping. I'd work on my book undisturbed and nobody could interrupt me. Not even Gil? No, not even Gil. And so the feeling of excitement struggled against a twinge of guilt.

A small wiggling boy sat behind me, pumping his feet and kicking the back of my seat with pitiless regularity. Nevertheless I decided to relax, to lean back in my window seat and gaze at shafts of sunlight as they slid across the wing as it sliced through the clouds, a sharp knife attacking a featherbed.

San Francisco appeared below, the Golden Gate, the bay, the hills, all so familiar, fraught with memories. There was Russian Hill, at the top of which stood the first house my parents occupied after arriving in the United States. The cable cars strained to make their way up and down the rise and fall of the city's streets and a jumble of narrow houses climbed to reach the tower on Telegraph Hill. I knew that on the other side of town stood our second house on Clay Street where Gil and I met and got married. My God, that was almost fifty-five years ago.

Gil! I closed my eyes and tried to quell the knot of fear that rose again in my chest. Gil, hold on, oh please hold on!

"Ladies and Gentlemen, we are approaching Seattle. We are going to fly over Puget Sound. You will be able see it on your left in a few minutes." The pilot knew what a magnificent sight he was presenting. The tone of his voice prepared us for something special, as if we were about to open a precious birthday gift. We had left the clouds and Puget Sound lay wide and shining in the sun below us. Large and small islands lay scattered along the coast, growing as we descended, and then lost from view as we hovered over the city with its own sea of streets and houses floating beneath us. The little boy behind me had eventually fallen asleep and now awoke with renewed vigor, howling in protest against his mother's efforts to ready him for the landing.

From the Seattle airport a shuttle bus took me to the ferry landing at Mulkiteo and from there the boat took me across the water, away from a life of daily business and worry to a place designed for peace and introspection.

Excerpts from my first letter home on April 8, 1999.

My dear Gil, and of course Rick, Bruce and Lex, (Ralph and his family were in Spain at this time.) One week has passed already. Melanie was right, it took all of this time to settle down. Only yesterday I was able to start writing for my memoir again. The day I arrived the weather was beautiful. The trip was easy and I was received with great friendliness.

The view of San Francisco from the plane brought all kinds of memories back and the sight of Puget Sound with all of the islands was breathtaking. In Seattle I caught the shuttle bus to Mulkiteo (Indian name), sharing it with six local people who had to be delivered to their homes first. So I had a great one hour ride all over Seattle. Arriving at the ferry pier I was dismayed to find that the ticket office was closed. Nobody had advised me to purchase tickets in advance, but they were still available at a house way up a steep hill, across the road. Me, with my suitcase, heavy purse and bulky coat. An angel appeared! A young woman seemed to notice my distress, stuck a ticket in my hand and ran up the hill to buy herself another one, for which I paid, of course. When we disembarked on the other side I saw her helping a short, substantial looking East-Indian lady with her luggage.

I, with my long green Loden coat together with the baggage-surrounded, bloomer-pantsed Indian lady, must have been a somewhat unusual sight a Clinton Harbor. Our eyes met and we each recognized a fellow Hedgebrooker. So Vibhuti Patel and I took to each other immediately. She is here for exactly the same time as I. We were picked up by a nice lady in a station wagon and upon our arrival at Hedgebrook were given a quick tour of the premises.

I wish you could see my wonderful cottage. Its name is The Cedars because it's all built from cedar wood. Gil, you would love to see its construction. All honey-colored beams on the inside. White walls. Only pegs, no nails are used. The architect had experience in working with the Amish in Pennsylvania. Each of the six cottages here is built from a different wood, one is oak, and one is fir, one cedar and another willow. Two houses are just named for their ambience: one is named Waterfall the other Owl. They are all distributed throughout this woodsy area so none of the occupants needs to intrude on their neighbors. I cannot see the other houses, but know that they can all be reached by a short two-minute walk. So, you see that I don't have to be afraid being alone, not even at night. Two other buildings are close by. One is the bathhouse and the other contains all kinds of storage items for the whole village. In the bathhouse are two great showers and an extra cubicle with a bathtub. A dressing table holds tissues and cotton balls, an array of various cosmetic samples, rubbing alcohol, talcum powder and individually wrapped little soap cakes. And now, the height of luxury, The Floor Is Heated From Underneath. This we don't even have at home.

You should see me hurrying back to my cottage in my robe and slippers along the narrow path under the trees. Coming from a hot shower, hair dripping, wet towel over my arm I am hurrying as fast as the bushes, the roots across the way and the slippery ground will let me. It is still quite chilly, thirty-seven degrees in the daytime, but the sun is shining and I am in a great mood.

You enter my little house through a door of beautiful wood that is hung by iron hinges. The iron handles are heavy and well shaped. The first thing you see is a wall of large colored rocks and a small iron stove (not pot-bellied, but square) that is standing on a bed of smaller rocks and pebbles; to the right of it the toilet and a small washbasin behind a sliding door.

From there you turn left into the living area that could not possibly be more tastefully and comfortably set up. It has a hot plate and a small refrigerator on one end of a broad countertop that runs along two of the walls and ends at an area that serves as my desk and my computer. Nothing is missing, from the can opener to the cd player/clock-radio. I learned how to heat my little stove with wood, although I do not really need it much, since they gave me the same electric oil heater I have at home. It is nice and cozy, though, when I manage to light the fire and it pops and crackles and flickers through the slits around the iron door.

A very steep carpeted ladder leads up to the loft that is almost filled by a double bed (down comforter!), a chest of drawers, a clothing rod and a small rocking chair in front of a tall stained-glass *window. You should see me climbing down from my loft in the morning, down the high hand-railed ladder backwards. Don't faint, Gil; it is perfectly safe. The only inconvenience is that I can't carry anything like clothes, laundry and certainly no books up or downstairs because I have to hold on to the rails with both of my hands. So going up I transport things by moving them from step to step and going down I just throw them over the banister with great gusto. Quite a satisfying enterprise.*

At six o'clock dinner is served at the farmhouse, the large building at the entrance to the compound. It contains the combined kitchen and dining area, a living room with a library and several other smaller rooms. The first thing we have to do upon entering the building is to remove our shoes and pick a pair of slippers out of a basket at the door. There are no shoes allowed in any room because the fine wood floors are easily scratched and the roads are muddy most of the time, especially now.

Assembling around the long wooden table I met the other women, all with university degrees and I having had my schooling cut off at age fifteen due to the Nazi threat. A bit intimidating, but I guess I have a fairly healthy ego. Vibhuti is a journalist for Newsweek, the international edition, and also works for the U. N. She too is writing her autobiography with a slant towards the history of her country, the same as I. She grew up in Bombay. Her father was very prominent in politics and she knew Gandhi and Nehru. Educated in English schools, she taught English literature in India and came to New York and the United Nations with her husband.

Gitana is thirty-two, short, sturdy, not yet fat, but soon. She has very short-cropped hair, a round face and small eyeglasses. I am really not quite sure what her profession is. She is writing a novel. She is super-bright, very nice, loves to have fun and is acting quite giddy. She is part South American.

Mari is half Japanese, thirty-seven and comes from San Francisco. She read some of her very sensitive and lovely poetry at night when we all congregated in the living room after dinner.

Hannah, in her twenties, is the youngest of the group. (My God, I should feel aged among these young women, but I don't really.) She lives in New York, works for a big publishing house and writes some sort of allegorically slanted fantasy with animals as the main characters. She reminds me of Izzy, being tall and slim, with dark hair and a very appealing, handsome face. (Hannah Tinti became a very successful novelist in later years).

Susan, a Jewish woman from New York, is fifty-nine, very intelligent, politically oriented, with the energy of a twenty year old and almost looking like one when you do not see her face close up. She is writing a book on her experiences in El Salvador where she worked in some Peace Corp-like capacity. How she gets much work done is a puzzle to me. She rented a bike and peddles all over the landscape, going to dance groups in neighboring communities, always on the move, always tense and seeing problems in absolutely everything.

The table is always nicely set with candles and flowers, the food most excellent. Three cooks alternate their services on different days and it seems as if they are competing with each other as to who can invent the best dishes, whether vegetarian or chicken or fish creations. After dinner on most evenings we congregate in the adjoining living room with its imposing iron potbelly stove and just talk, nibble M&Ms from a bowl that always stands on the coffee table and drink herb tea that we select from the kitchen.

Anything in the kitchen is available for the taking, except the contents of one pantry and one huge refrigerator. A normal sized fridge is open to all, juices, snacks, leftovers, etc. Two times already we've had readings at night. I think I kept my end up pretty well. Tonight is Gitana's last night here and she will read. I will read about the Hamlet performance in St. Gallen, since Gitana's passion is the theater.

A new woman came last night. Her name is Kate, tall, strong looking, but slender with a lot of spirit in her face. She teaches English and writing at a college in Portland. She is our second poet, to Mari's delight, who felt lonely up to now.

Five days later. Tuesday. Just came in from stretching my legs. Gorgeous weather! Walked around the property and marveled at the magnificent trees, particularly. All kinds of wild bushes and brambles in the undergrowth, tiny little flowers just peeping out. Everything starts to bud and grow. Bright green moss under the trees. Our resident cat sleeps on the bench in front of my door. She is blond, old and scrawny and accompanies us home after dinner when we tromp back to our houses with our flashlights. Since they obviously consider me to be the Ancient-One, somebody usually accompanies me to my door at night.

It is remarkable; anywhere else I would be uneasy about staying in a house all by myself and walking around in complete darkness, but I feel absolutely safe here. As a matter of fact on the first night I walked home by myself I missed my turnoff and wandered around in the forest with my flashlight not knowing where I was. That was a bit uncomfortable. I turned back, saw a house with a light in the window and decided to ask for help only to find that I was home. It was my own house.

It is still quite chilly, thirty-seven degrees in the daytime, but the sun is shining and I am in a great mood. Every morning I find a heap of firewood in front of my door delivered by Kate so I do not have to tromp to the shed to get it myself. Talk about being spoiled!

Now my Dear Ones, I better stop. The writing is going well. What a difference to be able to stay with it for so long.

Kisses for everyone
Gil, I miss you.

P.S. I just realized that in a few days my birthday is coming up. Another year under my belt! Enough already! Eighty two suits me fine. I wish to remain at just this stage. To whom do I apply? I came down to dinner last night and was received with happy-birthday balloons all over the ceiling and the long dining table strewn with M&Ms among the candles. On my place were presents: more M&Ms in a large jar, since they had discovered my passion for them during our evening reading sessions when there is always a bowl of them on the coffee table. Kate gave me a new roll of film for my camera and one of her poems. From Vibhuti I got a book with very nice whimsical watercolors by a French artist in which she had written the commentaries. There was a nice birthday card signed by everybody with a picture of a dachshund on it (guess why) and another jar, this time with candy corn in it, in commemoration of the story of Ralph and the candy corn.

(Here I shall allow myself to relate the ageless family story of Ralph and the candy corn. I was on a drive with Ralph, who may have been about 4 or 5 at that time. He was sitting in the passenger seat next to me munching on candy corn. I had to avoid an irrational driver bearing down on me by turning the wheel abruptly and swinging around a corner. The door next to Ralph burst open and if I had not grabbed one of his legs he would have fallen out. He was well on his way. I stopped the car and sat there in the middle of the street completely shocked and trembling. Ralph scrambled back into his seat and turned a furious little face at me, "You made me loose my candy corn!" Never mind that death had just barely passed us by.)

> There was also a card signed by the whole staff. We even got a bottle of champagne. So you see I was most adequately celebrated. Afterwards we had a reading in the living room with subsequent discussions until almost eleven thirty.
>
> These last days have been really spring weather, sunny. It is so nice to see more and more of the leaves on the trees and flower buds coming out every day. One does not notice such a change of seasons in Santa Barbara. What is amazing is that most of the plants growing around the Hedgebrook cottages have only been planted since the founding of the farm. There was nothing but a bare field before, abutting a stretch of forest way back towards a highway. I cannot imagine that these huge pines and cedars have not been here for a hundred years at least.
>
> There are small trees, bushes of hazelnuts and maple trees in the undergrowth. Cranberry, currants, blackberries and ferns grow among them and a host of twiggy and leafy stuff with flowers peeking out here and there. Three different ponds provide ample space for a chorus of frogs and even an otter supposedly has found its way to the water off and on. But I have not seen one. Deer have been walking past my window. Very early in the morning when it is still only half light at just about daybreak I can see them grazing on grasses and weeds in front of my door. I caught one with my camera the other day. He was peeking out of a thicket of undergrowth not too far from where I was hiding behind my curtains. I saw his ears watchfully cocked and did not move except for letting my finger click down on the shutter of the camera. It might have been too dark to catch an image, but I tried.

Across the road at the farmhouse, which stands at the entrance to Hedgebrook, there is someone else's property and it has llamas grazing on it, a strange sight indeed. The many rabbits around our place seem much more at home.

My work is going mostly well. Some days are more productive then others. I guess that is to be expected. Vibhuti informed me yesterday that we passed the halfway mark of our allotted time here and I told her to keep that to herself. I did not want to hear that. Not that I don't want to come home; it's just so very nice here.

Love to you all. How about some letters?
Me

It was May 6, 1999, shortly before dinner. I sat sideways at my desk with my feet up on a footstool, the writing board on my knees. It was a gray, cold day, but nice and warm in my cozy room. Outside the branches of the huge pine almost touched the window on my right, gently bowing to me in the wind, while the two broad cedars in the front performed a more ruffled dance. The little maple tree next to the entrance was skinny and naked when I arrived but was starting to sprout delicate red spiky leaves.

A knock came at my door. "Your husband is calling on the phone. It's urgent. You can take it in the shed." The wooden shed, where supplies are stored, stood just a few steps from my cabin and had a telephone hanging on the wall next to bins with toilet paper, kitchen towels and various tools. The light was dim and Gil's voice slow and hesitant.

I was anxious, "Hi Dear, what goes?"

"Well," a pause, I felt his breath and held mine, "I saw Dr. Koper yesterday. The cancer came back." The words were rung out of him. I closed my eyes. "I did not want to call and upset you," he said, "But Rick and everybody said I should."

I held the receiver tight, as if I could reach out to him on the other end of the line. "I'll be home tomorrow."

"I need you," he said. His voice sounded lost. I hung up and closed my eyes. Life stood still. I leaned my head against the cold, black case of the phone on the wall and only two words came to my mind, over and over, *That's it, that's it.* All other thoughts were suspended.

Next I found myself slowly walking up the narrow trail back to my cabin, almost stumbling over the big root that crossed the path.

Leaves that hung low on a maple tree brushed my forehead. A rabbit disappeared under the bushes.

When reality set in again there was a need for action. Friends from the other cabins gathered around. Martha packed the computer with great care; Kate collected my papers and books. Vibhuti took care of the clothes and several women sat up with me for a long time that night.

CHAPTER 32

Loss and Sorrow

Crossing the sound by ferry the next day, taking the limousine to the airport and then the flight home seemed to take no end. I had taken a book. I did not read. Rick picked me up from the plane. It was already dark.

I found Gil sitting in his favorite recliner next to his record player and TV. He threw the blanket off his lap and stood up to greet me. Obviously he had put on a fresh shirt over the pajama pants he wore that relieved the uncomfortable pressure of his regular slacks. He looked gray and tried to smile bravely.

"I am glad you are here," he said. Control, oh what controlled people we were. Only once did I see tears glinting in his eyes. Only once on another occasion did he turn to me and say, "We both know what goes, don't we?"

I looked up at him and all I could get out was a whispered "Yes." It took only a few seconds before we reached out and held each other and his eyes burned deeply into mine. It was his whole being that spoke and filled my heart forever, indelibly. Four weeks of daily trips to the Nuclear Center for radiation treatments followed, in addition to frequent office visits to three different specialists.

In the waiting room at the Center a baseball game was in progress on television. Husbands, wives or friends of patients were waiting to take their charges home after treatments. Comfortable sofas and chairs where clustered around low tables that held magazines and newspapers. A coffee machine dispensed its soothing aroma to no avail. The atmosphere was tense with a mixture of hope, fear and sad resignation. There I sat trying to read a book, trying to ignore the penetrating chatter of the TV announcer and trying in vain to concentrate on anything else then my anxiety. I watched the clock on the wall. One hour passed, another one.

The white-haired man sitting next to me kept one of his crossed legs tapping constantly up and down. A young girl who always sat by the door was ceaselessly filing her fingernails. There couldn't have been much left to file. The bustling volunteer tried to give me coffee. "How about a cookie then?" I took one to make her feel better.

After a while Gil got too weak to walk and I pushed him in a wheelchair. He was still a heavy man, as skinny as he had become. As we traversed the main waiting room to go directly to the treatment section, we passed the glass-enclosed reception desk and the rotund woman behind it. Gil had chatted with her before and of course knew all of the nurse's names by heart.

"Wave to Mary-Jo," he said, "It's her birthday." As in times past he told me what to do, but now my resentment was gone and only admiration was left, admiration for this desperately sick man, waving, smiling and joking with the nurses, trying to suppress the wince of pain when they removed his clothes before his treatment.

Another group of people kept me company in the smaller waiting room. Two women, one with a scarf around her bald head, the other wearing a concealing turban, sat next to each other and chatted. They had obviously formed a bond of shared experience, losing their hair from chemotherapy and radiation and talking about family concerns and hope for recovery. A sturdy man with the insignia Arrowhead Water emblazoned on the back of his shirt sat at a table against the wall earnestly working on a huge puzzle that was spread out before him. I imagined some nurse or orderly scrambling the pieces at the end of the day if and when anyone came close to putting it all together, just to sustain the challenge.

Time kept crawling along so very slowly. The daily trips for treatments exhausted Gil. At home he just sat in his chair, a blanket over his lap concealing the tubes and the bag that were strapped to his leg in place of his absent bladder. He listened to music a little, but usually fell asleep, even if it was one of his favorite pieces. He did not want to read or watch TV. "Too tiring," he would say. But he insisted that I read aloud some of my writing from Hedgebrook, so I did, a little at a time. How much he actually heard I do not know. His eyes were usually closed. Off and on he blinked them half open, nodded and said, "Go on, that's good."

Occasional visitors helped. Friends from Adult Education and from our reading group came. He perked up with these visits. Nurses from the Visiting Nurses Association, who came three times a week to check on him, adjust his appliances and give him a bath, were mostly cheerful women. He would joke and banter with them, briefly reviving his earlier life-affirming spirit, but would then sink back into his chair, exhausted.

Evening darkness fell late in that summer month. It was Sunday, the sixth of June and four weeks since I had returned from Hedgebrook.

"Read some more," he said and turned his head in my direction. "Get me to the bathroom first, though," he added. His face looked strained and then he pleaded, "Hurry!" and kicked the blanket off his legs. I grabbed the wheelchair, helped seat him and pushed him to the entrance of the water closet off our bedroom. He raised himself painfully, struggled towards the toilet and then suddenly his legs gave way. He collapsed, wedged upright in the narrow space between the wall and the bowl, the knees of his long legs almost touching his shoulders.

Was he conscious? I did not know. No sound came from his lips. Horrified, I tried to pull him up to a more comfortable position. It was impossible. I was alone and knew that I could not lift him. Rick was in Los Angeles for the day. I dialed 911, stated my case and rushed back to Gil. I tried to slide a small pillow between his head and the wall and to assure him that help was on the way. He did not respond. I ran outside.

The road was unlit, there was no moon to relieve the darkness and the oak-trees were black around me. It was still warm. The air held its breath. Headlights approached slowly down the lane towards me, obviously searching for the house. *Here, here* I yelled, waving frantically.

The paramedics took over. Two very large men eased him carefully out of his position and carried him to the bed. Only then did I see the vast black ooze under him that stained the carpet and the bed. They cleaned him up, checked him out thoroughly and administered injections and a transfusion. Gil left the home he loved for the last time. I left a note for Rick pinned to the front door and followed the ambulance.

The rest of that night and the week that followed remain very hazy in my mind. I spent my time at the hospital, sitting next to the bed or stretched out on the recliner late into the night. The first two days I went home to sleep. Bruce and Lex drove up from San Diego the next day. Our grandson Noah and his girlfriend Raquel came up from Los Angeles. Rick stayed at the hospital with me much of the time, but ran out a few times to go for a drive when his emotions overwhelmed him.

Friends came. Diane and Morrie Seidler appeared daily and sat with us. Mark Ferrer was there as often as his teaching schedule allowed. Other friends came, Lepska, Sophia and Mael Melvin, but often Gil was asleep. He woke up from time to time and even then his indomitable spirit came through. He made his little jokes with the nurses and delighted in seeing some of their pretty faces around him. Noah's girlfriend Raquel received an adoring smile from him. She was so touchingly sweet to him and we all loved her.

As the week wore on his speech faltered, his hands and arms did not work anymore, he was paralyzed and drifted in and out of consciousness. Swallowing became difficult and even water went down with difficulty in tiny sips.

"Beer," he whispered one day, "I want some beer."

We all looked incredulous.

"If he wants some beer he shall have it." Sharon Read dashed out of the room, returning after a short time with a six-pack of beer hidden under her jacket. With a teaspoon she served him beer from a paper cup until Morrie took over, carefully spooning the liquid out drop by drop. Gil's eyes were closed, but the expression on his face was one of utter delight. He kept pursing his lips and opening his mouth in anticipation of the next sip.

Sharon had been one of his classmates and a member of a close-knit group of friends attending the Adult Education class that Mark Ferrer taught for many years. I had always suspected that Sharon was in love with him, but now it was clear how deeply she felt. My heart went out to her. I hugged her and she wept and then rushed out and away. Sharon, the reserved lady, the bright and sometimes sarcastic one, how hard this must have been for her.

When evening turned into night I stretched out on the reclining chair next to Gil's bed and closed my eyes. The lights had been dimmed. I was left alone to rest. I could still hear a little cluster of friends talking quietly to each other outside my open door until everybody left. And then it was very quiet and even at the nurse's station across the corridor the atmosphere was subdued without the daytime's hectic activities. Just Gil's shallow breathing suffused the air.

My eyes were closed. I did not sleep. It all felt so unreal. I seemed to float in a hollow space, without thought or feeling.

A nurse's whispered voice, "Why don't you go home, Honey? Get a night's sleep in your own bed. He won't go yet. It'll be a while." I drove slowly through the dark and empty streets. I entered my house and it too was dark and empty. I did not undress. I did not go to bed. I sank into Gil's favorite armchair by his record player. The book he had tried to read lay on the floor half open with bent pages. I must have dozed off when the doorbell rang. Ralph and his family had rushed back from their vacation in Spain in response to Bruce's urgent call.

It was now the middle of the night. Ralph and Mary looked exhausted and little Leah was fast asleep snuggled against her papa's shoulder.

"What is his room number?" Ralph did not want to loose a minute. He and Mary dropped their bags and dashed away. Before I knew it I had little Leah on my lap breathing peacefully, completely undisturbed. I cared for her and let her sleep, even though I also wanted to go back to the hospital.

When my dear Gil passed away that night I was not there. I would have liked to hold his hand. Ralph said later that Gil did not respond to anything that went on around him and had his eyes closed, but that Ralph thought that he was aware of his son's presence. Holding his fathers hand he felt a small pressure answering the touch of his own, as if saying *I know you are here*.

Days of frantic activity followed. I needed to be busy. What should I do next? How will I lead my life from now on?

Rick offered to live with me. "Don't leave your house," he said, "We can manage together." Bruce would have liked me to move to San Diego to be near Lex and him.

Ralph said, "Come live with us. We have an apartment for you right in the house and your granddaughters will love having you close. This was an offer I could not refuse. Even with Rick, who frequently traveled for his photography, I could not stay in the house by myself. It had to be sold. It was a big step, but it had to be done.

Dismantling the household, sorting my books and giving many away to friends or the Salvation Army and donating most of Gil's large record collection to UCSB was not only exhausting but emotionally very difficult.

"You can't house hundreds of records. Where would you put them?" Ralph asked. "Anyway, all of this music is available on CD now." Still, it felt like I was discarding favorite books that were obviously much read, loved and a little shopworn and replacing them with brand new editions in pristine condition. It was just not the same.

I sat on the floor in our living room in front the two long shelves that held Gil's extensive record collection. Some of that beautiful music was spread over the carpet in front of me from de Lassus and Monteverdi to Shostakovich and Bartok to Bernstein and Copeland. The voices of great singers and performers were there, as well as folk music from many parts of the world. I put one of my favorites on the turntable, Victoria de Los Angeles in Faure's *Requiem*. Overwhelmed by grief and the beauty of the music I leaned my head against the shelves and closed my eyes. Tears formed beneath my lids, spilled over and ran down my cheeks. I could not stop them. I had to give in.

The house and garden had to be readied for showing and for sale. Walls were painted, windows washed, some bathroom tiles replaced. Our beautiful garden was in great need of rejuvenation. It had been totally neglected in all of the time that Gill was sick.

I hired a pleasant, energetic young woman who was a gardener and landscape designer. She had the most appropriate name for a gardener, Autumn Brook. She swore that it was the name she had been given at birth. She and her helpers went to work, raking, trimming and pruning, refurbishing and replanting whole areas that had simply been forgotten and died of thirst or were strangled by weeds.

Every weekend Bruce drove up from San Diego to be with me. This was truly a labor (and a long drive) of love. It was such a comfort. Rick was there too, of course, but he had several commitments to take photos of weddings and jewelry jobs in addition. He had not much time, but in the evening he was mostly home so I did not have to sleep alone in the house at night

Friends kept me busy. Invitations for lunch and dinner provided welcome distractions. The Seidlers took me to one of our subscription concerts at the Lobrero Theater. That was hard. Gil had always been in the seat next to me. Sometimes he had reached out to hold my hand, closing his eyes when a particular piece of music moved him. This time, as always, I felt his presence next to me, but when I looked he was not there.

I knew that Diane was watching me out of the corner of her eye, afraid that I might break down. So I held on. Seiji Ozawa did his best, but even his strings and horns could not blow the hurt away.

It was such a big job deciding what to give away and what to keep. Moving from a big house to a small apartment, from one life to another required a lot of sacrifice. Ralph and Mary wanted some of my furniture, which was to be shipped to Atlanta. I made a list of all of my pictures and the art collection. A few were for me to keep and the rest was to be divided among my sons. I knew that whatever went to Ralph I could still enjoy in Atlanta and Bruce and Lex would give a good home to all the treasures that came to them. Rick too was heir to many objects he coveted, but he was to live in a trailer and would have little space for anything. His brothers decided to store his belongings until he might decide to buy a house and retrieve what was his.

In the middle of September I put my house on the market. "Now let me see, we'll schedule an open house for . . ." Victor, the realtor, consulted his papers and marked a string of dates. Naturally, the interior of my home had to be impeccable, which meant that I hardly dared to live in it.

"Your house will be too unconventional for many buyers, but the garden and the land will be a big draw. I think we'll sell it fast." For three and sometimes four days a week groups of people poured into our living room, scattered in all directions through the rest of the house and then into the garden to leisurely saunter about as if it were a public park. Some even sat down on a bench to have a nice little chat. When they came back into the living room and moved towards the exit I picked up snatches of their conversations.

"I'd just tear it down and build a new one."

"Only one and a half bathrooms! Who could live with that?"

"But there is space for a tennis court, Johnny, don't you think?"

There goes my garden, I thought. Victor joined me for just a moment. He must have seen my unhappy face. "It would be best if you'd leave during viewing times, Felicia. I'll be here to take care of everything."

Victor was right. I got in the car and left. Most often I drove to the beach, parked and gazed at the ocean, watched small but long-legged birds stabbing their sharp beaks into the sand, finding something here and there that slipped down their gullets with a slight toss of their heads. I always had books in the car and read a little, but mostly I brooded and felt miserable. When the sun went down and the sky still glowed a little, ushering the evening shadows in, I decided that it was safe to go home.

Only four weeks passed before we had three potential buyers, all of whose bids came quite close to our asking price. I opted to give it to a young couple with children who were delighted with the garden and seemed to appreciate the house. I thought they would treat it well. On October 10th I accepted their offer and the next day escrow was set in motion. Ralph came from Atlanta to help resolve financial and practical matters. Then packing started in earnest.

Our old friend Jim had been ill at the same time as Gil. I heard from John, Jim's friend and partner of many years, that Jim was living out his last days at a hospital. It was the day before my departure. I felt that I could not leave without seeing Jim once more. He looked thin and pale but his mind was clear and he was still the old Jim smiling up at me from his pillow. His toupee was gone.

"They took my hair," was the only complaint I heard during my visit. I thought he looked much better without it, but I did not say so. We talked for quite a while, talked about Gil, the teahouse and the garden and the fact that his nurse was a bossy old dragon. The old Jim was still there. A good sign.

"I am so glad you came, honey."

"So am I Jim, so am I." Leaving, I looked back at him from the door. He smiled weakly, obviously tired from putting up such a good front for me. He tried to lift a shaky hand to his forehead in a gesture that wanted to be a military salute, remembering his years in the army. Those years had been the subject of so many of the stories he had repeatedly told us. I waved back at him and also, in my way, to Santa Barbara, saying goodbye to another chapter of my life. I learned that Jim had died three weeks after my visit.

CHAPTER 33

Atlanta

I arrived in Atlanta on the thirteenth of November 1999, just in time for Thanksgiving dinner at the end of the month. They all came to celebrate my arrival. Bruce, Lex and Zac came from San Diego, Rick from Santa Barbara and Noah from New York. And of course Ralph, Mary, Isabelle and little Leah were there. The whole family drew together.

Raising glasses of champagne around the dinner table we drank a toast to Gil, talked about how much he had meant to us and how much we missed him. We all agreed that his had been a good and fulfilling life, a perfect reason to celebrate. None of us had completely dry eyes and a few times I had to retire to my room for a few minutes to compose myself. Only Izzy let the tears roll down her cheeks.

Little Leah bounced from one to the other of the uncles and cousins, to big sister and Papa, trying to get attention and maybe a sip from someone's drink or a biscuit from the table. Those boring gown-ups just kept standing around with glasses in their hands, talking and talking instead of filling their plates and hers with that good food right there in front of them. I looked at her and wondered whether in later years she would remember her Grandpa who doted on her and disappeared from her life when she was only three years old.

Dinner was ready and Ralph and Mary brought in the turkey and set it on the table for all to admire. Rick proclaimed himself the master carver and did the job to perfection. Then he turned to me in spite of the fact that I had no part in preparing that bird and started to proclaim, "Fe, this is the best . . ."

Everybody fell in immediately and finished the sentence together, " . . . Turkey you've ever made." Without fail this heartfelt praise had been presented to me by my dear husband with great flourish at every Thanksgiving feast throughout the years. (I heard my father's favorite pronouncement as if floating in from somewhere in the sky, "Now *this* is a big celebration.") Then there was laughter in the room and a lively exchange of memories, of times almost forgotten and now remembered, of hurts and healing, squabbles and joys. I looked at all my children and grandchildren that were gathered around me and I did not feel alone anymore.

Nearly twelve years have passed since I arrived in Atlanta on November 13 and the calendar tells me that now the year is 2011. I am comfortably settled in my own apartment in Ralph and Mary's house. I am 94. I have trouble getting used to that. I still feel quite alive and am in good health in spite of having managed a series of spectacular falls over the last few years. One consequence of those falls was the need to relinquish my driver's license, which was a big blow. A cane is by force my constant companion now. I named it Pegasus, but, alas, it does not take me flying to a realm of poetic inspiration. It just keeps me from loosing my balance.

"Baby" Leah is now a bright and lively fourteen-year old. I never thought that I would see her grow up to her teen years. Isabelle is thirty-two, tall and lovely and my three boys are in there early sixties. It is hard to believe. If time could be arrested right here I would not complain.

I am sitting at my desk in front of the computer, a device that gave me some trouble at first, but that I eventually conquered (at least partially). I even managed to learn to type at my advanced age. I guess I am allowed to brag a little. Looking around my room I understand why one of my more orderly friends calls it cluttered. It is my nest now. Almost everything it contains, everything I brought with me from Santa Barbara and could not bear to leave behind, reminds me of some part of my life.

The walls are lined with paintings. Most of them are mine. There is a dreamy night scene of Washington Square in New York's Greenwich Village. It stems from my days at the Art Student's League, inspired by walks through the square on many a night, returning from class, envying the loving couples cuddling in the dark on wooden benches. An ice cream man's lighted wagon in the distance impersonates the moon.

Next to it hangs a funny little drawing, an homage to Toulouse Lautrec. It is of a couple swinging enthusiastically along the boards of a large public dancehall in New York where I had gone with my friend George, relishing the sights and sounds that filled that enormous space around us. A narrow casein painting, almost six feet tall, done mostly in gray and white tones hangs near my now much used recliner. I painted it while my mother was dying. When it was completed I discovered that instead of the abstract painting I thought I was creating, it had evolved into an otherworldly apparition, a floating, cloudlike figure, my mother's spirit.

Other paintings hang on my walls and they all have their stories. There is the elderly shoeshine man who had his stand in front of our bank in Montecito. I asked him to my studio and he sat for me patiently while I did a pastel drawing fairly quickly. When it was done he looked at it and shook his head in disapproval.

"You made me look like a bum," he grumbled. I promised to paint him the way he wanted to be seen, as a gentleman. So when he came back a few days later he was a gentleman, although he looked a little as if he had escaped from a somewhat earlier century. He was tall and groomed to perfection. A red vest showed under a long black jacket and a pearl gray tie held a white starched collar high up to his chin. In one hand he carried a slim, elegant cane and in the other a tall black top hat.

I painted him that way on a large canvas and enjoyed every minute of it. Thank God he approved. It was a good painting. Unfortunately it burned in the big Sycamore Canyon fire in the home of a good friend who had bought the painting and loved it. At least her life was saved.

My eyes land on a little canvas across from my desk. I painted it in Los Angeles when we lived on Elrita Drive in Laurel Canyon. I remember our garden swimming in sunlight with fleeting patches of gauzy shade from the branches of a leafy tree that brushed over grass and gravel when a light wind rose. I sat there one day with my paints and easel, gazing at the colors of a rosebush that stood near the gate. A flower in full bloom demanded my special attention.

On the small canvas balanced on my easel on the uneven path I tried to make the colors glow just as they shone in front of me. I worked and painted for one hour, for two, for three hours and more. Yet no flowers bloomed on my canvas. Instead there was a group of faces tucked together that seemed to unfold slowly like the petals of the rose. I had not planned this picture. It grew from . . . who knows from where?

Several years later we attended the opening of a group show in Santa Barbara, an event that is still so clear in my mind. My little picture had been accepted and hung between two very large wildly abstract canvasses on one of the main walls, looking like a chiuaua between two rottweilers.

"Who arranged that?" Gil grumbled.

"Oh Gil, it's fine. I like it there. Go look at the other paintings."

"Yours is way above any of them." He turned and grudgingly surveyed the other walls.

I found some friends and we chatted, but not for long. A nice looking elderly couple came bustling up to me. "We heard that you are the one who painted that lovely picture. We want to buy it. We love it." Did I ever feel flattered!

"It is not for sale. I am sorry," came a determined voice from behind me. "I am her husband and this painting belongs to me." My first reaction was outrage. How dare he take over and conduct my affairs without consulting me? But then I looked at his now beaming face and felt his arm around my shoulder. The painting and I were his property, his love. How could I not forgive him?

A black, dreamy African Pende mask, a present from my beloved brother Ralph, hangs on the wall near my desk. Next to it a weathered woodcarving looks down at me. Gil and I brought it back from one of our trips to Europe. It represents just the front part of an animal's head, the back of which is missing. With all probability it had been chopped off an elaborately decorated portal on the face of some ancient building and it shows the marks of an ax. My family has speculated about what kind of animal it was meant to represent. I believe that it is a bear with a big snuffling nose. On only one side of his face the lips are curled back over sharp looking teeth. Some say it shows a nasty snarl while others see it as an amused grin. I prefer the latter interpretation. Gil and I were so pleased to find this character at an outdoor flea market in Vienna. He was looking up at us from the pavement, thrown together with a heap of old copper pots and carpets. We called him Johannes Ohnesorg, meaning "John, Who Has No Worries," a name we found proudly painted on the window of a butcher shop nearby.

And now his weathered face conjures up a veritable stew of memories, bubbling and threatening to boil over. What to fish out? An impossible task. Up to now things were clear enough to call them up and give them voice, but here now I am confronted with such a jumble of recollections that it would take another few years to untangle and to present them in orderly fashion. At 94 how much time have I left?

I look back at a full life, a rich life, its wonders, its turbulence, heartbreaks and love and it feels good to share it with those who are close to me. I found an entry in one of my infrequently kept diaries dated Monday, February 3, 1958 written at our house on Cerro Gordo Street at the age of forty-one, which to me now seems so very young. I want to end my book with this little piece, because it still feels close to me.

A million ideas are racing through the day, a hundred images, sounds, songs and echoes vibrate throughout, never to be recaptured, never caught, only vaguely remembered, sometimes later, almost unrealized. I will try again to put some things down in writing, feebly grasping without too much confidence in my own strength and perseverance, but at least trying. It may not serve any other purpose than to amuse myself and maybe my offspring in later years.

Here I am, sitting at midnight in my brightly lit living room after the drawing class at the Kricheff's. Everybody sleeps, except the fleas on Scampy and Frou. Their hosts, or should I say their owners, are puffing away in peaceful sleep themselves, not counting an occasional hasty scratching-siege or hind-leg gnawing. The whole house seems to breathe in deep contented sleep. Even the rain is dripping off the roof more slowly now.

In me there lives a deep sense of gratitude for what I have. And if the thought creeps up that it can't last, who knows what's in store? What will the future bring? Such a thought born by what? Superstition fused with all the traditional, miserable, whining old ladies of fate? I can only shrug my shoulders and say: Yes, who knows what will be? But what we have now can never be taken from us; it becomes part of us, it becomes us. And if they take our own personal bodily atoms and blast them all to hell and fuse them with all the whirring busy-bodied atoms in the universe and nothing remains of us save for a faint occasional glimmer in some gifted Mars man's extrasensory perception, we might be able to whisper to him that at some point life was supremely good, warm, and definitely worthwhile.